STILL
GOD'S MAN

STILL GOD'S MAN

A Daily Devotional Guide
to Christlike Character

DON M. AYCOCK & MARK SUTTON

Kregel
Publications

Still God's Man: A Daily Devotional Guide to Christlike Character

© 2003 by Don M. Aycock and Mark Sutton

Published by Kregel Publications, a division of Kregel, Inc., P.O. Box 2607, Grand Rapids, MI 49501.

Cover design: John M. Lucas

Library of Congress Cataloging-in-Publication Data
Aycock, Don M.
    Still God's man: a daily devotional guide to Christlike character / by Don Aycock & Mark Sutton.
        p.   cm.
Sequel to: God's man.
Includes biographical references.
    1. Christian men—Prayer-books and devotions—English.
2. Devotional calendars. I. Sutton, Mark. II. Title.
BV4843.A93   2003
242'.642—dc22   2003022398

ISBN 0-8254-2001-6

Printed in the United States of America

03 04 05 06 07 / 5 4 3 2 1

I dedicate this book to
Ryan and Chris,
my young men,
who have made me more proud
than they will ever realize.
I love you guys.—DA

To Amy, Jennifer, and Sarah.
Your lives as dedicated Christians
are the greatest rewards I could hope to have as a father.
Thanks for being wonderful daughters!—MS

Spiritual Men

Men struggle. We all do.

Simple? Obvious? Perhaps, but that's often more an intellectual assent than an inner understanding. To struggle also implies that sometimes we fail.

I was in my thirties before I realized two important things about us men in our daily combats, failures, and victories. First, the level or degree of failure isn't the determining factor. It's the sensitivity to our failures. Our shortcomings (or to be more biblical, our sins) may appear minor to those around us. However, as we grow and yearn for more of God, we groan over those seemingly insignificant areas.

Second, although we want to live victoriously, few of us want to fight the battles to get there. Although we want to be spiritual overcomers, we want to triumph effortlessly. Life doesn't work that way because we can't live victoriously without fighting the battles that impede our growth.

One of the lessons we can learn from this helpful book is that Aycock and Sutton set patterns for us as we battle onward. They haven't always done things right themselves, and they show their human frailty. However, they point us to the biblical texts to encourage us in our own struggles and difficulties.

Another helpful thing in reading this book is that it can become a daily reminder that none of us is unique. Our situations differ, but our struggles—no matter how intimate or difficult—are remarkably similar.

As they point us to the great people of faith in the Bible, we remind ourselves that those who treaded the path in front of us have well marked it for those who follow.

In their own candid stories, we sense that Aycock and Sutton have learned to groan over their lack of spiritual progress. In the darkest hours of the night, they've cried out for God's loving forgiveness and yearned for a greater level of maturity and victory. As you read this book, that's the pattern these two men lay for us. Don Aycock and Mark Sutton know the human terrain. It's obvious that, like Jacob of old, they've wrestled with their own temptations. Setbacks have struck them in the face—just like the rest of us.

We sense that because they write with compassion as they urge us forward. The authors don't present themselves as superheroes or speak from lofty platforms. They also make it clear that those who open themselves to God convey consistency in the marketplace, in sermons, writings, and conversations. They don't shout their spirituality; they don't need to. They simply live it.

They also show that those who surge forward are often the first to doubt the positive witness in their own lives, but those who walk behind recognize that witness. It's as if we can see the invisible scars from their toughest battles. Genesis 32:31 says Jacob walked with a limp after his night-long fight with the Angel of God.

Unlike the patriarch, the scars aren't usually physical, but they're just as real. Maybe that's why this devotional book spoke to me. I believe it can also speak to other men. Both writers are battle-scarred. The messages flow with the poignancy of their own hard-learned lessons. Sometimes they didn't have answers and they made mistakes. They fought with ambition, desire, and all the other temptations the rest of us face.

In this book, they open doors for men to come into the light, to speak openly of failures, to confess their weaknesses, and also to accept God's loving, forgiving embrace.

—CECIL MURPHEY
1995 Gold Medallion Award Winner;
author of *Seeking God's Hidden Face:
When God Seems Absent* (InterVarsity Press)

Introduction

In 1998, Kregel Publications released *God's Man: A Daily Devotional Guide to Christlike Character.* More than forty different writers participated in the writing of that book. We used a thematic approach to issues with which men deal. We were successful with that first book, and it still sells well today, more than five years later. When Kregel Publications asked me (Don) to produce a second volume, I thought about it a long time before saying yes. My hesitancy had to do with the fact that I did not want simply to repeat what we had already done. Finally, I told the people at Kregel that I would do it on two conditions: first, that one other man and I would write it; and second, that we would use a chronological approach to the Bible.

Mark Sutton and I wrote what you will read in this book. I began with January and wrote every other month through November. Mark started with February and ended up with December. We began with Genesis 1:1 and followed the divine trail through the Bible, winding up in Revelation. What you will read here are the encounters with God of two men who try to be real and realistic. We are not super mystics, spiritual giants, or members of the intellectual elite. We are two men doing the best we can to serve God and love people.

We have had some enormous challenges while writing this book. Mark's beloved wife, Susan, courageously battled cancer but lost that war. She died just as this book was ready for the printer. Don left an established church over leadership issues and planted a new congregation. As you can see, neither of us is anything other than a guy pushing along while trying to make a living, serve God, and live up to his potential.

As you read this book, you will "hear" our separate voices. We have not tried to make ourselves sound exactly alike. Our distinct personalities, colored by our life experiences, emerge from the pages. That is the way it should be because, for good or bad, I am who I am and Mark is who he is. Neither of us is perfect; neither are we standing ten feet above reproof. We are simply two men who struggle each day to be men of God, good husbands, fathers, pastors, friends, and writers.

Thank you for taking this year-long journey with us. We hope that what you encounter along the way will be more than the words of two men; we hope that you will experience the living Word— Jesus, the living Lord. Be sure to read the suggested passage in your Bible each day. Not only will the day's devotion be clearer, you will gain a new understanding of your Bible.

We appreciate the support and encouragement of Dennis Hillman and Steve Barclift at Kregel Publications. Their entire staff has made this project possible.

Mark is the pastor of Brookwood Baptist Church in Shreveport, Louisiana. Don is the pastor of Liberty Baptist Church, a new start-up church in Palatka, Florida.

If you would like to contact us, please feel free to do so. You can reach us at the following e-mail addresses: Don Aycock, donaycock@kregel.com; Mark Sutton, marksutton@kregel.com.

Let us know how your journey goes.

—DON M. AYCOCK
Liberty Baptist Church
Palatka, Florida

STILL
GOD'S MAN

A New Beginning

Genesis 1:1

"In the beginning. . . ."
Those words have the refreshing sound of a mountain water-fall. Who doesn't long for a new beginning? One of the things I like to do at the end of each year is to think back over the previous twelve months and consider what went well and what did not go so well. I ask myself some hard questions like these: Am I into any habits that prevent my being what I want to be? Do I need to change any specific actions? Do any attitudes need work? Am I being dishonest with myself in any area of my life?

If you ask yourself enough questions like these, you will get either depressed or motivated! For me, and maybe for you, these questions are motivating. That is why I find Genesis 1:1 so refreshing. Imagine it. You can draw a line in the chronology of your life and say, "I'm starting over. From this day forward, I can change the course of my life by making some corrections."

One of the ways we can change is by spending some time each day in conversation with God. Reading this devotional book will be helpful, but prayer and Bible reading are essential. I know; you have tried that in the past but had trouble following through. You are in good company. But think of it this way. Developing a consistent devotional life is like investing small amounts of money over a long stretch of time and watching the magic of compound interest. Small investments can pay big dividends.

Make up your mind that you will get up fifteen minutes earlier, or keep the TV or radio off for a while, or stay up a bit later to get in your devotion time. You might not notice any difference at first, but stay with it. Let those powerful words *in the beginning* work for you.

Lord, thank You for the power of a new beginning.
Help me to remember that You were there when
the world and all that is in it began. You are here
now, too, through Your Spirit. Help me develop
the strength and resolve to spend time with You

*each day. Give me guidance as I grow in relation-
ship with You and others. Through the name of
Jesus, Amen.*

BE FILLED
Genesis 1:2

The description of the earth as "formless and empty" is a frightening picture. We don't do well with nothingness. Emptiness seems
like a death sentence. For some men, this description is not a statement about the cosmos but a comment on their lives—"formless
and empty." Does that describe you?

You might be surprised to learn that many men feel this way.
They have worked hard to achieve a certain position or status in
life. In the early years, all of the sacrifices seemed worthwhile. The
long days and sleepless nights, the time away from family, the hours
chiseled off the weekends—all of that seemed to be necessary for
reaching the goal. But what about now? Do you wish that you could
get those days back?

I know what I'm talking about. I entered the doctoral program,
moved our family to another state, and began a new pastorate when
my twin sons were nine months old. Talk about a challenge! I think
that I was a reasonably good father, but I know that the stresses
and demands of those four years were hard on all of us. I look back
at pictures of those days and remember them as time spent working harder than at any time before or since. I loved what I was
doing and really thrived. But I know, too, that my family sometimes got the leftovers.

You might know that feeling, too. One man said, "I spent years
climbing the ladder of success only to discover it was leaning
against the wrong wall." Look again at today's Bible verse. The
last part reads, "and the Spirit of God was hovering over the waters." That is what saves the day for us. God is hovering, ready to
bring creation out of chaos. Another word for that is salvation in
its fullest sense—wholeness, soundness, and unity.

Would you allow the Lord to do His work of bringing creation out of chaos in your life? The last words of our lives do not need to be *formless and empty.* Instead, our lives can include these words: *the Spirit of God was hovering.*

> *Thank You, Lord, for hovering over my life. At times, I seem to be a walking embodiment of "darkness was over the surface." But You have intervened both in creation and in my life. Give me strength, unity, and purpose. Through Jesus' name, Amen.*

JANUARY 3

GOD'S VERBS

Genesis 1

Do something unusual with today's passage from the Bible. Quickly scan chapter one of Genesis and look for the words *God said, God saw,* and *God created.* You might be surprised at what you find. Again and again you will see the biblical description of God as active, aware, and thoroughly engaged with His creation.

God says, "Let there be . . . , and there was." I love that! In times past, people wondered about the activity of God. Some people thought that He was like a watchmaker who made a cosmic watch, wound it up, and is content to sit back now and let it run down. But look again at today's text. God works at the unique task of creating all that is. His work culminates with the creation of humankind. When God saw His creation, He said that it was very good.

We men sometimes forget that God has given us the pattern of life in creation. We, too, are creators. We create families through reproduction. We create careers through training and hard work. We create communities by being actively engaged in the life of the community. We create churches by doing whatever it takes to make it an outpost of light in a dark world.

I have known many men who are passive. For whatever reason, they are not engaged in anything. They slide through life without ever seeming to touch it, much less change it. I don't mean that every guy has to be John Wayne, but we should look at life as a good challenge. God seems to give us life and says to us, "Here, let's see what you can do with this. Don't try to do it alone; I'll help you." God created the heavens and the earth. He is still active, working through His highest creation—humankind. That's you and me!

> *Lord, thank You for giving me life. Thank You for helping me to be part of Your creative process as I work to create a life for my family and me. May You look at me and say, "Very good." Through Christ, Amen.*

MY EVE
Genesis 2:20–25

Adam, the first of us men, looked around and didn't see anything in all of creation that interested him. Then God brought woman to him, and Adam said, "Wow! At last." Okay, that's a loose paraphrase of verse 25, but that's what it means. Eve had caught Adam's eye, and the rest is, as they say, history.

We men are made by God to be interested in women. Our biological and neurological makeup causes us to act that way. Some scientists speak of our brains being "hardwired" for this kind of attraction. After all, if not for this sort of mutual attraction, we would not be here. Of course, this interest in the opposite sex can get us into trouble if we are not careful. We all know people who have shattered their lives by thinking with their hormones rather than with their brains.

Don't miss the intention of God for our well-being in relationships. I am blessed in having friends of both genders, but there is only one exclusive relationship of marriage for Carla and me. The "one flesh" idea is one of life's most satisfying relationships. All concepts of promiscuous sexuality are rejected out of hand.

When I perform weddings, I often use a paraphrase of this biblical image. Dr. J. R. Sampey was a seminary president three-quarters of a century ago. He paraphrased today's biblical passage this way: "The woman wasn't made from the man's head to rule over him, or from his feet to be trampled; but from his side to be equal, from under his arm to be protected, and close to his heart to be beloved."

If you are married, thank God for your wife. Treat her as the treasure she is. We all have our faults, but grace has put us together for our mutual well-being. Look at your wife and say again, "Wow!"

Lord, thank You for my "Eve." She is my beloved, and I will do whatever it takes to protect her, love her, and help her to grow in Your image. I am so blessed to have her. May I always act with grace and tenderness toward her, the way You act toward me. In Jesus' name, Amen.

JANUARY 5

DOWNFALL
Genesis 3:1–19

This selection of Scripture is not the original "Dr. Dolittle" with talking animals. It is a starkly realistic picture of Adam, Eve, Don, Mark, and every other human being. It shows the way we think and the actions we choose. Do you doubt it? Consider the ways you have thought yourself into trouble in the past. You were taught when you were a child that certain behaviors were not permitted. But what did you do? You did the exact thing that you were told *not* to do! Something in our nature rebels against all authority, even the authority of God.

When our twin sons were little, I sometimes said something like this: "Boys, it's been raining and the yard is wet. Don't play in the mud." They would look at me as if to say, "Hey, thanks Dad. We hadn't thought of that." Think about your own family. Doesn't it work that way?

Genesis 3 gives the devastating picture of human rebellion, choice, sin, and the terrible aftermath. We are all part of it. Even when we commit our lives to Christ and try to live for Him, we still find ourselves immersed in a culture of rebellion. That is why we have such a need to be in a strong church to help us with our weaknesses and failures. That is why, of all places on earth, the church should not play games but face sin and its consequences squarely.

The good news of the gospel is that God has done something about our rebellion. He has taken it on Himself through Christ Jesus. Are you rebelling against Him? Are you still trying to do life your way? Haven't you realized that the fate of every Adam is the same (see v. 19)? Commit your life to God. He will help you with a serious attitude adjustment.

Lord, You know my heart. Sometimes I love You and want nothing more than to follow You. But there is also another part of me. Sometimes I want to do it all my way. I try to ignore You as if You did not matter. Help me, Lord, to be more consistent in my love for You and in my conduct. I need You. Be close to me today. Through the Lord Jesus, Amen.

JANUARY 6

My Brother's Keeper
Genesis 4:1–16

The question came in the aftermath of treachery. Cain had killed his brother Abel. Read the first seven verses of Genesis 4. You can see disaster building. Abel seems to be the "good" son whereas Cain has much to live up to. You have seen that old story haven't you? Maybe you have lived it. One child earns straight A's whereas the other child barely makes it through school. One brother excels at athletics whereas the other child can hardly walk through the house without stumbling.

But sometimes we set ourselves up for failure. We ignore warnings. We chafe at correction. We get ticked at suggestions for improvement. Cain had his chances. Verse six tells of a pretty good lesson. The teacher was the Lord Himself! He said to Cain, "If you do what is right, will you not be accepted?" That is a big "if." *If you do what is right. If you listen. If you pay attention. If you control your anger. If, if, if.* Those lessons are still coming our way to keep us from disaster. Can you recall times when you were offered a lesson but refused to learn?

So Cain sloughed off the warnings and cooked up a plot to get his brother away from the rest of the family. While the two of them were out in the field together, Cain seized his opportunity. He murdered his brother Abel. This was sibling rivalry pushed to its absurd conclusion. Abel's blood was hardly dry before the voice of the teacher came to Cain again: "Where is your brother?" Isn't it strange how we think we can get away with our sin? Cain had no answer, only another question: "Am I my brother's keeper?"

You already know the answer to that question. Yes! When I consider my life and my responsibilities, I come up against that "yes" over and over. People all around me—my brothers—are in need. Do I really have any responsibilities to them? You already know the answer.

Who is your Abel?

Lord, You know me too well. You know the ways I've tried to wiggle out of my responsibilities. But, in Your grace, You have given me another chance. So help me to do right. Help me to take care of my brothers. Help me to be a good son. Through Christ, Amen.

JANUARY 7

I ENVY NOAH

Genesis 6:11–22

I admit it. I'm envious of Noah. Why? Genesis 6:22 states, "Noah did everything just as God commanded him." I wish I did that. Can you see yourself as being right on target with every decision you make? Could you imagine your decisions and actions getting the divine nod of approval?

Noah started building an ark before the rain came. His country-men thought he was crazy. Some of his own family members might have laughed at him. But Noah kept sawing and hammering. His audience was not the crowd that laughed. Noah's sole concern was God.

I have a tough time with that. Do you? I am pulled in so many directions. I have a job, bills to pay, and a family to take care of. Many things pull at me. You know how it is. There is never enough time. So I end up spinning like a weathervane in a storm. Then I read about Noah again and try to slow down.

The word *multitasking* is used often these days. It is the ability to do several things at the same time. I was driving to my office re-cently when I came up behind a lady who was driving, brushing her hair, and talking on a cell phone. I kept my distance as I laughed at her. But then I looked at my schedule and laughed at myself.

What is our number one need? It is to be like Noah—to do ev-erything that God commands. That is difficult, but it is possible.

Lord, You see my dilemma. I love You more than I can tell, but I am pulled in many directions. I ask for Your help in determining what is most important in the midst of what is merely impor-tant. Let me be Your man. In Christ, Amen.

JANUARY 8

When God Makes a Promise

Genesis 9:1–17

The word *covenant* is an important term in the Bible. Its basic meaning is "agreement." God offered covenants with various groups and individuals in the Bible. In today's passage, He made an agreement with Noah. The covenant was an iron-clad guaran-tee that God would keep His part of the agreement. Noah could count on the fact that the Lord always keeps His word.

The covenant even had a sign to remind both parties of its exist-ence—a rainbow. In verse 16 God says, "Whenever the rainbow appears in the clouds, I will see it and remember the everlasting covenant between God and all living creatures of every kind on the earth." I like that idea of a covenant sign. In fact, I wear one on the third finger of my left hand. It is the covenant that I have with my wife. I see that sign and remember our agreement made on a November afternoon in 1973. We have gone through three decades of marriage and have reared twin sons who are now almost out on their own. We have moved around the country and have faced enormous pressures of every imaginable type. But we are still together and more in love today than on that afternoon in 1973.

How are you doing with your covenants in life? With your wife? With your kids? On your job? In your relationship to God? Is it time for a tune-up? We will have the opportunity to think more about covenants as we move through this book. For now, use the following prayer as a guide for reflection and action.

Thanks, Lord, for the signs of Your steady love and unbreakable promises. The rainbows above and the signs below remind us to keep up our side of the agreements. For Jesus' sake, Amen.

JANUARY 9

DELIVERY IN THE NURSING HOME
Genesis 21:1–7

Imagine opening your morning newspaper and seeing these headlines: "Nursing Home Resident Delivers Child." We would wonder all sorts of things: the name of the father, the condition of the mother, the health of a baby born to someone in her ninetieth year, and so on.

Abraham and Sarah were certainly old enough to live in a nursing home had one existed then. Abraham was one hundred years old when Isaac was born. No wonder they named him Isaac, which means "he laughs." But who was laughing? The father, certainly, because of his age, and Sarah because until then she had seen only dried up breasts and an empty womb. She said, "God has brought me laughter, and everyone who hears about this will laugh with me" (v. 6). It was a party! And why not? It's not every day that a child arrives to people who are old enough to be great-great grandparents. If it happened to you or me, we would laugh too.

I remember the birth of my twin sons. I still remember the warm tears trickling down into my mask as I watched the surgeon take them from Carla's womb during a C-section. The first sight of those reddish writhing boys filled me with such great joy that I laughed and cried at the same time. It was one of the greatest emotional experiences of my life. Do you remember those experiences? Not every man can. Some guys had to be away at work during the birth of their children. Others stayed in the waiting room, afraid of what they would see. I watched the surgery performed on Carla. Far from being revolting, it was one of my life's most precious sights.

Sarah laughed. Abraham laughed. The community of Israel laughed. Imagine—a baby being born to a centenarian. That's something to howl about. Can you laugh with joy at your family? Can you celebrate their baby steps? Do you love looking at their pictures of days gone by? Outside of my salvation in Christ, being married to Carla and being the father of Chris and Ryan are the greatest joys of my life. Nothing in my ministry even comes close. I laugh when I think of how God has blessed me. How about you?

Lord, I can see them bent over in laughter—
Sarah and Abraham rolling in the sand for joy.
Thanks for the overwhelming joy of celebrating
our families. Some of the experiences are anything
but fun. Some of them nearly kill us. But You
have never abandoned us, so we laugh and say,
"Thank You."

JANUARY 10

STEALING A BLESSING
Genesis 27:1–40

Jacob and Esau. It could have been Don and Glenn. Or Bill and Jack. Or any other two male names you could insert here. The story is about two brothers so desperate to be somebody that they get into a power struggle that threatens to crush their family. In that era, a family passed its birthright from the father to the oldest son. It passed in the form of a blessing that was usually given verbally. Once the verbal blessing was spoken, it could never be taken back. That was the dilemma that Esau faced. His younger brother, Jacob, schemed to steal the birthright, the control of the family wealth and future. The father, Isaac, was tricked into giving it to the wrong son. In this case, the schemers did not need a firm of lawyers to cook up a plot worthy of John Grisham. All they needed was to cook up a pot of stew and to use a simple costume to fool the old blind patriarch. Isaac thought that Jacob was Esau because of the trick, so he laid the family blessing on him.

I love the way Isaac spoke to Jacob (thinking that he was Esau): "Ah, the smell of my son is like the smell of a field that the LORD has blessed" (v. 27). Did Jacob think that he needed to resort to deception to have his father touch him and bless him? My twin sons are in college as I work on this book. Recently, one of them was home on spring break. He and I drove to Atlanta for him to look at a medical school. I loved being with my son and spending a few days in close quarters with him. When he left to go back to school, his mother and I hugged him. I smelled his soap and found it so easy to bless and love him. That same day, our other son called. He had gone to Oxford, England, to check out a doctoral program there. I found myself wishing that I could hug him, too.

God brought good out of the family mess of Isaac. But I don't want to rely on His needing to redeem my relations with my family. I should take care of that myself. Do you have children? Bless and love them. Sometimes it is hard to do so, but stick with it. Our children are too important to let them wonder if we love them.

Lord, in Your Son Jesus You showed us how much You love us. You gave Your blessing to Him, and He, in turn, showered it on us. Father, sometimes our family life goes wrong. But remind us that in the midst of chaos You add the blessing of Your presence. Let us understand. Let us feel loved.
Amen.

MEETING YOUR PAST

Genesis 32:1–21

I got an e-mail recently that began this way: "Don, you probably don't remember me, but I remember you!" That got my attention. The writer went on to say, "I'm Kim . . . from Melville, La. You preached a revival in our church in Melville in 1971. Just wanted to say that I was a teenager when you preached at my home church, and you said something that I've never forgotten. I've heard others say it since then, but I heard you say it first . . . 'What you do speaks so loudly that I can't hear what you say.' I've used the line myself a few times!" That e-mail came to me thirty-one years after I spoke those words. I remember the church and the experience but not those particular words. What an amazing thing to have your past come into the present and pat you on the back.

The past has a pesky way of coming back to us often. Something we did years ago pops up in the least expected way. That was Jacob's experience with his brother Esau. Jacob had swindled Esau twice! Now events were bringing them together. Jacob was about to meet his past. How do you think he felt? Genesis 32 tells us about the preparation he made to face Esau. All in all, Jacob knew that his life was in danger. He was "in great fear and distress" (v. 7). He should have been! All of the lies, treachery, and swindles were catching up with him. They always do.

You already know that and could add your experiences here. But the past does not have to bedevil us. It can bless us. Our choices can be like bank deposits, earning interest for future spending. Jacob made some very bad decisions in his life. Maybe you have too. If so, admit it and do what you can to make them right. Sometimes all you can do is ask for forgiveness. That is what Jacob ended up doing.

The e-mail I got from Kim ended this way: "Just wanted you to know that, probably without knowing it, you had a great influence on my life." Thanks Kim. You never know when you might meet your past.

Thanks, Lord, for the reminder of a relationship built, a word rightly spoken, a life influenced.

Help us make our decisions in ways that will
build a livable future. Forgive us where we fail.
Strengthen us along the journey. Through our
Lord Jesus, Amen.

JANUARY 12

BETTER THAN THE PWE

Genesis 32:22–32

I never wrestled my father. He was forty when I was born, so by the time I got big enough to wrestle, Dad thought that he was too old for that sort of thing. But when my boys came along, I made sure there was plenty of time and room for that playful sport. The house we moved into when they were eight had a huge den. We bought an area carpet and spent many happy hours tumbling, grabbing, sweating, and sometimes bleeding, on that carpet. Whew! They were rough little fellows!

I think about those experiences when I read about Jacob wrestling beside the river Jabbok. But his match was no giggle-filled pastime. Jacob was in a fight with "a man." People have given many interpretations to that description. Just who was that man? This much is clear—Jacob was in the fight of his life. His opponent turned out to be God! The Bible says that the man could not overpower Jacob. Does that mean that God will not overrule our stubbornness and wrongheaded thinking? Like Jacob, our actions have consequences. Even the Lord will not force us to do what we are not willing to do.

Jacob wrestled God and in the process was crippled. Do you see the pattern? Our opposition to what God is doing in our lives damages us more than God. I admit that I limp a bit because of some of my past decisions and attitudes. My finances are not what they could be because I did not pay attention as I should have. Some of my relationships are not as close as they could be. Even my relationship to God suffers at times. How about you? Do you feel the stiffness in your spiritual joints? Do you creak when you get up? Are you still in hand-to-hand combat with the Father?

I laugh when I see the antics of professional wrestling entertainers

(PWE). But I don't laugh when I see the GWF—the God Wrestling Federation. Who belongs to that group? We all do. So did Jacob. That is why his name was changed to Israel, "he struggles with God." Let us make up our minds that we will call off the match, acknowledge that God is the victor, and join Him in His work.

Lord, You and I have had some great wrestling matches, haven't we? I struggle so often with knowing You, or with doing the right thing, or with loving as I should. As hard as it is to do so, I invite you to cripple me if that is what You need to do to get my attention. I'll limp to Your glory. Through Christ, Amen.

JANUARY 13

RECONCILIATION FOILED

Genesis 33:1–20

I have an older brother. When we were children, we never got along very well. Only later did I come to think of my brother as an okay guy. He lives in Texas, and I live in Florida, so we do not get to see each other much. When we get together now, we find that we enjoy many of the same things, especially fishing.

Jacob and Esau were brothers. Jacob, the younger, had tricked Esau many times. In today's Bible text, they seemed to be on the road to reconciliation. Jacob humbled himself to Esau and gave him many gifts. The older brother at first did not want to accept them because he had done well. But at last he accepted them as a sign of making up with his younger brother. Esau invited Jacob's entire family to go with him to his home in Seir. Jacob agreed but said that he could not drive his herds at a fast pace. He told Esau to go back home and wait. Jacob would come later. But as soon as Esau left, Jacob reverted to his old tricks. Verses 16–17 read, "So that day Esau started on his way back to Seir. Jacob, however, went to Succoth, where he built a place for himself and made shelters for his livestock."

Had he intended to trick Esau all along? Or did he simply change his mind? He seems to have gone through a charade to trick Esau one more time. That is a tragedy because reconciliation takes two parties. How did Esau feel when he finally realized that Jacob had done it to him again? Could there ever be reconciliation after that? Do you have someone with whom you need to be reconciled? Can you take the first steps? When you begin this process, you never know if it will be successful. One person might genuinely want it whereas the other person might not. If you initiate the process, you might not succeed. But if you do not begin, you definitely will not get anywhere.

Lord, You know that our relationships are often messy. We bump into people around us and have friction with even the ones we love the most. Help us to have the courage to reconcile with those from whom we are separated. Let us forgive others as You have forgiven us. Through Christ, Amen.

JANUARY 14

Spoiled
Genesis 37:1–36

Jacob had many sons, including Joseph. When Joseph was seventeen, he had a dream that seemed to have his older brothers bowing down to him in homage. When he told his dream, his older brothers were not amused; they were murderously angry. These older brothers thought of Joseph as just a spoiled brat, and they were not about to play games with his fantasy. They thought up a plot to have Joseph sold as a slave to a group of Midianites. They, in turn, sold him as a slave to a man named Potiphar, the captain of the guard for Pharaoh.

Joseph went from being the second youngest child in a large family to being a slave in another country. What a transformation that must have been. But many of us know that swift transformation. You pour yourself into a job for years, and then one day the supervisor hands you a pink slip. Just like that you are let go. One day you had an office and a secretary, but the next day you are packing your personal items and trying to find a way to deal with the maelstrom of emotions you feel.

Maybe you have given a decade to build your marriage, but she still wants out. One day you go home to your house with the large front yard and the larger mortgage, but the next day you find your way to a tiny one-bedroom apartment. How can things change so quickly? How can anyone deal with such changes?

Joseph's story is unique in its details but not in its emotion. Most of us know about sibling rivalry and about all of the mixed feelings that come with it. Most of us also know that relationships and situations can spiral out of control so fast they make us dizzy. If you find yourself caught up in events that seem beyond your powers to guide them, take strength in the fact that God has not abandoned you either. He is still there with you even in an unemployment line or a new apartment.

Lord, things happen so fast. You know how it went. One day this, the next day that. One day I thought I was going this way, then suddenly I am going another way. How did all that happen? Help me deal with the realities of my life. Give me strength for this part of the journey. Through Christ, Amen.

JANUARY 15

TRUTH OR CONSEQUENCES
Genesis 42:1–38

Young Joseph was in Egypt as a slave. His older brothers, who should have been looking out for him, sold him to get rid of him. Their father, Jacob, was brokenhearted over what he thought was the death of his son. An entire family was in tatters because of the crime. Famine covered the land where Jacob's family lived, so they must travel far to seek food. Little did they know that they would find reconciliation.

This story sounds like it came out of the *National Inquirer* instead of the Bible. Jealousy, intrigue, lies, murder—they are all part of the story of Joseph and his brothers. Many men can identify with it. Many of us have had rocky relationships with our birth families. I know a man whose parents divorced when he was young. He went for fifteen years without seeing his father. I was present when they reconciled. The joy of that occasion could not completely erase the pain those years of separation had caused. Another man grew up in foster homes and carries with him a kind of vacuum in his heart regarding relationships. Still another man accidentally shot his brother when they were children. Now, years later, he cannot talk about that experience without great emotional pain.

Joseph had been dealt a heavy hand, but he played it well. Genesis 42 informs us that he could have ordered his brothers' execution because of his position. Instead, he toyed with them a bit and worked out a plan to bring the family back together. Isn't that amazing? He tried to reconcile with the very people who had betrayed him. What was the controlling factor in that? It was his belief that God was somehow in the process. What the brothers had intended for spite God had intended for good.

Trust that God is with you today, no matter what you are going through.

O God, my faith that You are here right now is sometimes weak. At times, You seem far away. Help me to realize that You are working in the circumstances of my life. No matter what others might intend, You intend good. I will count on that fact. Through Jesus my Lord, Amen.

JANUARY 16

BLESSING MY FAMILY
Genesis 49:1–28

Joseph finally succeeded in getting his scattered family together. They joined him in Egypt during a great famine. The father of all of those raucous brothers, Jacob, gathered all of his sons to give them his blessing before he died. One by one, the old man brought his sons before him and gave each his blessing.

When you read these blessings, you wonder what sort of blessings they were. Some seemed to be caustic, such as the ones for Reuben, Simeon, and Levi. Others were so short as to be mysterious, such as the one for Naphtali. But each one was a word from the father to the son that gave power and liberty. That is what a blessing is; it is something that empowers.

Did your father bless you? Mine did, though seldom with words. Dad was a toolpusher (the foreman on a drilling rig). One day, when I was about ten, a truck from a chemical supply company came lumbering down the board road on its way to the drilling site. The driver turned around and began backing up to the supply house. He could not see everything clearly and backed his truck into the radiator of one of the large diesel engines used to pump the drilling fluids. The truck driver stopped when he felt the bump and jumped out to see what had happened. He saw me standing there watching the accident. Dad came running over. Before Dad could say a word, the truck driver said, "That kid over there was in my way. I didn't want to run over him, so I had to swing around him. That's why I hit the pump. It's his fault."

I was stunned, but before I could think to speak, I saw my father get right up into the face of the driver. He yelled over the roar of the rig noise, "I saw exactly what happened. He was standing over here way out of your way. He didn't have anything to do with it. You're just a bad driver who just tore up my radiator. It's *your* fault, and your company is going to pay for getting it fixed. Got it?" The driver just nodded, pulled his truck out of the pierced radiator, and unloaded his supplies. Later, Dad told me, "I know that wasn't your fault, so don't worry about it. And if anyone ever tries to blame you for something like that again, you come tell me. We'll get it straight in a hurry." That was a blessing. It gave me power and the knowledge that I was loved.

I have always tried to do that with my family. I don't always get it right, but I try. Bless your family right now. Don't wait for a deathbed blessing.

You have blessed me, Lord. I want to bless my family in turn. Let my words and actions be power, love, and liberty to them. In Christ, Amen.

BURYING MY FATHER

Genesis 49:29–50:14

Jacob, the last of the great patriarchs, died in old age. His life had been rich and full. It was challenged, pushed, stretched, and sometimes miserable, but Jacob had really lived. Then, when his time came, he "was gathered to his people" (v. 33). I love that phrase. It gives the sense of purposeful homecoming rather than senseless death.

Joseph and his brothers grieved for Jacob. The biblical scene seems unusual to Americans. We are used to having death handled by the professionals. It seems unreal. But the fact is always there. For most of us men, to lose a father is a great blow. I know. Some men have a strained relationship with their father. Their death seems not to raise even a ripple on the emotional sea. But the truth is that all men want to have a close relationship with their fathers.

My father died of lung cancer when he was seventy-five. He had struggled with that disease for a year. He had surgery that seemed to arrest it for a while, but it came back with a vengeance. I remember going to visit him in the hospital during those last weeks. He got progressively weaker and could hardly talk. My twin sons were about six at the time. He tried to talk to them, but it was difficult. I could see the life ebb from him with each visit. When the call came that he had died, I was sad but not surprised. We had never had a close relationship in the sense that I would tell him all of my personal problems and dreams. Dad was an oilfield toolpusher—as tough as shoe leather—but he had his "soft" side. I loved and respected him and still miss him.

He drilled oil wells in England for a top-secret project during World War II. I have a book titled *The Secret of Sherwood Forest* that tells about that work. It has his name and picture in it. Recently, I showed my sons that book. It was good to see Dad young and strong.

How is it between you and your father? Is he still living? If so, do whatever you can to get close to him. If he is gone, remember those positive parts of your relationship. If that is impossible, thank God that He is your heavenly Father.

Most of us will bury our fathers. That is the life to which God appoints us. But think of the heavenly reunion to come!

Lord, I thank you for my father. He was such a unique guy. Smart. Tough. Sometimes tender. His dumb jokes and stinky cigars were so much a part of him. Thanks for the legacy I have from him. Thank You that I still have a father—a heavenly Father—You. In Christ, Amen.

JANUARY 18

Unknown

Exodus 1

A friend received a "pink slip" recently. The company that had employed him for years had been going through some changes. New managers were brought in to streamline the company. The older employees—who called themselves the "gray dogs"—thought that they were safe because of their experience and tenure. Management did not agree. Many of the most experienced people were terminated. They were unwanted.

Change happens. The book of Genesis ends with Joseph and his family firmly established in Egypt. Then Exodus begins with the Egyptians beginning to be suspicious of the Hebrews. They were too numerous. Verse 8 speaks of a new king who did not know about Joseph. Generations had passed. The wonderful efficiency that Joseph had brought to Pharaoh was lost in history. Joseph? Who is that? Besides, what has he done for us lately?

We wince when we read those words. We like to think that once we establish ourselves we are set for life. But the truth is sometimes brutally different. We have to win our successes many times. Riding a wave of achievement will last only so long, then it's time to get on the next wave and do it all over again. That is difficult. Change in America happens so fast that we can hardly keep up. Whatever our work might be, we feel that we are running hard just to keep up. The Chrysler Corporation nearly went bankrupt in the late 1960s and early 1970s. They had been resting on the laurels of past achievement and did not spend time or money thinking about the future. Finally, they woke up and launched a campaign to reposition their company as a leader.

There is always a new leader who does not know Joseph. We have to keep up with change and resist the temptation of living off past achievement. That is where our faith comes in. God is actively working in His world. He knows what we face. Trust Him to give you strength for the journey. Lean on Him during times of crises. Pharaoh did not know about Joseph, but God did.

Lord, the world seems to be spinning faster and faster. You know what I face at work. You know that at times I can hardly keep up, much less get ahead. But I will trust You, and I will be diligent in my work. Give me strength for the journey. Through Christ, Amen.

JANUARY 19

A Mistake

Exodus 2:11–25

Have you ever made a mistake so huge that you thought you could not live it down? We all have made enormous mistakes. So did Moses. He grew up in wealth and privilege. He lived in the palace of pharaoh, but he knew that he was a Hebrew, not an Egyptian. One day, Moses saw an Egyptian beating one of his people, so in the white-hot blaze of anger Moses killed the Egyptian and hid his body in the sand. Just like that, through that one terrible act, Moses became a wanted man. Pharaoh tried to kill him, but he ran away and was separated from his people for many years.

Sad, isn't it? We can spend a lifetime building a career and a family only to have it damaged by one senseless act. One night with another woman. One dip into the company funds. One act of violence. I know a man who confessed that he had broken every one of the Ten Commandments except murder. He was not sure about that one, though, because he fought in World War II and did not know if killing the enemy counted.

Are you running from something in your past? Do you think no one knows? A man sat in my study one day and confessed the wasted years of his life—drinking heavily, ignoring his family, failing to plan for the future. The gist of the conversation was his sense of shame at having let down everyone, including God. I reminded him that God already knew everything that he had confessed to me and that God would like to hear the man's confession. This huge man sat crying and pouring out his failures to God and asking Jesus into his life. Later he said, "I feel like ten tons have been lifted from my shoulders!"

You cannot run fast enough to escape God. You cannot busy yourself enough to make up for your mistakes alone. The good news of the gospel is that you do not equal your mistakes. You are more than your blunders and sins. Confess it all to God and ask for forgiveness. If you have injured someone, you might need to make some restitution. Remember, the Lord wants you whole and well. That comes with forgiveness and moving beyond your mistakes.

Lord, You know, don't You? You are aware of everything I've ever done that is sin in Your sight. Every mistake, every blunder, every intentional act of cruelty—You see it all. Would You forgive me and cleanse me? I ask Your pardon in Jesus' name, Amen.

JANUARY 20

BUSHED

Exodus 3:1–9

Moses was bushed. He had been running from his past. The murder of an Egyptian had him on the run for years. Then one day Moses was "bushed" in another way—God appeared to him in the form of a bush that seemed to burn but was not consumed in the process. God decided to reveal Himself to Moses in this most unusual way.

Encounters with God have ways of taking on a life of their own. I wrote these words while vacationing in Key West, Florida. While watching the sun set in the Gulf, I thought of Moses and his encounter with God. I do not know exactly what the bush looked like to Moses, but I could easily see why he felt attracted to it. Something about the encounter spoke to Moses and seemed godlike. Have you had such an experience?

Your encounter with God may have come in various ways. Maybe it came while watching an especially gorgeous sunset, but maybe it came when you were closing a special business deal, or running a sander over a fine piece of lumber, or serving a meal in a homeless shelter, or meeting someone who seemed godlike. Meetings with God can come in various ways, but they point to the same direction—to pay attention. Elizabeth Barrett Browning once wrote, "Earth's crammed with heaven and every common bush afire with God."[1]

God uses various ways to get our attention. You are reading this book because you want to give God your attention. You might have mixed feelings about that. You might not know what to do, or you might wonder what you are getting yourself into. That is okay. Everyone struggles with those feelings. The important thing to remember is this: when you see the bush flaming, pay attention!

Lord, burn brightly before me. Let Your radiance be a beacon for my attention. Teach me to take off my shoes in reverence in Your presence. Through the power of Jesus, Amen.

JANUARY 21

PLAGUED

Exodus 8–11

You can hardly read the accounts of the plagues without wondering, *What was Pharaoh thinking?* The story is well known. Moses went to the leader of Egypt, demanding that the Hebrews be allowed to leave the country. What had begun as a welcoming of strangers under Joseph had ended up becoming outright slavery.

---

1. Elizabeth Barrett Browning, "Aurora Leigh" Book VII, 821–22.

But God saw the trouble of His people and sent Moses to lead them to freedom.

When Moses spoke to Pharaoh about releasing the Hebrews, the king wanted to know why he should do such a thing. After finally promising to release the Hebrews, Pharaoh changed his mind—several times. Chapters 8–11 of Exodus tell the story of the plagues and their purpose. Through them, God was trying to get the king's attention. A plague would come upon Egypt, Pharaoh would agree to let the Hebrews go, the problem would pass, and then the king would change his mind. Then another plague would come to get his attention again!

All of this makes me wonder about the lengths to which God is willing to go to get my attention. I do not see the plagues as "punishment" as such. They seem to be incidents designed to get the king's attention so that God could communicate to him. But Pharaoh kept ignoring the message. Before I get too haughty, I wonder how many of God's messages *I* have ignored. I have had my share of problems, of course, but nothing like a series of plagues. Even so, I wonder what God has been trying to say to me.

I do not think that every form of trouble that comes to us is divine punishment, but I do think that God can use every experience to communicate to us. Are you going through a trying experience now? Has your house seemed to be consumed by plagues? Do you feel like old Pharaoh, wondering where the next disaster might come from? Our lives are filled with trials and problems. There is no way to avoid them. What we need to do is to ensure that we are not bringing them on ourselves through stubbornness and disobedience. If you are guiltless and trouble comes anyway, ask where the voice of God might be in it. It's funny how the Lord shows up in the most unexpected places.

Thank you, Lord, for being there in all experiences, especially the trying ones. At times I feel abandoned or, at least, lonely. Help me to remember that You are with me always, especially during the rough times. Keep me close. I need You.
In Christ, Amen.

THE BIG TEN
(PART 1)
Exodus 20:1–17

A series of roadside billboards have appeared all over the country. They are communications from God and say things like, "Keep using my name in vain and I'll make the commute longer"; and "What part of 'Thou shall not' don't you understand?" I laughed when I first saw them. The idea of God coming to communicate with puny mortals like me seems funny. But that is precisely what happened.

Moses led his people out of Egyptian oppression, but the people were an unruly mob of ex-slaves. They needed something to draw them together and form them into a cohesive group. Moses was given the Law—what we call the Ten Commandments—to give to the people. Those laws helped the people know that they belonged to God. It pulled them together and helped to define them.

We might think of the Ten Commandments as God's way of spoiling all of our fun. In one way they are! But in a far more significant way they show us the way to God's rule and help us understand who we are. Consider the first one: "I am the LORD your God, . . . You shall have no other gods before me." That helps us know that God is unique—special and unlike any other so-called gods. Because that is true, we have a unique relationship with Him. The second commandment has to do with keeping our ideas about God pure and ever growing. If we could reduce Him to a statue in idolatry, God would not be much of a deity.

The third commandment is about keeping God's name holy—pure, special, and unpolluted. The greatest blasphemy is not a four-letter word. It is attaching God's name to some ungodly enterprise and claiming His leadership for something that is not of Him. The fourth commandment reminds us that we are designed for a pace that includes rest and reflection. Our 24/7 world seems to drive us all to distraction. God says, "Take the seventh day and rest and worship."

Commandment five is a clear word to care for our aging parents. That might mean having them in our home, if possible, but the best care might be in a facility designed to care for them. No family is perfect, but do the best you can.

> *God, I have heard You through the Ten Commandments. I have not done a good job with all of them. Give me the will to keep trying and to realize that I'll never keep them perfectly. Only through Christ do I have any hope. Through Him, save me. Amen.*

JANUARY 23

THE BIG TEN (PART 2)
Exodus 20:1–17

The Ten Commandments are God's word to His people about living in relationship with Him and with other people. Let's look at the next five.

Commandment six seems clear enough: do not murder. But people are still debating the meaning of those words. For example, does murder include the taking of all human life, including capital punishment? This, and other debates, should not force us off track here. We are clear enough about the intent—life is to be respected and protected. Period. I have no right to take your life nor you mine.

Many people think that the seventh commandment is out of date. "Hey, what's a little adultery? Everybody does it!" Some of you reading this book would give anything to be able to reverse some poor decisions in this regard. The Bible makes the sanctity of marriage absolute. I saw a cartoon once that had a teenager asking his grandfather a question about safe sex: "When you were young, what did you wear for protection?" The older man smiled and said, "A wedding ring."

Command eight establishes the fact that what is mine is not yours. I have had things stolen from me, and the experience always leaves me upset. I worked to earn those items; the thief did not.

The ninth commandment forces us to be honest. Real honesty has to come from the inside, of course, but this one helps us know that the great Judge of the universe will not overlook dishonesty. We can so easily injure people by telling lies about them.

The last commandment is about keeping our greed in check. It is a matter of our spirit. The Scripture has much to say about being satisfied with what we have. If you need something else, create value for someone else by earning it. Don't expect someone to earn it for you.

The Ten Commandments are still in effect because we always need guidance in our thinking and our actions.

Thank You, Lord, for giving us these guidelines that help us gauge our lives according to Your design. Give us strength for the journey. Through Christ, Amen.

JANUARY 24

BOVINE THEOLOGY

Exodus 32:19–24

The story is as old as humankind. Moses went up to Mount Sinai to commune with God. He was gone a long time—much longer than anyone expected. The people began to go a little mad. They spoke harshly against Moses, and then they had a party! Aaron took jewelry from the people and fashioned a calf from the gold. He showed it to the people and said, "Here is your god."

When Moses finally returned, he confronted the people, especially his brother Aaron. Aaron's defense was the classic sidestep: "They gave me the gold, and I threw it into the fire, and out came this calf!" (v. 24). Life with no consequences!

I've been guilty of this sort of thinking, and you have too. Just do whatever you want—give in to the pressures around you. If you get caught and have to account for it, hey, it's no big deal. Just blame the system, or the leader, or God. Slither and slide, but don't ever take responsibility. "It's not my fault!" That is what we have taught an entire generation to say.

But wake up! It is our responsibility. I spoke with a friend recently who was having trouble in his marriage. His difficulty has been an enormous wake-up call to him. To his credit, he said, "I realize that 90 percent of our difficulties have been my fault. I'm committed to do whatever it takes to try to make this right." He knows he is late, but at least he is not sidestepping.

I wish I could have seen the expression on Moses' face when Aaron spoke those maddeningly silly words: "I threw it into the fire, and out came this calf!" We had better be careful what we throw into life's fire. We might be surprised at what will come out.

Lord, I've been careless with what I've thrown into the fire. More than that, Lord, I've tried to dance around the consequences. Help me to wake up! Help me to sow only what I want to reap. Forgive my silliness and my sin. Restore me, for Christ's sake. Amen.

JANUARY 25

WORSHIP MATTERS
Exodus 40:1–33

Worship really matters. We sometimes have the fuzzy idea that worship is just sending up "good thoughts" toward God and that nothing more specific matters. But read today's passage carefully. Moses set up the tabernacle with great care and specific instructions. The proverb is true: "God is in the details." We read about all of the preparations and wonder what that might have to do with us in the twenty-first century. It has to do with our attitude.

For the early Hebrews, worship was serious business. God was not some far-away deity. He was the liberator who had led them out of slavery. He was present, active, and worthy of their best. That fact pulls me up short, especially when I consider a worship service that I recently attended.

It was poorly planned. People forgot several parts of the service and had to try to make it up as they went along. The pastor was elderly and fell down the steps coming from the dais. The music leader called on all single people to stand, then asked them to come up and join the choir! The pastor's sermon rambled all over the place, and I had trouble following him. All in all, it was a disaster. What disturbed me more was that no one else seemed to notice. I wondered if worship was that haphazard every week.

Worship is not an option for a disciple of Jesus. It is our filling-station, our place to get the spiritual batteries recharged. Worship is getting outside of ourselves long enough for God to get inside. Then worship becomes an act of adoration. I want to offer God my best. That includes my preparation and my attitude. Moses was careful with the matters of God. How are you doing with them?

Don't be careless with things divine. God deserves our best. Okay?

I confess, Lord, that I've been too quick in my attitude and actions. I have not always given You the best I have to offer. Forgive me and help me offer You my best. You deserve my time and atten-tion. I offer them both freely. Please accept them as my offering. In Christ, Amen.

JANUARY 26

RESPONSIBILITIES OF FREEDOM
Leviticus 1

The book of Leviticus picks up where Exodus ends. The first seven chapters are all about different offerings. The people were to offer them as symbols of both their identity as God's people and their devotion. The offerings helped to set them apart as different from the people around them.

Modern readers tend to get bogged down in Leviticus because of all of the seemingly obsolete practices. But what were those all about? They were the ways the early Hebrews expressed their re-sponsibilities of freedom. For them, freedom was not only free *from* but also free *for.* They had shaken off the shackles of the Egyptians, and now they were willingly becoming identified with the Lord. They were His people, and that meant acting in certain ways.

The modern mind-set suggests that we are free to do anything we wish. But unless people have guidelines for behavior and goals to pursue, life seems empty. Look around you. Our streets are filled with people who have no goals, no dreams, no standards of ethical behavior. They are "free," but look where it gets them.

Freedom is costly. It requires a disciplined approach to living, including worship and devotion. Read Leviticus 17–19. You will see all sorts of prescriptions for the free life. When you know the wrong path, you are then free to take the right path.

We are still early in the year—late January. How are you doing with your devotional life? Do you need to remember the responsibilities of freedom and be more diligent? Maybe you are doing okay, and you deserve a pat on the back and an "Atta boy!" Consider it given. God loves you more than you can imagine. In return, He wants us to be good men. As hard as that might be, it is worth the effort.

Lord, help me use my freedom for Your honor and not for anything that will injure anyone. I want to be a good man—Your man. Give me the strength to get out of any situation I might be in that is slavery, and help me move toward free-dom. In Christ, Amen

JANUARY 27

THE DREADED "T" WORD

Leviticus 27:30–34

I can give you a word that is sure to cause sweat to form on your upper lip and a trembling to start down your right arm. What is that word? *Tithe.* People seem to dread that word because it dredges up images of guilt, pain, deprivation, and all sorts of other bad feelings. But should it?

The biblical picture of the tithe is of a healthy respect for God and His provisions. The tithe was a sign that people realized that everything came from God. Giving ten percent back as an act of respect had several clear goals. First, it was an act of worship. Second, it gave a sense of perspective to the person giving it. Third, it helped to cure the greed impulse in the tither.

Is tithing still a valid act of obedience today? Yes! I have heard many discussions and read studies by people who suggest that tithing is an Old Testament concept and, therefore, no longer valid. They say that Jesus never said, "Thou shalt tithe." No, He did not. He assumed that people would tithe. His trouble was not with the act of tithing but with people who played games with it. Jesus was looking for a willing heart in every act of worship.

Let me introduce you to Esther, a woman who was a member of the church where I first began my ministry. Esther and her two small children attended regularly and gave to the offering each week. One day, she asked to speak to me after church. She said, "I feel bad that I can't give a full tithe of 10 percent to the church." She explained that she did not work outside the home. Her husband gave her a strict amount to run the household. He was not a Christian and did not give Esther anything for church. When she went shopping, she used every cents-off coupon she could. Whatever money she saved that way she gave to the church. It amounted to a few dollars a week.

She wanted to give more but could not. I think the Lord understands and accepts her offering with pleasure. Most people are not in her situation. We could give more but simply do not. What about you? Where is your heart regarding God's tithe?

Lord, You know my heart. I have gotten myself into situations that are not healthy spiritually or financially. Help me learn to take responsibility for everything in my life. Help me honor You with a tithe as a sign of my love. In Jesus' name, Amen.

JANUARY 28

BEING GOD'S PEOPLE
Numbers

You will notice that I have not given you a specific text for today. Instead, I merely pointed you to the book of Numbers. Before you panic, stay with me for a minute. Thumb through this forbidding-looking book, and you will see names of tribes, their arrangements in the camps, chapters of regulations, tests of various sorts, and other elements of tribal life. The point of all this is that God was forging this motley group into His special people.

Do not underestimate the chaos of coming out of Egyptian slavery and forming into a nation. It was a messy process. The people failed time and again. God led them, sometimes rewarding, sometimes punishing. But, all in all, He was shaping the people into a special group that would be His.

The Lord is still doing this. He takes men like you and me and shapes us into the kinds of people He can use. He makes us ready to serve in His current special group, the church. Again, do not underestimate the difficulty of that task. God shapes us, leads us, teaches us, guides us, and often says to us, "No, this is not the way." In that process, we are becoming men He can use. Do you sometimes find that you have trouble being shaped? Join the club! The book of Numbers gives us a picture of what it means to be God's people, but it is not a pretty picture. Like those early Hebrews, we are still kicking and screaming as we go.

In chapter 13, a group of spies went into the land of Canaan and returned with their report. Ten of the group thought that the task of taking that land was too difficult for them. Only two, Joshua and Caleb, thought that it was possible. That is the kind of odds we still face today. Many opinions are against us, and obstacles litter the path like boulders on a ledge. But our job as men of God is to press on, ignoring the naysayers, and be what God can help make us.

Forward, march!

> *Lord, You know my challenges. I'm often like the men in Numbers—unsure, reluctant, and even rebellious. Help shape and form me, Lord. I am Yours, and I want to be what You can make me. Through Christ, Amen.*

THE SUCCESSION DILEMMA

Numbers 27:12–23

Have you ever had to fill the shoes of a big man? A really big man? Some of us have tried. Maybe it was your father's shoes you tried to fill. Or maybe it was someone at work who seemed like a giant to everyone and then they looked to you. In today's Bible reading, Joshua was chosen to take the place of Moses. How could anyone hope to succeed in such a task?

It was Moses who led the children of Israel out of Egypt. He kept them in check as they moved, sometimes hauntingly slowly, through the desert. He interceded with God when they got too full of themselves and lost touch with the Lord. To many of the people, Moses was like God Himself. He was the only leader many of them had ever known. I have heard people speak of their feelings when Franklin Roosevelt died in office. Because he was in his fourth term as president, many people had not known any other president.

Can you imagine how Joshua felt at being selected to pick up where Moses had left off? He was aided because God told Moses, "Give him some of your authority so the whole Israelite community will obey him" (v. 20). That and the help of God got Joshua through that pressure-cooker transition.

Every man comes to a time when he picks up where others left off. For some people, that time comes early; for others it comes late. My father had to quit school when he was in the seventh grade and go to work. He was able to make a good living for his family, but he missed much of his childhood. His situation did not seem to bother him. He accepted the challenge and did well.

What has been transferred to your shoulders? What do you need to hoist and carry because it's your turn? Do you have a wife who is your responsibility? Do you have a child who looks to you for leadership and support? You have some big shoes to fill. That is okay. Your feet are large enough.

Lord, the burden seems heavy at times. I wonder if I
can shoulder the load. But You have given me the grace
to carry on. Help me not to stumble. In Christ, Amen.

JANUARY 30

THE GREAT DISCOVERY
Deuteronomy 6:4–9

One of the great passages of the Old Testament is today's text because it gives the people of God a target toward which to move. They lived in a land of many so-called gods. The great discovery of the Jews was that there was one, and only one, God. This passage of Scripture is called the Shema and begins with these unforgettable words: "Hear, O Israel: The LORD our God, the LORD is one" (v. 4).

I call this the great discovery because it was the great unifying idea for the Jews. God was one, solitary, not fragmented into hundreds of deities. He is the creator of all that existed and the sustainer of His people. This does not really speak to what Christians call the Trinity. The way God deals with His people today is through the Father, Son, and Holy Spirit. Those ideas were refined in the New Testament. For our purposes today, we can see that religion took a great leap forward when the people realized that only one God exists.

Now what does all of this have to do with men? This: we still need a strong, unifying principle in our lives. We get so busy and feel pulled in so many different directions. The centrifugal forces of life seem to spin us away from the center to the outer edges. When I feel pushed and strained, squeezed and squashed, I need to remember that at the center is God. I doubt seriously that anyone reading this book does not understand what I mean. Nearly everybody I know seems spun out!

When you are driven away from the center of your life, pause and remember the ancient Hebrew affirmation that brought a nation into being and held it together: The LORD is one. Because He is, we are to love Him "with all your heart and with all your soul and with all your strength." In addition, we are to teach our children about this center of living. God is an invited guest in our home as we talk to our household about Him. His name is upon our "doorframes" and "gates," that is, we live in a constant awareness of His presence in our lives. That is good news. God, the only Deity, wants to be close to us.

*Thank You, Lord, for Your closeness. I invite You
to be at home in my life and in my house. Help
me always to remember when the pressures of life
get me down that You are there at the center of
everything. I always have a spiritual home to
which to return. In Jesus' name, Amen.*

SAYING GOOD-BYE TO A GIANT

Deuteronomy 34

It is never easy to say good-bye to a giant. The Hebrews must
have felt that way when Moses died. He had been everything to
them—leader, visionary guide, defender, interpreter of God's will—
everything. The book of Deuteronomy ends with a fitting tribute:
"Since then, no prophet has risen in Israel like Moses, whom the
LORD knew face to face. . . . For no one has ever shown the mighty
power or performed the awesome deeds that Moses did in the sight
of all Israel" (vv. 10, 12).

You and I have had to say good-bye to some giants in our lives.
I think of a man who was a caring mentor to me. He was always
interested in what was on my mind and loved to talk about my
plans and dreams. I had him speak in my church and simply loved
being around him. When the time came for him to retire, I felt like
crying. He moved out of state but still kept in touch. I once flew
out to Texas to visit him after he retired. He took me around his
new area, and we talked for hours about everything. In my mind,
he was a giant.

I think about a teacher I once had. He had been a scholar of
unequaled depth. He knew everyone in religion and politics. His
achievements filled books. I took a class with him once and felt
intimidated the whole time, but he was very kind to me. I went to
his house and visited with him several times and marveled at the
depth of his knowledge and the breadth of his spirit. When he died,
I attended his funeral and wept. He was a giant.

Sooner or later, we all have to bury our giants. The consolation
is in knowing that what they were to us we can be to someone else.

I don't mean that we try to be what we are not. But we can show interest in others and let them know that we love and respect them. Who knows? Maybe in their eyes we will be giants.

Thank You for putting those great people in our paths, Father. They have blessed us and helped make us who we are. Help us be that for someone coming along behind us. Through our Savior, Amen.

FEBRUARY 1

WHOM WILL YOU SERVE?
Joshua 1:8–9

The sheet of paper is no bigger than a postcard. It is slightly pinkish—and extremely valuable. This piece of paper is so important that it was exhibited around the country for several months before being auctioned in London. Its final price brought more than $5 million to the paper's owner!

What makes this small piece of paper so valuable? After all, the only thing on it is a light sketch of a rearing horse and rider. The value comes from the person who drew it. The artist is none other than Leonardo da Vinci. The sketch is a preparatory study for the Italian artist's first great composition, *The Adoration of the Magi*. Of the five-hundred-year-old sheet, a spokesman for Christie's auction house said, "It is probably the most important drawing by the artist to come to auction in nearly a century. It is very powerful."

Take a closer look at your Bible. In appearance, it is merely a book. Yet it is powerful because it contains all of the revealed truth of God! Within its pages you will find treasures far more valuable than a five-hundred-year-old sketch by da Vinci. The written Word of God reveals the living Word of God—Jesus.

At the dawn of Joshua's leadership of Israel, God promised him greatness and success—*if Joshua soaked himself in the Scripture and followed God's commandments.* His willingness to do so assured Israel of victory in the Promised Land.

What kind of man are you? The promises that God made to

Joshua are equally available for your own life. You might never lead a nation, but you may very well lead a family, a Bible class, an accountability group. Your dedication to God's Word will make you more effective in every area of your life. If you've not yet done so, commit to making the Bible a powerful part of your everyday life.

Dear Father, thank You for the promises contained in the Bible. Help me develop a hunger for Scripture. I commit to reading Your Word every day and applying its principles to my life. May I become the leader and the man You want me to be. In Jesus' name, Amen.

FEBRUARY 2

TOTAL DEDICATION
Joshua 3:5

You've probably never heard of Mrs. Lillian O'Donahue. She lived in Australia and was a telephone operator in the days before automated telephone service. She was far off the beaten track; her office was in a small white building miles down a dusty road. No one would think that Mrs. O'Donahue could ever make a difference in the world, much less a critical space voyage. Yet that is just what she did.

During a NASA space mission in 1964, a vital communications link between one of the key satellite dishes and a tracking station near Adelaide broke down. Technicians searched frantically for a viable option to help the astronauts miles above Earth's surface. They discovered Mrs. Lillian O'Donahue and her ancient equipment just in time.

Through one long, difficult night, this dedicated woman carefully recorded strings of coded messages from one outpost and passed them on to the next. Every time the Gemini craft flew over the southern skies, the fate of the entire mission lay in Mrs. O'Donahue's hands. As we now know from history, the back-road telephone operator fulfilled her mission faithfully and successfully. Her reward? Mrs. O'Donahue made six dollars in overtime money.[1]

When ordinary men and women dedicate themselves, they are capable of accomplishing extraordinary deeds. Take, for example, the men and women under Joshua's command. Today's passage sees them consecrating themselves to God before a major encounter with the enemy. Because they dedicated themselves wholly to the Lord, they watched the walls of Jericho crumble to dust.

What does God want to do with your life? Give yourself to Him completely, and He will work through you to accomplish mighty things. You probably won't pull down a city's walls. But God might use you to build up your brothers in Christ, heal marriages, or strengthen your church.

Dear Lord, I want to be used by You and for You to make a difference in this world. I give You every area of my life and ask You to cleanse me completely. In Jesus' name, Amen.

CREATING ANCHORS FOR YOUR FAMILY
Joshua 4:21–23

The stones stood in the middle of the Jordan River for years. A young boy passing by with his father might ask, "How in the world did those twelve huge stones get piled up in the middle of a river?"

What would be the father's response? He could have said, "We don't have time to talk about this right now. I've got to hurry to Jerusalem." Or he might have said, "I don't know. Ask your mother."

But if the father counted himself a follower of Jehovah—if he obeyed God's instructions—he would have stopped, taken the boy by the hand, and explained the miracle of God's drying up the Jordan just long enough for the Israelites to cross. He would tell

---

1. Bill Bryson, *In a Sunburned Country* (New York: Broadway Books, 2000), 301.

his son that those stones were a reminder of the power and majesty of God in the life of each person.

Fathers, God has placed children in your household so that you might nurture them spiritually. It is your responsibility to tell them the great stories of the Bible. You are the one who should be taking a strong part in helping them understand what Jesus Christ can mean to their lives. Those little ones are looking to you for guidance. By your habits and deeds, show them the power of God to transform lives.

Heavenly Father, help me to take seriously my role as spiritual leader in this house. May my daily actions and words lead my children unerringly toward a relationship with You. In Jesus' name, Amen.

FEBRUARY 4

DEALING WITH OBSTACLES
Joshua 6:20

Bronko Nagurski played on the early Chicago Bears football team. The Bears had a reputation for tough, gritty players, and Bronko stood as the toughest of them all. Broken tackles and shattered teeth seemed common when Bronko ran with the ball.

The Bears' owner, George Halas, loved to tell about the time Bronko took the ball, tucked his head down, and blasted through the opposition like they were kindling. Rumbling into the end zone, he kept going with his head down—until he hit the brick wall of Wrigley Field. When he returned to the sidelines, he admitted to the coach, "That last guy gave me a pretty good lick!"[1]

Whether brick walls or the walls of Jericho, all of us have to face hard obstacles from time to time in our life. We can turn away from them in fear, or we can face them in faith. God has promised to be with us every step of the way through this world. If we trust Him at every turn, we'll discover that some walls crumble, some hit us

---

1. Scott Simon, *Home and Away* (New York: Hyperion, 2000), 80.

with a pretty good lick, but none ultimately can destroy us. God's presence assures us of the strength to meet—and defeat—every wall that Satan can raise against us.

God, help me to trust You with this day. Help me remember that no matter what happens, Your presence means that I can meet it with confidence. In Jesus' name, Amen.

FEBRUARY 5

THE POWER OF FORGIVENESS
Joshua 6:25

Forgiveness. It's a wonderful, miraculous gift. We've just read about a prostitute who lived in a city getting ready to be destroyed. Talk about a lose-lose situation! Yet, God saw her heart and offered her a second chance. Rahab, at the risk of being killed by the city's inhabitants, helped the Israelites and so received a new life, a new people, and a new Savior. This prostitute-turned-godly-woman became one of the ancestors of Jesus Christ!

Forgiveness. We all need it. Maybe you've done something that has ruined your reputation, your Christian witness—maybe even hurt your family. God can forgive you today, no matter what you've done. Admit that you need help, receive God's pardon, and then change your habits. He can still use you for His kingdom. The God of the Second Chance wants to help you today.

Father, I acknowledge my sins to You. I do not try to hide them or blame them on anyone else. Please forgive me completely and help me to serve You once again. In Jesus' name, Amen.

GREED OR GOD?

Joshua 7:11–12

The third-grade teacher was demonstrating a math problem for her students. "Johnny," she asked, "if you had three pieces of candy and I asked you for one of them, how many would you have left?"

"I'd still have three, teacher," responded Johnny.

Greed. Selfishness. If we're not careful, these qualities can ruin our life. Business best-sellers may promote the value of these dubious attributes, but God's Word commands us to stay far away from them.

In today's Scripture passage, Joshua and the Israelites received a vivid lesson from God on the destructive properties of greed and selfishness. Someone in the Israeli camp had taken something from Jericho and kept it for himself. It should have been sacrificed to God. The result cost the Israelites a battle that they should have won, resulting in the loss of lives and confidence. In response to Joshua's anguished cry of "Why did this happen to us?" God told His people that they cannot have a right relationship with Him while withholding for themselves that which is rightfully His.

Flash forward to the last book in the Old Testament. Through Malachi the prophet, God says,

> "Will a man rob God? Yet you rob me.
> "But you ask, 'How do we rob you?'
> "In tithes and offerings. . . . Bring the whole tithe into the storehouse, that there may be food in my house. Test me in this," says the LORD Almighty, "and see if I will not throw open the floodgates of heaven and pour out so much blessing that you will not have room enough for it." (Malachi 3:8, 10)

What are you withholding from God? If you want victory in every area of your life, you'll give God first place in your money and time. Make sure you're not stealing from the Lord that which is His. Let Him have control of your checkbook and your priorities.

*Heavenly Father, Help me to care more about You
than I do about money and the acquisition of
"things." Right now, before Your throne, I give
you the key to every area of my life. In Jesus'
name, Amen.*

REMAINING FAITHFUL
Joshua 14:10–12

*And now, behold, the LORD has kept me alive, as He said, these
forty-five years, ever since the LORD spoke this word to Moses
while Israel wandered in the wilderness; and now, here I am
this day, eighty-five years old. As yet I am as strong this day
as I was on the day that Moses sent me; just as my strength
was then, so now is my strength for war, both for going out
and for coming in. Now therefore, give me this mountain of
which the LORD spoke in that day; for you heard in that day
how the Anakim were there, and that the cities were great and
fortified. It may be that the LORD will be with me, and I shall
be able to drive them out as the LORD said. (NKJV)*

The preceding words were spoken by Caleb. At eighty-five, he
could have retired. Instead, we find this man asking for a mountain
to subdue! Caleb should be a model for men everywhere. Like him,
we need to be faithful to God all of the way to the end of our lives.

Some of us have known men who started off living for the Lord,
but are now, for one reason or another, no longer serving Him. It
matters not what spectacular successes a man might have had in
the past while serving God. We are in a marathon, not a sprint.
And our goal should be that as we draw our last breath we can say,
"I remained faithful." Caleb did it. And so can you.

*God, please help me to remain faithful through-
out my life. May nothing I face be as important
to me as my relationship with You. In Jesus'
name, Amen.*

GOD'S PROMISES AND YOUR LIFE
Joshua 21:43–45

Are you interested in buying some real estate? Recently, John MacLeod had some for sale. Was it a house? Well . . . it was at least that. Was it a farm? Partly, yes.

In reality, MacLeod put up an entire mountain range for sale in Scotland! Part of the Inner Hebrides, these mountains cover about thirty-five square miles. They contain more than fourteen miles of coastline, two salmon rivers, a licensed campsite, a sheep farm, a farmhouse, cottages, and other farm buildings. All of this could be had for a paltry $16 million. MacLeod said that he would use the money to keep his castle (Dunvegan Castle) in good shape.[1]

Let's face it, few of us can afford anything close to a $16 million mountain range. But, believe it or not, we can have something far better! Look once more at verse 45 in the preceding passage. God kept every one of His promises to the children of Israel.

The Bible tells us that God "is the same yesterday and today and forever" (Heb. 13:8). His hundreds of promises to Christians are waiting to impact *your life.* The same God who faithfully kept all of His promises to the Israelites will also act mightily in your life. You need only trust in Him and claim those promises. Remember: "Without faith it is impossible to please God, because anyone who comes to him must believe that he exists and that he rewards those who earnestly seek him" (Heb. 11:6).

Seek God's face. Claim His promises. And believe that the Lord will be faithful in answering those promises in your life—beginning today.

Heavenly Father, please forgive my sometimes lack of faith. Help me to read Your Word and discover Your promises to believers. May I claim those promises for my own life, and may You receive glory for everything You do for me. In Jesus' name, Amen.

---

1. Nytimes.com, 22 March 2000.

FEBRUARY 9

STAYING ON THE PATH
Joshua 23:6–8

The twenty-three-year-old African lived in a village in Ghana. He and several of his friends asked the local *jujuman*—or witch doctor—to make them invincible to bullets. After smearing his body with a concoction of herbs every day for two weeks, the young man was ready to try out the potion.

He volunteered to be shot at by one of his friends to test the potency of the witch doctor's brew. You can guess the rest of the story. One of the other men fetched a rifle and shot the Ghanaian. The young man died instantly, in spite of the potion and the witch doctor's assurance. Angry residents seized the *jujuman* and beat him severely. Had a village elder not interceded, the witch doctor also would have been dead.[1]

Will we never learn? False gods and fake leaders might sound compelling. Many people might even follow their teachings. But God tells us that our hope, health, and prosperity rest in following—completely—God's commands. When we "turn aside to the right or to the left" (Deut. 5:32), we leave the path of God's protection. This departure leaves us open to deadly temptations that Satan can fire at our unprotected life.

Are you leaving the path of God's protection in some area? Ask God's forgiveness, turn away from it, and allow God's mercy and grace to restore you.

Lord, You know my areas of weakness. Help me to stay close to You, instead of trying to make it through this life on my own. Protect me from Satan's temptations as I trust in You daily. In Jesus' name, Amen.

---

1. Excite.com/news, 15 March 2001.

A LINE IN THE SAND
Joshua 24:15

But as for me and my house, we will serve the LORD. (NKJV)

There comes a time in the life of every man when he must draw a line in the sand and say, "This is my boundary. Beyond this, I will not go." Losers never draw boundaries. Some people say they're going to, but the weeks turn into months, which then become years, and nothing has changed. There's no discipline, no values, and no boundaries that safeguard their lives or the lives of their loved ones.

The statement at the top of this page came from the lips of Joshua near the end of his life. He had been a successful leader of Israel, following God's commandments and helping the Israelites conquer the Promised Land. Now, with the prospect of his earthly life ending, this great man of God renewed his *total commitment* to Jehovah. Others can do what they please, but Joshua's line in the sand was God's will.

Where are your boundaries in life? Have you drawn a line in the sand that says to your family, your business, and your church, "Here is where I stand. My allegiance is to God and to God alone"? Proverbs 1:7 says, "The fear of the LORD is the beginning of knowledge." Letting God's boundaries be yours enables your life to fall under His mighty protection.

If you haven't done so, I encourage you to draw that line—set those boundaries—today.

Heavenly Father, may I allow your Son, Jesus Christ, to be my Lord as well as my Savior. May I stand for the things for which You stand. May I oppose the evil that You abhor. And may I love others in the way You love them. In Jesus' name, Amen.

YOUR COMMITMENT TO GOD'S WORD
Judges 1:28

If you were in charge of a library at a university and had a space problem, with no option of adding shelves, what would you do with your books? A university library in Australia was faced with this very problem. Established in 1989, the University of Western Sydney has experienced fourfold growth of its student body. An unknown official thought that he had a brilliant idea for storing the surplus books cheaply. He buried thousands of books . . . in the ground . . . without protective covering!

The university has only just now discovered the ruined tomes. "Instead of being stored which would have been most appropriate, some idiot got rid of surplus books by burying them," University of Western Sydney spokesman Steven Matchett told reporters. Fully ten thousand books had been ruined because of this incident.[1]

Burying books in the ground ensures that they will be both ignored and destroyed. In essence, that's exactly what the Israelites did with God's commands. As we begin the book of Judges, we see the children of Israel failing to obey God's commands concerning those who did not believe in Jehovah. They were supposed to put out of their land all unbelievers so that their sons and daughters might not be contaminated by pagan beliefs. Instead, the Israelites compromised, leaving their enemies in the land as slaves.

History tells us that this burying of God's commands had horrible consequences for the Israelites. Their unwillingness to follow the Lord completely resulted in their land's being polluted by unbelief and forced them to fight many unnecessary wars.

We have a way of ignoring truths that we don't like. We can bury them through apathy, anger, or unbelief. Ignoring God's commands, however, will always bring us wars that we don't want to fight and situations that we wish we weren't in. The solution, of course, is to drive all sin from our lives. Let's decide that we will

---

1. Excite.com/news, 21 March 2001.

no longer keep the Bible buried through neglect. Let's allow God's Word to light our path each day.

Dear God, may I not ignore the truths contained in the Bible. Help me to accept Your wisdom, love, and power as the guide for my life today. In Jesus' name, Amen.

FEBRUARY 12

GOD OR SELF?

Judges 2:10–12

Modern art is garbage . . . really! When Emmanuel Asare went into work at the Eyestorm Gallery in west London, he was confronted by a mess. A pile of empty beer bottles, dirty ashtrays, coffee cups, and candy wrappers left over from a party launching a new exhibit was strewn around the museum. Asare cleaned up the place and threw everything into the garbage bin.

There was only one problem: the "mess" was the exhibit! Damien Hirst, a controversial artist, had taken garbage and arranged it into what he claimed was his latest creation. Gallery employees hastily retrieved the items from the garbage and, using photos, recreated the exhibit.

Hirst said the misunderstanding over his work was "fantastic, very funny." As for Asare, he remained unrepentant. "As soon as I clapped eyes on it, I sighed because there was so much mess," the cleaner said. "I didn't think for a second that it was a work of art. It didn't much look like art to me."[1]

Garbage as art—doesn't that phrase describe modern man's attempt to create his own morality! We've just read a Scripture passage that could describe today's generation. The Israelites who were born after Joshua's death forgot the Lord. Their own attempts to control their lives angered God. A whole generation learned—the hard way—the futility of trying to worship God while also honoring other false gods.

---

1. Excite.com, 19 October 2001.

What about you? Have you forgotten God? Do you allow God to have all of your life, or do you let Him have only a portion? Do you try to make God share space in your life with wrong habits or relationships? Today, remember that Jesus Christ died to pay for all of your sins—sins that have no business continuing to abide in your life. He desires to keep you free from sin, free from compromise, and free to possess an abundant life.

Lord, may I remember what You've done for me, both on the Cross and in my everyday life. I renounce anything that I've been putting in front of my allegiance to You. Cleanse me and direct my life today. In Jesus' name, Amen.

FEBRUARY 13

CONQUERING FEAR
Judges 7:8–9

Not long ago, Delta Flight 458 took off from Atlanta on its way to Newark. Shortly afterward, panic began to spread in the cabin. Two "Middle Eastern men" seemed to be causing a disturbance, according to the passengers. The pilot, notified of the incident, landed the plane in Charlotte, North Carolina. Passengers deplaned, and officials checked out the two men.

Instead of a disturbance, embarrassed officials discovered that the men were Orthodox Jews who had been in the process of saying their prayers! The other passengers, perhaps a bit embarrassed, reboarded the plane, and the flight continued without incident.[1]

Fear—it is one of the most powerful forces that any of us can face. As men, we don't like to admit that we're afraid. But if we're honest, we can sometimes feel fear right behind us, elevating our blood pressure as it breathes down our neck. We wonder if our jobs will continue to be there for us, if our health will hold out, or any of a number of other things over which we have no control.

On the other hand, we know that "perfect love casts out fear"

1. Excite.com, 15 October 2001.

(1 John 4:18 NKJV). God invites us to let Him give us His peace—in every circumstance. Because God loves us, lives in us, and empowers us every day, we need to remember that nothing has the strength to overcome us when we stay in God's will.

"Get up, go down against the camp, because I am going to give it into your hands " (Judges 7:9). Gideon refused to let fear rule his life. With God at his side, he and a handful of men overcame a vast army. Gideon took God at His word. Will you do the same? Today, ask God to give you victory and freedom over your fears. Trust in Him to give you the wisdom and strength to handle any difficulty that comes your way. And finally, trust that the Lord will guide you into a wonderful future.

Heavenly Father, I ask that You give me victory
over my fears. Help me to trust in Your power.
May I look to Your strength, not my weaknesses.
In Jesus' name, Amen.

FEBRUARY 14

POISON OR PEACE?

Ju∂ges 13:16—20

With terrorist attacks around the world in recent history, everyone is on edge. When a retiree in a town near Berlin, Germany, received an unusual gift just before Christmas, he became suspicious. Police, bomb squads, and experts in chemical and biological hazards swarmed his residence to safeguard a package with the word *poison* marked on it.

Tension mounted as the experts debated how to handle the package. Then, one of the officers saw that the box had come from the United States. He also remembered his English lessons in school and solved the problem for everyone. It turns out that the German word for "poison" is *gift*. And, *gift* was the word stamped on the package from the United States—so that everyone would know that the contents were safe![1]

---

1. Excite.com, 15 October 2001.

All of us have misunderstood a situation from time to time. It might cause us only a momentary embarrassment. At other times, however, it can radically affect our lives negatively. Like the couple in the preceding Scripture, sometimes we might be in the presence of God and not even realize it!

The next time your family is gathered around you, realize that God might want you to take time to help them focus upon Him through a family altar. At church, remember that God desires you to seek His presence with all of your heart. When you are on the job, look for opportunities to grow in Christ and witness for Him.

This life is not meant to be poison. Instead, it is a gift from God. So don't miss the daily presence of your heavenly Father. Use each moment to worship Him and learn from Him.

God, help me to see Your presence in my life today. Give me the wisdom to lead my family to focus upon You and to learn from You. In Jesus' name, Amen.

FEBRUARY 15

TRIALS, FEAR, AND FAITH
Judges 15:11–20

What are you facing right now that you believe is impossible? What looms before your eyes, threatening to rob you of hope and joy? What fears dominate your life? One of the principles that God teaches us is that in Christ we can do far more, put up with far more, and resist far more than we ever imagined. Remember the adage: "Eat a live toad first thing in the morning, and nothing worse can happen to you all day long." In other words, face your difficulties and fears; don't run from them.

Take Samson, for example. That great judge led his people successfully against the Philistines for more than twenty years. His ability to perform great feats of strength could operate only when "the Spirit of the LORD came upon him."

What was true for Samson is also true for you and me.

I encourage you to look in a new way at the great difficulties facing you. Think of them as opportunities for God to make you stronger. Realize that God might be using the trials as a way of moving you—physically or spiritually—to the place where He can better use you.

My wife and I were church planters in France several years ago. God was blessing our new church, and in a country where few evangelicals exist, we were seeing people come to Christ. As the church began to get on a firm footing, we came back to the United States on furlough. One afternoon, not long before we were scheduled to return to the field, we received a phone call that rocked our world. Our oldest daughter had flunked the medical exam that all furloughing missionaries and their children must take. We could not return to the place to which we believed that God had called us.

What would happen to the young church and even younger believers? What would we do with our lives? How would this situation affect our oldest daughter? These and other questions flooded our minds during the next several weeks. In the midst of this time of uncertainty, however, one thing became certain: God was still in control.

On the same day that we had to let our church know that we would not be returning, a missionary couple on the other side of the world—who *just happened* to be fluent in French—called our mission board to tell them that they felt led to move to France! Our church would continue to have a pastor. The Lord allowed us to begin a new work in south Louisiana that quickly became one of the largest churches in the area. And, although it took a number of years and several hospital stays, God eventually healed our daughter.

Through all of our trials, we discovered that the Lord helped us and sustained us. As I tell others, I also tell you: it is no cliché—God's grace is sufficient.

Father, help me to trust in You to take care of my deepest fears and greatest problems. I want to let You be in charge of whatever I face today. Give me Your wisdom to make right decisions and Your strength to fight the spiritual battles. Thank You for hearing this prayer. In Jesus' name, Amen.

THE IMPORTANCE OF DEALING WITH SIN
Ju∂ges 16:4–20

The man sat across my desk from me, weeping. He had once been a great force for good in our city. Youth had flocked to him; people came to Christ as a result of his ministry; families became stronger through his counsel. But one area of his life remained untamed. No one knew about it—at first. Because the man refused to deal with the one, key weakness—because he ignored it, thinking that his ministry and gifts would cover it up—Satan used it to destroy his influence and, for a time, his life.

He showed deep remorse, but it was too late to stop his reaping the consequences of his sin. He promised to reform, but it could not bring him back to his former level of ministry. And the terrible aspect of the whole, sordid mess is that it could have been avoided. None of it had to happen. If the sin had been dealt with early on, the man would never have seen his influence for good plummet.

The great news is that after a period of several years of getting his life straight, this man is once again living for God. But the pain he went through and the lives he hurt will always haunt him.

Learn the lesson of Samson and of this former minister: don't let sin continue to live in your life unchecked. The good you do for God can never make up for continuing, unconfessed sin. If something is hindering your Christian life today, give it to God. Admit that you have sinned. Don't rationalize it as being normal or okay. Let the Lord cleanse you and make you stronger in your ability to deal with sin and help others.

*Dear Lord, I don't want to hide anything from
You. Please deal with every area of my life:
thoughts, habits, relationships, and goals. Reveal
any wrongdoing of which I might be guilty, then
take it out of my life and cleanse me once again.
May I be totally Your servant. In Jesus' name,
Amen.*

VICTORY OVER BITTERNESS
Judges 16:21–31

"Donald" (name changed) hated church. He also hated Christians, preachers, and African-Americans. But one Sunday, this bitter man learned that his wife's church was hosting a black saxophone player for a concert. Donald might have hated blacks, but he loved saxophone music. So he did something rare: Donald decided to attend church for just that one time.

After the concert, the saxophone player explained how a person could be cleansed of his sins and have the certainty of heaven when he died. Music started playing, the invitation began . . . and then everything changed—for the service, for the church, and for Donald.

Before anyone could really understand what was happening, Donald left his seat and made his way toward the altar. The church family, many of whom had prayed for Donald for a number of years, spontaneously broke out into applause! And a man who had hated blacks and Christians came to know Jesus as Savior, led there by a black Christian. Today, Donald is still on fire for God. His witness has brought others into the kingdom. And God has transformed Donald's hatred into love for others and for his Savior.

God redeemed Samson's life, even after he'd blundered. God redeemed Donald's life in spite of his hatred. And God can redeem your life right now. No matter what you've done, no matter how far you've strayed, God will cleanse you as He promised in His Word. Give everything to Him right now, and let God reshape your life for His glory and your peace.

Dear God, I don't want to stay the way I am. Please cleanse me, strengthen me, and use me once again. I humble myself before You and ask forgiveness for my sins. Redeem my life that I might live for You. In Jesus' name, Amen.

KNOCKED OUT BY LIFE

Judges 17:1–6

One of the most embarrassing moments I've experienced happened, thank goodness, with only two witnesses: my wife and a six-month-old puppy. This "puppy" was growing at an alarming rate. She had eaten us out of house and home, and was fast becoming too big for the pen we had in the backyard. Her strength was, and is, incredible. Combine that with a love of jumping up on people and licking every area of their face she can reach, and you have the ingredients for my downfall.

Late one evening, Susan reminded me that the dog had not been fed. Our youngest daughter, who usually took care of that chore, was spending the night elsewhere, so the job fell to me. I turned on the lights in the backyard, let Daisy out of her pen to exercise a bit, and went to get her some food. The next thing I knew, Susan was standing over me, screaming my name and crying!

"What happened?" I asked. And why was I lying on the ground with our new puppy delightedly licking me?

It seems that the dog had decided to play with me while my back was turned. Susan said that Daisy had taken off and, running full tilt, clipped me perfectly in the back of my knees. Susan watched me go up in the air and land heavily on my side. I never knew what hit me. But I surely wasn't going to tell my friends that I'd been knocked unconscious by a six-month-old puppy!

Sometimes the unlikeliest things can set our lives back. Take, for example, verse 6 in today's key passage: "In those days Israel had no king; everyone did as he saw fit." Israel had received the five books of Moses containing their laws, the Ten Commandments, and how their society was to be run. But at that stage in Israel's history, the Law had been set aside and forgotten. Instead, each person lived his life as he saw fit, deciding which laws he would or would not follow.

Does that remind you of America in the twenty-first century?

Because no one had a reliable authority outside their own experiences, the smallest events were upsetting them, "knocking them out." Stealing money from parents, making an idol, installing pagan priests in the land of Israel—the people of God were no longer living for God. They had descended into spiritual anarchy and confusion.

What about your own daily walk? Let's take an inventory. Look for the little areas that you have not yet given to God. They like to hide from close inspection. They want you to overlook them and underestimate them. But those "little puppies" are Satan's time bombs, waiting to detonate at the most inappropriate moment and cause ruin to your life.

Don't let life knock you out. Don't let the unexpected flatten you because you're unprepared. Let Christ have the central place in your thoughts. Keep reading the Bible every day. Meditate upon what you've read. Memorize Scripture and apply it to your life. In this way, you'll stay on an even keel even when those unexpected surprises come crashing into your life. With Christ as the center of your existence, you'll be able to keep balanced in a topsy-turvy world.

Heavenly Father, I know that nothing can happen to me today that is not completely known to You already. Help me to trust in You, no matter what occurs. Prepare me for each day's challenges by placing Your Word in my heart and mind. In Jesus' name, Amen.

FEBRUARY 19

HOW DID I GET HERE?
Judges 17:6–13

"How did we get here?"

I found myself on the side of the highway in my van, facing the opposite direction from where I'd been intending to go! We had been traveling toward Amarillo, Texas, with traffic fairly thick but flowing nicely. Then we hit "black ice." Totally unexpected and impossible to see, it took the traction from our tires and sent everyone around me spinning out of control. As I fought for control of the van, I could see cars crashing into each other and running into ditches. When I heard gravel crunch under my tires, I hit the brakes hard, figuring that I was off the ice and onto something firm. Sure enough, the vehicle shuddered to a stop. But we had turned completely around and now faced the oncoming traffic. Needless to say, the rest of our journey proceeded at a much more cautious pace!

Today's Bible passage deals with a Levite who became a priest, not for Jehovah, but for an idol! Judges 18:30 tells us that he was actually Moses' grandson, Jonathan, the son of Gershom. How could Jonathan have ever come to such a place? His grandfather had been responsible for bringing an entire people out of slavery and giving them access to almighty God. Now, he found himself ignoring God's clear commands and worshiping a piece of silver instead of the Creator of the world.

"How did I get here?"

I hear that question all of the time. People find themselves in situations and environments in which they never intended to be. Their lives, wrecked and ruined, stand as mute testimony to the terrible power of sin to derail us if we're not careful. Turned around and disoriented, we can quickly lead ourselves and those who depend upon us in the wrong direction and into dangerous areas.

"How did I get here?"

For Moses' grandson and for us, it usually happens in a series of small steps that eventually culminates in a tragedy. Jonathan, along with his people, had forsaken God's instructions. Every day they moved farther from God's standards. Walk away from God long enough, and you find yourself lost and in unfamiliar territory.

Are you walking with, toward, or away from God? If your family follows you, where will they find themselves: close to God or in an area where they are liable to be hurt spiritually? Decide that you will follow God's path, God's will, and God's commandments. Doing so ensures your peace and a rich, full life.

God, I know that many paths present themselves to me every day. Help me to follow You and You alone. May I lead others in the right direction as well. Thank You for the Bible. May it become my guide and authority. In Jesus' name, Amen.

GODLY FRIENDS
Ju∂ges 18:1–6

How do you go about making decisions? When you come to a crossroads in life, how do you determine which way to go?

Most of us have some friends with whom we hang out from time to time. Maybe we talk to them. Or it could be that we watch how others in our situation have reacted, and we try to do the same thing. But how do we know that we're making the right decision?

In today's passage of Scripture, some people from the tribe of Dan needed advice. On the surface, what they did seemed like a good idea: they asked a priest if God was going to bless their efforts. But this question caused a problem. As we saw yesterday, that man was a pagan priest who was trying to mix worship of God and worship of idols. His advice assuring the Danites of the Lord's approval had horrendous results. It plunged the nation of Israel into civil war and, eventually, established a center for idol worship that sapped the nation of its spiritual strength!

Advice, whether good or bad, can have long-term consequences.

A number of years ago, I lived in a town just outside of Paris, France. Learning to get around in a foreign metropolis is a challenge, to say the least. I knew one way to get from the center of Paris to my home in the suburbs, and I followed it every day without fail. Then one afternoon, during rush hour, I came to my exit and discovered it closed! As I slowed down, a gendarme impatiently whistled at me and waved me on. One thought pounded in my head: if I miss this exit, I'll be completely lost. In a moment of desperation, I did something unbelievable. Stopping the car, I got out, locked it, climbed up on the hood, sat down, and folded my arms!

I thought the policeman would have a heart attack. He screamed at me, gesturing violently. I explained, in English (I didn't yet speak French) that I didn't understand what he was saying but that I wasn't going anywhere until someone gave me correct directions to my home in Massy.

The gendarme wheeled around and spoke briefly into a walkie-talkie. A police car pulled up a few minutes later. The driver got out and came over to me. In heavily accented English, he explained that two exits farther would also lead me to my destination. Then, putting his arm around me, he pleaded, "Now, please go!"

I went.

The directions proved correct. I reached home safely. Good advice had produced good results.

In your own life, it is imperative that you find godly friends who are mature in the Lord. These are the people to whom you should be turning for advice. God's Word and God's people form an unbeatable combination for helping you to determine God's will.

If you've been unsure as to the rightness of your life's destination, I encourage you to pull over, stop going in the wrong direction, and ask God to be your source of strength, wisdom, and direction. His advice can radically improve your life—forever.

Dear God, may I learn how to trust in You for direction in my life. Help me to turn to You first when I need advice or help. Throughout this day, I ask You to be my guide. In Jesus' name, Amen.

FEBRUARY 21

ROBBERY VERSUS REWARDS
Judges 18:14–26

The thieves had planned their robbery to perfection. They had scouted out a school in South Africa for weeks, and they knew that the principal kept a large amount of money in the office safe. Breaking into the office late one afternoon, they forced the principal to open the safe and give them the money. They then put the stolen loot into a briefcase and escaped.

When the gang finally got to their hideout, they gathered around the briefcase to divide their ill-gotten gains. The leader eagerly opened the briefcase, reached into the very bottom and came up with a handful of . . . homework! The thieves had grabbed the wrong briefcase! Back at the school, police carefully put the money into a new safe and students had a new excuse as to why they wouldn't have their homework turned in the next day.

Committing robbery is bad. But robbing someone and ending up empty-handed is just plain stupid.

In reality, that's exactly what happened to the Danites in today's Scripture. They robbed a man named Micah. But what they stole from him didn't enrich them; it hurt them. A pagan priest and worthless idols will never make a positive difference in anyone's life. For the Danites, it made them only more enemies and created more problems.

God's Word has some clear warnings for those who cut corners and hurt others in their greed to get "more." "These men lie in wait for their own blood; they waylay only themselves! Such is the end of all who go after ill-gotten gain; it takes away the lives of those who get it" (Prov. 1:18–19).

Many a man has spent his life working every spare minute, only to turn around one day and discover that he's lost a relationship with his family, his friends, or his God. Ensure that what you're working hard for will stand the test of time. The souls of your children, your spouse, and your friends and neighbors will last forever. Major on helping them discover the richness of a Christ-filled life. In the process, you'll receive the truly valuable benefits of a relationship with God, riches that no one can steal and that the world cannot duplicate.

Heavenly Father, help me to so order my life that
I am working for that which is truly valuable.
Keep my ethics solid and my morals high. In
Jesus' name, Amen.

FEBRUARY 22

GOING RIGHT IN A WRONG WORLD

Judges 20:1–10

Here are the headlines for one evening, gleaned from the newswires: "L.A. woman survives 9 days stranded on the floor of apartment"; "Secretary fleeces boss using erasable ink"; "Unborn baby saves mother from deadly bullet"; "Six brides-to-be among dead in house collapse."

What do you do when everything in your life turns upside down? How do you continue when it seems that nothing is going right? The Israelites in today's passage were in danger of losing their love of each other and their identity as a nation because of gross sin. To their credit, they refused to hide their heads in the sand and ignore their problems. Instead, they faced a terrible situation head-on and eventually brought some joy out of terrible sorrow.

How is your life faring these days? If you think that all hope is gone, I encourage you to look up, down, and within. Look up because God is still on His throne, watching over the world. Look down at the Bible. Wonderful Scripture passages will encourage and inspire you. And finally, look within your heart. If you know Christ as Savior, He is living *in* you, *with* you, and *through* you. He will give you the strength to come solidly through whatever difficulty faces you. Remember this: the sorrow will one day pass; the joy will always remain.

Father, I turn to You right now. I give You all of my life, my problems, and my failures. Help me to trust in You to bring good out of heartache, and give me the strength to stand for You in the midst of difficult times. In Jesus' name, Amen.

FEBRUARY 23

FRIENDS OR GOD?

Judges 20:9–14

The young father sat weeping in my office. Brilliant, gifted, married with a new child, he should have been happy. Instead, he wept because a problem with drugs threatened to tear apart everything he held dear. As we talked, it became evident that he was ready to turn his life around—except for one thing.

"I'm committing my life to Jesus," he said. "Church attendance will be a priority every week. My wife and I are also going to be a part of a small group Bible study. Surely that's enough to turn my life around."

I hesitated a moment before responding, wanting to say the right thing. "All of what you've just said is absolutely wonderful. And, of course, giving your life to Christ is the first step in a wonderful adventure that will never end. But there's one more thing. If you're going to escape the pull of drugs, you're going to have to change your friends. They still do drugs, and being with them will create a powerful temptation for you every time you're with them."

He was already shaking his head. "They're my friends. I can't leave them. I would be disloyal if I gave them up." Nothing I said could dissuade him. And before long, he found himself back into the drug scene, hooked worse than ever.

This story, however, has a happy ending. The young father finally realized that Jesus, not his friends, demanded his ultimate loyalty. He cut himself off from old temptations and forged new relationships. Today, he and his wife are growing in the Lord.

We've been reading in Judges about a war that should never have happened. The Benjamites were defending family and friends who had done a despicable act. Instead of being loyal to old friendships, they should have been loyal to righteousness. Their refusal to put God ahead of family ties caused thousands of people to die.

What about your friends? Are they leading the kind of lives that would please God? Are they pulling you closer to the Lord, or are they pushing you farther away from Him? Satan will use anything and anyone he can to keep us from living as we should for Christ. Don't let friendships keep you from being the Christian you should be. Ask God to help you develop relationships that will help you be a strong force for good.

Lord, You know my heart. Please show me if some of the relationships that I'm holding on to are making me weak. Help me to give up old friendships that might be tempting to me. Guide me into finding godly men who can help me become more like Jesus. In Jesus' name, Amen.

THE END OF THE STORY

Judges 20:29–44

It's not often that we get to see the end of the story.

A man leaves his wife and family for a younger woman and seems, to all the world, to be perfectly happy. A businessman offers bribes, treats his workers shabbily, and makes a fortune. We wonder where the justice is in such actions. Why do these immoral criminals get away with what they've done?

They haven't. It's just that their story has not yet been completed.

We've been reading the account of the men of Gibeah for the last several days. In the preceding passage, the consequences of the sins that they committed finally came due. In the manner of evil that was not dealt with, the consequences had grown far worse than anyone could have imagined. That is the end of the story, and it destroyed more than twenty-five thousand lives.

Sin and death *always* go together.

Whether in the Old Testament or in this second month of the year, actions that at first seem so wonderful—even powerful—will *always* lead to destruction. That's why it is critical that you and I deal promptly with any sin that the Lord reveals in our lives.

Because the end of the story is coming.

The great news is that you get to choose how the story will conclude! Keep your life close to God, regardless of how others might act, and your story will end in triumph. You'll see God on His throne, and you'll hear Him say, "Well done, my good and faithful servant." Until then, stay close to God, feet planted firmly on the path of righteousness.

Heavenly Father, help me not to get caught up in the seduction of temporary successes. Let Your Spirit guide me every day, keeping my feet from evil. As my family watches my life unfold, may I show them the influence that a godly man can have on this world. And may the story of my life end in faithfulness to You. In Jesus' name, Amen.

FEBRUARY 25

GOD'S LOVE AND YOU

Ruth 1:1–16

I stood at the front of the church, a twenty-one-year-old man scared to death! The organ swelled, the back doors opened, and my bride started down the aisle. I thought that I would faint before she finally reached me, and we turned to face the preacher—my father.

Then, the unbelievable happened—my dad forgot my name! I wasn't the only man there who was nervous that day. The great event—my marriage to Susan—began a commitment that has endured for more than thirty years. Through three children, sicknesses, jobs on two continents, and battles with cancer, our love has deepened and grown. But the whole story began with a commitment: "I do."

Today, we've begun reading one of the great love stories in the Bible. Ruth, the foreigner; Ruth, the poor widow who had nothing, ended up marrying a wonderful Israelite. In doing so, she became an ancestor of King David and of Jesus, the Messiah. But it all began with a commitment: "Where you go I will go. . . . Your people will be my people and your God my God" (v. 16).

Have you made a commitment to God? Renew that commitment today. Strengthen your ties to the Lord. He desires to do much good through you. Blessings so wonderful that you cannot imagine them await you. But, it all starts with commitment: "Lord, take control of all of my life. I give myself to you."

Have you done this? If not, will you do it today?

Heavenly Father, I commit my life to You. Give me the strength to live for You daily. May what I do honor You and bring glory to You. And may I never forget Your love for me and my commitment to You. In Jesus' name, Amen.

MATURE LOVE
Ruth 2:1–12

Ah, Judy! Her eyes captured mine the instant we met. My heart beat so hard I thought it would come out of my chest. And when she spoke to me, I trembled all over. I just knew that true love was mine. Alas, Judy soon grew tired of me and turned to Craig, my best friend! I still remember coming home that afternoon and yelling, "I hate the second grade!"

We are in the process of reading one of the world's great love stories. Chapter 2 of Ruth introduces Boaz to this remarkable woman. She came to his attention because of her kindness to Naomi, her mother-in-law. As Boaz watched Ruth day in and day out, he was convinced that her actions revealed a woman worth getting to know.

Judy or Ruth? A seven-year-old's fickle emotions or a mature relationship based on kindness and love in action? What kind of love are you showing to those around you?

Paul reminds us in Ephesians that we men are to love our wives as Christ loved the church and gave Himself for it. Mature, Ruth-type love. Whether you are married or single, the way you react to the people you love says much about you. If you are constant in the way you treat others, regardless of how they are treating you, your behavior reveals a mature, godly love. Ruth and Boaz began a lineage that brought Christ to earth. Your love should also point the way to the Savior.

God, help me to love those around me with a
godly, mature love. May I not react in selfishness
or insist on my own rights. Through my love, may
those closest to me see Christ. In Jesus' name,
Amen.

EYES ON THE GOAL
Ruth 3:1–11

Have you ever been on a diet? I have—many times. I agree with the person who said, "The third day of a diet is the easiest because by that time you're off of it!"

Doctors tell us the person who loses weight and then keeps it off usually follows the same scenario: a true change in eating habits, regular exercise, and weighing himself almost daily.

In other words, those who truly lose weight don't run after every fad diet or the latest food craze. They keep their eyes on the goal.

In today's passage of the world's greatest love story, we see Ruth coming to Boaz for protection. Evidently, he was much older than she was because he said in verse 10, "The LORD bless you, my daughter. . . . This kindness is greater than that which you showed earlier: You have not run after the younger men, whether rich or poor."

Ruth won great honor and a wonderful husband because she refused to be distracted by youth, beauty, or wealth. All of those attributes could have been hers, but if she had run after them, Ruth would have been settling for less than the best. Instead, Ruth kept her eyes on the goal.

God has promised each of us wonderful gifts if we follow Him. Instead, some men run after the things of the world because they look flashy, feel good, or are popular with others. If you're one of those men, I encourage you to quit settling for less than the best. Center all of your attention upon a right relationship with Jesus Christ. And then . . .

Keep your eyes on the goal.

Heavenly Father, I want to make Jesus the Lord of my life. Help me not to be distracted by any activities, relationships, or habits that would keep me from living fully for You. Help me to keep my eyes upon You alone. In Jesus' name, Amen.

JESUS CHRIST, REDEEMER
Ruth 4:1–17

When I was a little boy growing up in Hot Springs, Arkansas, I heard many stories about my uncle, who lived in Chicago. He was a rich, successful businessman. He had a great personality, told amazing stories from his own experiences, and always brought his nephews and nieces presents on the rare occasions when he visited.

One afternoon, while I was playing on my grandparents' front porch, I watched as a huge, white Cadillac pulled up to the curb. A man I'd never seen before got out and approached the house. "You're my uncle from Chicago!" I blurted out.

The man looked surprised. "How did you know who I am?" he asked. "I didn't tell anyone I was coming."

About that time, my grandfather heard the commotion and came outside to meet his brother. As I looked from one man to the other, I explained, "You had to be my uncle from Chicago. You look just like Grandpa Joe!"

Relatives often resemble one another. An entire family can have the same speech pattern, same color hair, or same facial characteristics.

As we conclude the book of Ruth today, we see Boaz, the "kinsman-redeemer," ready to marry Ruth and protect both her and Naomi. To be able to accomplish this, Boaz had to be related to Naomi's family, rich and powerful enough to purchase land in Naomi's and Ruth's names, and willing to marry Ruth so that a future family line could be assured.

Jesus Christ is our "kinsman-redeemer." The Bible tells us that Christ looked like us and talked like us while He was on earth. That's because He is related to us. Jesus called Himself the Son of Man many times. But Jesus is powerful enough that He could redeem you and me from the slave block of sin. The great news is that He was also willing to do that, going to the Cross so that we might have freedom from Satan and a new life in Christ.

Today, take a moment to thank God for sending us Jesus Christ, our "kinsman-redeemer."

*Dear God, thank You for the gift of Your son,
Jesus Christ. Thank You for redeeming us forever
through the sacrifice of His blood on the Cross.
May my thoughts and actions show clearly that I
love You and stand for You every day. In Jesus'
name, Amen.*

MARCH 1

THE POWER OF FAMILY
1 Samuel 1:1–8

Nothing has the power to bless or curse us more than our family. Those who have a strong, loving family can face nearly any challenge or crisis. When you know that, despite whatever life hands out, you have a support system, you are buoyed and steadied. But the opposite is just as true. If you do not have a supporting family behind you, everything in life becomes doubly difficult. One man explained his life without a loving family this way: "It's like trying to swim across the Mississippi River with a piano tied on your back!"

In today's text, poor Elkanah lived in a household that was torn by strife. He had two wives—not an unusual custom in the Old Testament. One wife, Peninnah, had children. The other wife, Hannah, had no children—a sign of shame in her time. The situation was difficult enough, but imagine what might have been if the family had pulled together in love and unity. The women could have aided each other. Elkanah could have been a loving support to them. But look at how the Bible describes their situation: "Because the LORD had closed her womb, her rival kept provoking her in order to irritate her. This went on year after year" (vv. 6–7). Don't you know that was a fun home to visit!

Do you see the pattern there? There was a situation—the barrenness of Hannah. But the situation was not the main tragedy. The main issue was the friction between the women. One chose to use the situation as a club against the other. It was an act of hostility and meanness. But it did not have to be that way. Ultimately, God intervened to help with the family situation. Think how much strife could have been prevented if the parties had agreed to work together instead of against each other.

Our families are very much dependent on our input. If yours is not everything you hope for, do not give up. Continue to pray. Continue to work toward reconciliation among everyone.

I need help, Lord, to keep our family together.
Give me strength and wisdom to help
_____ and _____ to get
along for all of our sakes. I count on You, Father.
In Christ, Amen.

MARCH 2

DEDICATING THE FAMILY
1 Samuel 1:9–28

Family is so very important. That has always been the case. From the fog of ancient history this truth stands out: without family, we're in trouble. Elkanah and his wife Hannah were childless together. Elkanah had children with his other wife but not with Hannah. That was a bitter situation, especially for Hannah.

That godly woman prayed and prayed for years. She went to the old priest Eli and prayed so fervently that he thought she was drunk! Hannah explained her dilemma, and the elderly priest gave her a blessing. Things happened. The Bible puts it this way: "So in the course of time Hannah conceived and gave birth to a son. She named him Samuel, saying, 'Because I asked the LORD for him'" (v. 20). The name Samuel sounds like the Hebrew word meaning "heard of God."

We would think that Hannah's life was fulfilled with the birth of her son. But look at what happened next. She had dedicated the child to God, so she took him back to Eli to be reared in the temple. From that point, the child would grow up in the service of God under Eli's care.

The point of this account is that we can still dedicate our family to God. No, we cannot take a child to the church and tell the pastor, "Here, he's yours now." What we can do is in our attitude and prayer life say to the Lord, "This child is a gift from You. I dedicate him to You. Use him as You wish." My wife and I did that with our children. That does not mean that they will become pastors or missionaries. One is pursuing a medical career and the other is working in computer science. But they can belong to God wherever they are.

It is not too late. Dedicate your family to God. Even if they are grown, offer them up in regular prayer and dedication. The Lord can use everyone everywhere.

> *Lord, take my family and add Your blessing to each of their lives. You know our situation. Not everything is perfect, but use us anyway. In Christ's name, Amen.*

MARCH 3

TROUBLE IN THE FAMILY
1 Samuel 2:12—25

When our family is in trouble, nothing else seems to matter. Some of you reading these words will wince at the remembrance of your own situation. You might feel as though a wedge has been driven between you and your wife. You might realize that a child has rejected you and your values. Nothing hurts like the pain of family discord.

Hannah had dedicated young Samuel to the service of God under Eli's leadership. That sounds fine—until we realize that Eli did not do such a wonderful job of rearing his own children. Today's text shows that Eli's boys were arrogant and disrespectful of both Eli and God. "The sin of the young men was very great in the LORD's sight, for they were treating the LORD's offering with contempt" (v. 17). Their father tried to intervene and straighten the boys out. You can already guess the outcome. What happens when we speak to our children? Often, they do the exact opposite of what we want them to do. "His sons, however, did not listen to their father's rebuke" (v. 25).

What are we to do when our family gets into trouble? First, don't panic. Remember that no family is perfect. Ask the Lord for wisdom and guidance. Deal with love and patience no matter what. If necessary, get outside help. Family counselors are helpful in sorting out difficulties. Do not hesitate to get help if you need it. When one of our sons was a high school senior, he was always upset and hostile. I finally took him to a counselor who worked with him for several months to help him settle down and get over his attitude. I do not consider my taking him there a failure. I consider it a success.

Whatever it takes, do what you can for your family. All sacrifices are worth the effort.

Help us, Lord, with our families. They mean everything to us, but You know how difficult things can be. Give us wisdom and patience. Whatever it takes to have a stable family we will do. Through Christ, Amen.

MARCH 4

SYMBOLIZING GOD'S PRESENCE
1 Samuel 4:1–11

How do you symbolize God's presence? What object, relationship, or feeling could make you believe that God is here, right now? These are not idle questions. From biblical days, people have wanted something to let them know that God was with them. Devotion to Him, although necessary, sometimes seems insufficient by itself. That is where religious symbols come in. These symbols are like signposts, pointing beyond themselves to a greater reality.

Moses brought the tablets of stone containing the Ten Commandments down from Mount Sinai. He placed them in a special box called the ark of the covenant. If you have ever seen the movie *Raiders of the Lost Ark,* you will at least know a Hollywood version of what it looked like. To the Hebrews, that ark was the symbol of God's very presence with them. When the ark was present, God was present. That is why the capture of the ark by the Philistine army seemed to be such a disaster. It was as if the reality of God was being taken away.

The greatest symbol that Christians have today is the cross. It exists in many forms, shapes, textures, and materials. Some of them are mere jewelry, but I have always been surprised that people would wear a hangman's noose or an electric chair around their necks. That is what the cross is—a symbol of death. But, of course, it means more than death. The Christian cross is the symbol of hope, life, courage, and God's great "yes" to us.

The next time you see a cross, think of it as a sign pointing to something beyond itself. Death is not the last word because the Cross is empty. The Savior who hung there is alive and will someday return. Let the symbol of God's power inspire and encourage you.

Speak to me in the powerful symbol of faith,
Lord. Let Your presence in my life be a constant
that keeps me going and gives me strength.
Through Christ, Amen.

MARCH 5

CHANCE OR CHOICE?
1 Samuel 6:1–9

On July 29, 2000, I awoke and realized that I was being lifted onto a stretcher. At first, I could not understand what was happening. A few minutes before, a friend and I had been cutting a broken limb from an oak tree in my backyard. Part of it was on the ground; the rest of it was still attached to the tree. We each had a chain saw and worked our way from the end on the ground closer and closer to the tree. That's when it happened. The part that was attached to the tree broke off and fell. The smaller part reared up and hit my legs, knocking me to the ground. Then the larger part hit the ground, bounced up over my friend, and came down on the left half of my head. Just that quickly I had a fractured skull and a blood clot on my brain.

What followed was three weeks of hospitalization, two surgeries on my head, pain like I have never known before, and physical and speech therapy. I was out of my pulpit for two months.

When I went back, my schedule was severely limited for several months.

Why did all of that happen? That is a natural question that many people ask when unusual things happen. But the short answer is, "I don't know." Actually, I never asked that question. I never once felt singled out, punished, attacked, or anything else. It was just an accident. Things happen. I don't leap to any premature conclusions.

In today's passage, the Philistines returned the ark of the covenant to the Israelites. They had experienced turmoil in their land while they had the ark. They placed it on a cart, hitched it to a pair of oxen, and let it go wherever the animals took it. They said that if it went one direction, then God was responsible for their trouble. If it went the other way, then everything had happened by "chance."

God or chance. That is often the choice in life. I believe that God is present in all circumstances—not directly as the cause of everything, but there as Lord of all circumstances. Would you trust Him with your circumstances?

Lord, I do trust You. Whatever happens to me, I will believe that You are here with me. We live in a fallen world where bad things happen. But You are redeeming us out of this world. Thank You for the grace. In Christ, Amen.

MARCH 6

BLESSED
1 Samuel 10:1–8

Have you ever been blessed? I don't mean in some fuzzy nonspecific way. I mean in a personal, specific, and emotional way. If you have ever been chosen quarterback on your recess team, you have been blessed. If the girl you proposed to said "yes," you were blessed. If you received a promotion or a raise, you were blessed.

I have had such blessings on several occasions and can tell you that each time is touching. In one of my pastorates, we went through a rough time regarding personnel issues. In one meeting, the leader of that meeting had my wife and me sit in the middle of a circle and people joined hands. One man placed his hands on my shoulders and prayed for us. That was the last thing I expected in that meeting, but believe me, I was blessed! I drew strength, comfort, and resolve from that experience.

The prophet Samuel anointed Saul as king. The process of anointing was a ceremony of blessing. Saul drew from it what I had from my experience. Not everyone will have an experience like Saul's, of course, but everyone can receive the hand of God upon him. Our salvation through faith in Christ is a time where God puts His blessing upon us. We are chosen. We are touched. We are wanted. No matter what anyone else might think, we are God's men.

Saul had a tough time with his blessing. When the time came for his public anointing as king, he was hiding among the baggage. The people had to find him. That's the way life is sometimes. We are almost embarrassed to receive God's blessing. But who are we to turn down what God has offered?

Lord, You have blessed me. You chose me to be part of Your kingdom. I am both thrilled and embarrassed. How could You choose the likes of me? But You did, and I will make the most of Your choice. Thank You, in Jesus' name, Amen.

MARCH 7

STANDING THE TEST OF TIME
I Samuel 12:1–3

Have you ever thought about your last words? When you wrap up your life, what do you want to say? Will you think about the work you didn't do? The meeting you did not attend? The customers you did not win?

Samuel, the old prophet of Israel, looked back over his life and thought about what to say to his people. He asked the people to remember his life and how he had treated people. He testified that he had not cheated anyone or oppressed them or taken bribes. In other words, he had lived with integrity. He was as good as his word.

I love that idea. The grit in Samuel's life was enough to say, "Look at my life, and see if it adds up." I have known many people who have lived that way. My father was one of them. When he said "yes," he meant yes. When he said "no," nothing on earth could move him. When I was a child, I thought that his way of life was too rigid and harsh. I know better now.

The world needs more people who can reach the end and say, "I've done it right." I do not mean that they are perfect. No one is. But they live consistently. Nothing is more damaging to a man's reputation than the charge that he is a hypocrite. To claim to be one thing while actually being another is absurd. Faith gives us the courage to live what we say and say what we live. That is what Samuel had done. That is what I want to do. What about you?

Lord, give me the strength to live right all the days of my life. Through Christ, Amen.

DON'T GET THE BIG HEAD
1 Samuel 13:1–14

An older relative used to have an expression for people she thought were acting arrogant. She would say, "Don't get the big head." I have always laughed about that expression, but I understand it. Our heads swell with pride and arrogance when we see ourselves as better than others.

King Saul found his army in an important battle. He wanted the aid of God, but did not know how to ask for it. Because the prophet Samuel was absent from the battlefield, Saul offered burnt offerings himself. The problem was that only an authorized person could do so. In this case, that person was Samuel, not Saul. The prophet's rebuke to Saul is stark: "Your kingdom will not endure" (v. 14).

This might seem like an incredibly harsh judgment, but remember the context. God was establishing His nation out of a rather motley group. The people had to stick together if they were going to get anything done. When King Saul took it upon himself to perform the priestly function of the offering, he was intruding upon the province of God's man. It is not that Samuel was better than Saul; he was simply called by God to a different function.

The Christian gospel tells us that we are all alike in God's sight. But that does not mean that each person can do anything he pleases. God calls us to Himself and gives each of us work to do and gifts to use. I cannot do everything you can, nor can you do everything I can. This is not an excuse for not trying our best, but it is a recognition that God still appoints people to His work.

Are you serving God to the best of your understanding and ability? If so, great! But remember—"Don't get the big head."

Help me, Lord, to stay humble and to remember who I am. You have called me, and I will remember that I work for You. In Christ, Amen.

MARCH 9

REJECT
1 Samuel 15:17–35

A word that is hard to say or hear is *reject*. We do not like to think of anything as not being good enough, but we realize that some things must be perfect to be useful. When I take my car to the shop to be repaired, I do not want the mechanic to use parts that have the word *reject* stamped on them. What good would that do me?

Even harder to think about is a person who is a reject. I do not mean to be harsh or judgmental here. The fact is simply that some people have chosen a path in life that leads to disaster. King Saul in today's Bible reading is such a person. God had chosen him to be the king of Israel, but Saul did not succeed. He took upon himself some duties that were meant for only God's prophets. Because of his arrogance, Saul ended up being a reject. The last sentence in 1 Samuel 15:35 summarizes his tragic life: "And the LORD was grieved that he had made Saul king over Israel." Even God was sorry that Saul had failed so completely.

We could get depressed if we took that incident too personally. Who among us does not feel like a failure in some aspects of life? I know some businessmen who are successful in their work, but their home life is a wreck. I know some guys who are okay at home, but their careers are a shambles. Life does not have to be either/or, of course. I am merely pointing out that most of us feel not quite up to par in some area of life.

Here is the good news: in Jesus Christ, no one needs to be a reject. We can all accept Him as our Savior and live as His servants. To be included is the greatest blessing in life. Don't be a reject.

Lord, thank You for accepting me. I am not all that I should be, but I am better than I once was. Keep me moving, Lord, and growing for You. In Jesus' name, Amen.

CHOSEN

1 Samuel 16:1–13

What a great joy to be chosen! In school, we played ball. The captains of our teams chose players. Do you remember how it felt as they looked around at the potential team? My heart used to race, and my palms got sweaty. Then I'd hear those wonderful words: "I choose Don."

As tough as it is to be rejected, so it is as sweet to be chosen. We go through life being chosen. We go to school and get chosen to receive a degree. We find a mate who chooses us back. We enter the job market and hear those wonderful words of choice: "You're hired." Children come along, and we feel chosen by God to be the father of these precious bundles of possibility.

King Saul was rejected by God because of his arrogance. Young David was chosen to be his successor. How do you step into a king's sandals? The task would be overwhelming, but David grew into the responsibility. Therein is the key to life. We grow into the positions we take on. I remember bringing our twin sons home from the hospital eight days after they were born. We placed them in their bassinets on the living room floor, and I looked at Carla and asked, "Well, now what?" I did not know how to be a father, but I learned.

What do you feel "chosen" to do? Be a success at work? Have a great family life? Serve God in special ways? Write a book? Build a house? When we do what we feel we should be doing, we often feel chosen by something greater than ourselves to do that task. That is the way God deals with us. The Lord has chosen you. Enjoy the privilege.

You have chosen us for salvation, Father, and we are so grateful. You have blessed us with so much in life, and we feel privileged. Help us keep our eyes on You all of our journey. In Christ, Amen.

MARCH 11

HOW TO FIGHT A GIANT
I Samuel 17:1–50

You have been up against them, and so have I. Giants—people or forces that loom large on the horizon and make us want to shrink back. A friend wanted to start his own business. His enthusiasm was matched by the number of frustrations with regulations, cash flow, and personnel. He finally got it up and running but was amazed by how difficult it was. I know another man who had a construction business. One of his subcontractors on a major job skipped town without paying his bills. The IRS got involved, and the man ended up going bankrupt.

How do you fight a giant? Look at what young David did when he faced Goliath. First, he volunteered for the job. He did not let his fears stop him. Next, he refused to go out in another man's armor. Saul meant well when he offered his armor to David, but it just did not fit the lad. No one has the exact formula for success for us.

Next, David prayed for God's strength and wisdom. The fact that he prayed did not mean that David could sit back then and do nothing. He still had to go out and face Goliath. Also, David chose his weapons carefully. He picked up five smooth stones for his sling. One of them proved to be lethal.

If you are like most men, you are facing some giants of your own. Your giant might be the bank that seems to be a black hole, the job that is unfulfilling, a wife who is distant, or a child who is rebellious. Maybe it is all of the above! But do not give up. Life's greatest prizes go to the marathon runner, not the sprinter. Face your giants. You will take great pleasure in seeing them fall.

Lord, as with David of old, give me courage and wisdom as I face my giants. You know what they are. Help me with each one. I will do my part in this battle as You do Your part. Thanks for the victory, no matter what. In Christ, Amen.

MARCH 12

GRAY DOG VERSUS NEW PUPPY
1 Samuel 18:1—16

The green-eyed monster of jealousy has crept up on many a man. You work yourself silly to master a skill and build a career. You become one of the "old gray dogs" in your field. You do every-thing the right way, but you might not go as far as you had dreamed. Then along comes a new guy who does not know half what you know. He is a "new puppy." But he gets the promotion and the raise. You feel as though you've gotten the shaft.

Is this a new situation of the twenty-first century? Hardly. Look at what happened after David killed Goliath. He got all of the glory. That was fine—except that people began taunting King Saul with David's victory. They sang, "Saul has slain his thousands, and David his ten thousands." The Scripture says, "Saul was very angry; this refrain galled him" (vv. 7–8). No kidding! It would gall anyone.

I have been there. Have you? This passage should make us very aware of how we talk to people and how we treat everyone. Sure, success should be rewarded, even if it is just with a card or a pat on the back. But does someone's success mean that others need to feel like failures? In a car race, only one driver will cross the finish line first, but are the other drivers failures? Of course not! They were at least in the race.

Even churches can be bad about creating an environment in

which some people are elevated whereas others are made to feel irrelevant. Let's get this clear right now: no one is irrelevant or unwanted in the kingdom of God. The Lord will raise up a David now and then, and people will flock to him. But we need Sauls to keep things moving.

Are you a "gray dog" or a "new puppy"? Either way, you need the other.

Keep me from jealousy, envy, or feelings of superiority, Lord. Whatever I am, I am Yours, and that's good enough for me. In Christ, Amen.

MARCH 13

FRIENDS (PART 1)

1 Samuel 20:16–17

When Stuart Miller began research for his book *Men and Friendship*, most people thought that he was working on a book about homosexuality.[1] But Miller was asking the question that many men raise, "Why don't I have many close friends?" After spending years searching for answers, Miller concluded that genuine friendship is hard to find. "True friendship must also be true engagement with the friend—a very frequent mutual holding in the mind and heart. Though the centrifugal pressures of modern life limit the frequency of the physical presence of friends, engagement makes physical proximity less of a problem. Male friendship can thus be thought of as a place in a man's inner being, a space in his life, that is daily occupied by another man, a place that is regularly charged with love, concern, hurt. Engagement means emotional involvement."[2]

The rise of groups such as Promise Keepers is, in part, the result of men wanting more from life and relationships than just golfing buddies. They want close relationships with other men. They want love and friendship. In *Confessions*, St. Augustine wrote, "Men go forth to wonder at the heights of mountains, the huge waves of the

---

1. Stuart Miller, *Men and Friendship* (Boston: Houghton Mifflin, 1983), 2.
2. Ibid., 191.

sea, the broad flow of the rivers, the vast compass of the ocean, the courses of the stars; and they pass by themselves without wondering." To wonder means to accept ourselves and our full capacity to love others and to express that love. That is often difficult to do. We're afraid that we might seem to be weak or foolish to others if we open ourselves to love. But what other option exists? To remain suspicious and unloving?

David and Jonathan were friends. They loved each other. That is a fact that some guys have trouble with, but they should not be troubled. I have friends whom I love. Nothing about it is perverse. It is a gift of God, and I appreciate my friends. If you have a friend, treasure that man. Spend some time with him. Let him know that you care. You will both be better for it.

Thanks for my friends, Lord, and thanks that
there is a friend who sticks closer than a brother.
In the name of that Friend, Amen.

MARCH 14

Friends (Part 2)

1 Samuel 20:16–17

When I was growing up, I had many friends but one special one. His name was Milton. He and I were almost inseparable. We lived a half mile apart in a rural area of south Louisiana. Woods, swamps, a bayou, and pastures for cattle were all around us, and we knew every square inch of them. Together, Milton and I hunted, fished, went to school, played basketball at school and softball at home, and threw cow "muffins" at each other. We once lined up tin cans on the little road in front of our houses so that cars would have to slow down when they got there. We waited in the palmetto bushes and shot out their taillights with BB guns. (I've regretted this many times since!)

We swung from vines out over Bayou Des Canes, giving our Tarzan yells as we let go and hit the water. We climbed small pines and grabbed the tops of those saplings and jumped out so that the trees bent, and we got an "elevator" ride down. Sometimes the tops snapped off, and our ride down was faster than we wanted! Milton and I picked mayhaws (a small fruit that grows in Louisiana swamps) and rode around in boats during flood times. He had a huge abandoned sawdust pile behind his house, and we spent many hours tunneling through the sawdust with old stockings over our heads to keep the sawdust out of our eyes and noses. We were friends, and friends will do anything with, or for, friends.

Milton and I do not see each other very often now. We have gone our separate ways, as adults do, although I still hold him in high esteem. That relationship taught me some important things about friendship.

Lord, thanks for the good friends I have had during my life. Thanks for the friends I now have. Bless them in Jesus' name, Amen.

MARCH 15

SPARE A LIFE
1 Samuel 24

It sounds like something out of Hollywood. A villain is trying to hunt down the hero. Then the bad guy lets down his guard for a minute and gives the good guy a chance to kill him. But the hero is a man of conscience. He lets the villain know that he could have ended his life but has let him live. The two men finally reconcile.

Hollywood? Hardly. This is right out of the Bible. Saul had been furious with his young protégé, David. The young man had captured the hearts of the people, and Saul was jealous. He vowed to hunt David down and kill him. David and his men hid in a cave. Saul came in to "relieve himself." While he was doing his business, David got close enough to cut off a piece of Saul's robe. David had caught him with his pants down and could have easily overpowered him. Instead, David let him live and leave the cave. What happened next is amazing.

David called out to Saul and asked for a settling of their differences. Saul wept when he heard the request. He agreed to cease the hostilities. What could have ended in bloodshed wound up with peace between two groups.

Does that sound like a fairy tale? Is such an outcome possible today? Too many of us wear our feelings on our sleeves and get bent out of shape for the wrong reasons. Few of us have someone literally out to kill us. What we have is a competitor who might be trying to take our business or win a promotion over us. Yes, you have to protect yourself in many situations, but think of the ways you might be able to call off the war. I would much rather have a colleague than an enemy. How about you?

Give us grace enough to be strong, Lord, strong enough to make the first move toward reconciliation with an enemy. Help us make peace and not war. Through Jesus' name, Amen.

MARCH 16

Taking Our Own Life
1 Samuel 31

A friend of mine is killing himself—slowly. He is not taking arsenic or drawing up an elaborate plan to put a .44 to his head. He is killing himself with a knife and a fork. Another guy is murdering himself with a small white cylinder that he regularly sets on fire and places in his mouth. Still another is committing suicide every time he pours fluid from a bottle and shoots it down. Another places a needle in his arm and relaxes as the chemical takes effect. Another flops in front of the TV with a can of beer and a bag of potato chips and never moves.

Each one is dying slowly. What about you? In today's Bible reading, King Saul was wounded and did not want his enemies to get the pleasure of killing him. Instead, he placed the tip of his sword to his body and fell on it and died. Many a wounded man has felt like dying. One man I know lost his job after pouring his life into that company. But times changed, and he was given his walking papers. He was wounded so badly that he felt like dying.

May I give you a word of grace today? God knows exactly where you are and what you are up against. Exactly! Others are facing situation like yours, but some of their situations are worse. As bad as your situation might be, your circumstances are not hopeless. Call on God for strength and guidance. Ask Him for patience and wisdom as you go through this situation.

One thing I ask of you. Do not kill yourself. God needs you. That is why He made you. Others need you. Put away the bottle or the needle. Be careful with the knife and the fork. Skip the momentary high of the cigarette or the drugs. Get moving and get motivated. Don't fall on your own sword.

> *Lord, You do know what I'm up against. Sometimes I feel like dying. But give me life—give me life. You are the life-giver and sustainer. I trust You and ask for Your help, guidance, wisdom, and strength. Help me make it one more day. Through Jesus' name, Amen.*

MARCH 17

GONE BUT NOT FORGOTTEN
2 Samuel 1:17–27

I conducted a funeral service a while back for a fellow whom I did not know well. I asked his family about him and got some amazing stories about his life. His family and friends loved him and missed him. As they told stories about Jim, they got animated and laughed and cried. They missed their companion and openly wept over his departure.

We guys sometimes have trouble with our grief. We lose friends and family and do not know what to do. But any loss brings the same grief—loss of a job, of our health, of our status. Never underestimate the power of loss.

When you read today's selection from the Bible, you might wonder what is going on. Saul had hunted David like an animal and tried to kill him. Yet, when David heard of the death of Saul, he mourned his loss. After all, Saul had been the king and now was dead. David refused simply to "forget" Saul. He wrote a song of lamentation and taught it to his people. They sang it in honor of their fallen king.

Have you ever wondered what people will sing in your honor? Let us hope it won't be like the old country song "Thank God and Greyhound She's Gone." We are writing our mourning song right now. Our relationships with our friends, the way we treat our family, our attitude toward God and His work—all of those variables go into the song that people will sing about us.

David sang, "How the mighty have fallen!" Although we might expect him to say, "Good riddance," he mourned. Life is precious. Value it and live it to your full potential. Amaze your friends. Make them sing a great song over you when you are gone.

Thank You, Lord, for giving me the opportunities that I have. My family is precious to me, my friends are a delight, my work is challenging, and my future is secure in You. Accept my gratitude in Christ, Amen.

MARCH 18

COME TO THE DANCE
2 Samuel 6:12–22

When I was a teenager, the little church I attended had a debate. Could a Christian dance? You might laugh when you think about that weighty discussion, but at the time it was important. Some people thought that dancing was a sin, no matter what; others thought that as long as it was supervised, dancing was fine.

You can imagine my surprise when I read about David's dancing in the Bible! Today's Scripture reading tells the story. The ark of the covenant, containing the tablets that Moses brought down from Mount Sinai, was returned to the people of God. When it arrived in Jerusalem, David was ecstatic. That word *ecstatic* means literally "to stand outside of oneself." We all have had occasions when we got so caught up in the excitement of an event that we got carried away. I have seen it happen at ball games many times.

David got caught up in the thrill of the ark's arrival. He danced with joy and abandon. His wife, Michal, the daughter of Saul, saw his display and thought that it was vulgar. She and David had a sharp argument about it. David's defense was simple: "I will celebrate before the LORD" (v. 21).

Have you noticed that someone always wants to dump cold water on people who are energetic and enthusiastic? "Don't get too excited," they say. "Be just like everyone else. Don't call attention to yourself." But David was right. Sometimes we express ourselves before God in ways that might not be very "dignified" to some people, but that expression is heartfelt and meant as an offering.

Love God with all of your heart. Give yourself as an offering to Him. Enjoy the pleasure of His presence. Come to the dance.

Lord, You know how much I love You. Everything about me, including my emotions, belong to You. Accept even my dance as an acceptable gift. Through Christ, Amen.

MARCH 19

THE PROMISE
2 Samuel 7:1–17

"Cross my heart and hope to die." That was the phrase boys used to seal a promise when I was a child. It meant that we were really serious about what we were saying. If you crossed your heart, you simply had to tell the truth! The consequences would be unbearably awful if you broke your word.

What if God Himself made a promise to you? Do you think that you could trust that promise? Nathan, the prophet, went to King David with a word from God. In essence, the Lord said to David that his kingdom would forever stand and that God would never take His love away from David. What must it have been like to hear that word from Nathan?

Neither you nor I have heard anything quite like that, but we certainly do have some promises from the Lord. He promises to save us when we call out to Him. He promises to give His Spirit to be with us in all of our trials and joys. And God promises to take us to be with Him for all of eternity when our time in this life is over.

I can well imagine that some guys reading these words question these promises. Some of you are going through the most incredible trials: possible financial ruin, eminent death in the family, crisis after crisis. All of this comes crashing down over you as if you were caught in a landslide. Has God abandoned you? No, I do not think so. We are never promised that we will not face trouble. What we are promised is that God will be with us in our trouble. That makes all of the difference in the world.

No matter what you might be facing, hold on to God's presence with you. Draw from His strength. He has given you a promise, and He keeps His word.

You do keep Your promises, Lord, and I thank You that I can trust in them. Help me to draw strength from You. You know exactly what I am facing. Give me grace and resolve to get through this time with Your peace. In Jesus' name, Amen.

MARCH 20

EVERY MAN'S WEAKNESS
2 Samuel 11

David and Bathsheba. Those three words speak volumes that send a shudder through every man. We know the story. David, young and powerful, lets his attention wander from business to a woman. The problem is that the woman was another man's wife! Even if you did not know the story, you can already see disaster coming. Disaster it was, too.

King David, who could have had anything legitimately, ends up wanting the one thing that he cannot have. That sounds like the plot of a made-for-TV movie. The dilemma is as old as humankind. Part of our condition is that we often want what is not for us. Wars are fought over such matters. Lives are ruined because of such things. Theologians speak of "original sin." That means that all of us have a built-in rebellious streak. We grasp for the very things that hurt us.

We men have the potential to get carried away with David's problem. If we let our minds and eyes wander from home, we will build our own fantasy island on which we will be left stranded and alone. Is it worth it? I have known too many men who have ruined their careers, their families, and their spiritual lives because they got involved with women who were not their wives. Proverbs says that is like scooping burning coals into your lap; you will get burned (see Prov. 6:27).

Every man has this struggle to some extent. You must take responsibility for your thoughts and actions. Cultivate your own garden. Stay on the straight and narrow. Never listen to the excuse, "Everybody's doing it." No, they are not. You have nothing to gain and everything to lose.

Lord, help me keep my eyes, hands, thoughts, and actions at home. Help me to want what I already have. In Jesus' name, Amen.

MARCH 21

THE SACRIFICE FACTOR
2 Samuel 24:18–25

Golfing great Arnold Palmer once said, "Every man wants to hit hard." I take that in several ways, not just on the golf course. We want to do something in life that matters and makes a contribution. We want to participate in something that really stretches us and calls forth our best.

King David, late in life, wanted to build an altar for sacrificing to God. He offered to buy a piece of property from a man named Araunah. This man offered to give the site to the king. But David said something that gets to the heart of devotion: "I will not sacrifice to the LORD my God burnt offerings that cost me nothing" (v. 24).

Ease and simplicity were not qualities for which David looked. He had learned early that he had to be responsible for himself and his actions. He did not want someone else acting for him, especially when it came to worship. Twenty-first-century men should not miss that lesson. Our devotion to the Lord should be such that it costs us something—time, effort, cash—our very selves. Why? When we put out our best, we grow. We appreciate the real cost of effort. Too many times, I have seen men dabble in something related to the church instead of going at it full tilt. Organizations such as Promise Keepers encourage men to get at it with full momentum.

Like Arnold Palmer, do you want to hit hard? Give the Lord your best—something that really costs you. Feel the stretch. Experience the pain. But marvel in the growth. What costs, gives.

Lord, I do want to sacrifice to You. I am not satisfied to dabble and play games. I vow before You to give You the best of which I am capable. Help me keep that vow. Through Christ, Amen.

MARCH 22

PASSING THE TORCH
I Kings 1:28–31

Letting go is difficult. We gain some little authority or position, and we squeeze it for fear of losing control. How many men have the idea that in their job nobody but they can do it right? I once worked for a guy who thought that the world would stop if he did not do his thing every day. He was difficult to work for and alienated all of his employees. Even as a young man I realized that plenty of people could do a better job than he could.

But it's hard to let go. Consider King David. In the twilight of life, he had to choose a successor. Plenty of contenders were around. But, under the leadership of God, he chose his son Solomon to succeed him. That set off a series of events that would change the nation.

Where are you in life? Are you at a position to rise and take on new challenges or in the process of passing the torch to others? Part of what we need to do is train others to take up the fight and to become leaders in their own right. Many men are involved in a mentor program of some sort. They intentionally give themselves to younger protégés for the sake of the future.

In what are you sinking your life? What is your best investment?

Your portfolio might be full of people rather than stocks. If so, then you have passed the torch well.

Help me to invest in people, Lord. Help me be ready to pass the torch to others when their time comes. You have blessed me in more ways than I can count. Let me show others how that happens. In Christ, Amen.

MARCH 23

GETTING WHAT YOU ASK FOR

1 Kings 3

Sometimes you get what you ask for. That sounds so simple, but often we are afraid to ask for what we really want. If you could ask for anything, what would it be? A bank account that makes Bill Gates seem like a pauper? The ability to persuade people and nations? Better relationships with your family?

Imagine what would happen if God Himself said to you, "Ask for whatever you want Me to give you." That is what happened to young King Solomon in a dream. I can imagine the look on his face as he considered the possibilities. Maybe he thought of the very things you and I might think of. Then he gave an unexpected answer— "give me wisdom." Solomon realized that he needed the ability to think clearly and act decisively. God's reply was that Solomon would get not only wisdom but also, as a bonus, riches and honor.

We would do well to remember Solomon's request as we approach the Lord in prayer. I have heard people pray for many things and situations but rarely wisdom and insight. The ability to do that stems from a humble heart and a dedicated spirit.

Do you believe that God still answers prayer for wisdom? I believe that, and I pray for it regularly. I do not know if I have any more wisdom than the average guy, but I do know that I am hungry for all that God has for me.

What are you wise enough to want?

Give me, too, a discerning heart, Lord. Help me

know the better things of life—the life of the Spirit. Grant that I would know Your will and Word and would have the sense to put them into effect. Through Jesus, Amen.

A Dangerous Detour

1 Kings 11:1–13

He had it all—wealth beyond his imagination, the respect of the nations, and the blessings of God. But with all of that, he wanted still more. He was Solomon, the king who ruled Israel after David. His power began to lead him on a dangerous detour that took him away from God. He had seven hundred wives, many of whom were not of his faith. The Lord had specifically told Solomon and others to stay away from such women: "You must not intermarry with them, because they will surely turn your hearts after their gods" (v. 2). Hey, Solomon was rich and powerful. What would be the harm of just a little rebellion?

Does that sound familiar? We could all fill in the blanks of the question "What could be the harm in a little _____?" We already know the answer too. A *lot* could be wrong with it! We are all like Solomon in that we do not make such detours all at once; we do it gradually, just a little at a time here and there. "Aw, it won't hurt if I do this just this one time." "No one will know if I don't do my best today." We know better.

The Lord was decisive in His reaction to Solomon's defection: "The LORD became angry with Solomon because his heart had turned away from the LORD, the God of Israel, who had appeared to him twice" (v. 9). Turning away from God happens slowly, but it always has the same result.

Which way are you facing?

Help me stay focused on Your way, Lord, and not turn aside to detours. I am so easily dragged away from You. Help me to stay close. Through Jesus, Amen.

PAYDAY SOMEDAY

1 Kings 21

When I was a college student, an old gentleman came to my church to preach. He wore a white suit and preached from 1 Kings 21 a sermon that he called, "Payday Someday." That preacher was R. G. Lee, a well-known pastor who preached that sermon more than a thousand times. People flocked to hear him tell the story of a conniving king who stole the only possession of a common man—his vineyard.

That story is about a king named Ahab who, along with his wife Jezebel, had a man named Naboth killed so they could get his vineyard. Did they think that they did not already have enough property and possessions? The human spirit is always reaching out, saying, "More! More!"

Ahab had not counted on the fact that God was watching the entire process. He sent the prophet Elijah to Ahab to say, "I am going to bring disaster on you" (v. 21). In telling this story, the writer of 1 Kings adds, "(There was never a man like Ahab, who sold himself to do evil in the eyes of the LORD, urged on by Jezebel his wife. He behaved in the vilest manner by going after idols, like the Amorites the LORD drove out before Israel.)" (vv. 25–26).

That phrase haunts me—"sold himself to do evil." We sell ourselves whenever we try to do something against God's will. The consequences are always certain to come, either quickly or slowly. That is why R. G. Lee called his sermon "Payday Someday." Jezebel and Ahab earned a payday for what they did. And the bill came due sooner than they expected.

Lord, deliver me from my innate sinful desire that always tempts me to want what I cannot have. Through Christ, Amen.

DEATH IN THE POT
2 Kings 4:38–41

We guys are like the servant of Elisha who was sent out to gather the makings of a stew for the prophets. He gathered some herbs and other "fixings" but came across a wild vine. He took some of the gourds from it and put them into the stew also. When the group sat down to eat, they cried out, "There is death in the pot!"

I have gathered some death. Haven't you? I would never intentionally do anything to poison anyone, but some of the attitudes that I have gathered through life end up being poison. How about a stubborn, self-seeking mind-set? What about an insistence on doing things my way? The list could go on and on, but you get the point. Not everything we bring home is good for us.

When my children were little, I was sometimes too harsh with them. Somewhere I had gotten the idea that they were supposed to be different because they were *my* kids. Where did I get that idea? It was like death to them sometimes. I would do many things differently if I had them to do over.

What do you take home that is like death to your family? What attitude do you need to soften or change altogether? What actions could you modify to bring health to the people closest to you? Elisha told his servant to put some flour into the pot. It changed the chemistry of the stew and made it edible. That one ingredient made the difference between life and death.

For us, that one ingredient is faith in God and obedience to His way. That really will change death in the pot to satisfying nourishment.

Lord, I've brought home with me way too much poison from the world. Forgive me, and give me wisdom to separate what gives life from what brings death. Take my faith and let it be the ingredient that changes death to life. Through Jesus, who gives life, Amen.

A BANQUET OF CONSEQUENCES

2 Kings 17

A wise observer of life once noted that sooner or later every man sits down at a banquet of consequences. Throughout life, every person has been preparing the meal and setting the table. Then the time comes to dine on what he has cooked up.

This happens in not only individual lives but also groups. In today's reading, the nation of Israel fell to Shalmaneser of Assyria. The writer of 2 Kings gives the reasons in 17:14–23. He pointed out that although the Lord was gracious to the nation, "they would not listen and were as stiff-necked as their fathers, who did not trust in the LORD their God" (v. 14). Also, "they forsook all the commands of the LORD their God" (v. 16). Furthermore, "they bowed down to all the starry hosts, and they worshiped Baal" (v. 16).

As I read this list of failures, I cannot help but look at it on two levels, one personal and the other national. On a personal basis, I realize that some of my life choices were not very good, and they are still paying unwanted dividends today. I set the table, and now I get to dine there! On a national basis, I understand that some of our nation's choices also are consequence-laden. For example, people will debate for years the circumstances of September 11, 2001.

In all of this, I look to one thing that helps—the grace of God. Yes, you and I live with the aftermath of some of our choices. But grace means that they need not mean ultimate failure. Grace brings life from disaster and hope from despair. That is worth holding onto and living for.

As I sit down at this table of consequences, Lord, would You be my guest and help me by Your grace? Through Christ, my Lord, Amen.

RESTORED

2 Kings 22:1–13

Have you ever rummaged through your attic or your basement and found something you had forgotten that was important to you? You look at that picture or hold that object, and your mind floods with memories that put a smile on your lips or a lump in your throat. You wonder how you could have forgotten about it because it was so important.

King Josiah started a program of restoring the temple in Jerusalem, which had been neglected. In the process of the restoration, workmen found a book that had also been neglected. It was the "Book of the Law." Scholars believe that it was the book of Deuteronomy, or at least key portions of it. When Josiah heard its content, he was personally grieved, and then he led his people in a process of national reformation.

The Word of God has that power over us. How could anyone stand up to its strength and act unmoved? Many men today ignore the Bible and act as if it were nothing but a dusty collection of ancient tales. But it has the power to restore men and nations to their proper relationship with God. A man came to me recently to talk about his life. He had not attended church in years but finally had begun to come with his wife. As the Scripture was read and preached, it seemed to reach into this man's very soul and shake him. He wept as he talked about the wasted years during which he had ignored God's Word.

Do you need restoration? Like Josiah, do you need to be shaken out of your ruts? Open your heart to God. He will draw you close and use His word to restore you.

My prayer is for restoration, Lord. You know my heart. Fill it to overflowing with Your love and grace. In Jesus' name, Amen.

ON SECOND THOUGHT
1 Chronicles 29:26–30

Readers of the Bible are often confused about the layout of the books of Samuel, Kings, and Chronicles. Why repeat things over and over? Samuel and Kings tell the story of the nation of Israel *before* the Babylonian captivity, which lasted seventy years. The books of Chronicles tell the national story *after* the captivity. The perspective of each is different. The people had learned a great lesson. In telling the life of David, for example, nothing is said in Chronicles about his shameful affair with Bathsheba.

Most of us can look back on events in life and realize that our perspective has shifted somewhat. I think about things about which I once bragged, but now, on second thought, I realize that I had nothing to brag about. Instead, I feel ashamed of some of the things I did. You know that feeling, too, don't you?

One of the great aspects of life is that we are not condemned to make the same mistakes repeatedly. We can learn. Some lessons are more painful than others, but at least we get a second thought about events, people, and decisions. Some of the things I once thought were disasters have taught me some of life's most important lessons. On the other hand, some of the things that I once thought were blessings now give me second thoughts.

At the end of 1 Chronicles, we read of David, "He died at a good old age, having enjoyed long life, wealth and honor. His son Solomon succeeded him as king" (v. 28). That is not a bad summary of his or anyone's life. In looking back, some things are better not said. Thank God for the opportunity of a second thought.

You have taught me some life lessons, Lord, as I looked back and reflected on my actions and attitudes. Help me learn going forward. Through Christ, Amen.

CARE OF GOD'S HOUSE
2 Chronicles 2:1–11

I have always been amazed in reading about the minute care that Solomon took in constructing the temple. The money is impressive, but I have always been more captivated by his utter commitment to detail. He wanted the exact materials—logs, gold, and silver—and workmen—painters, craftsmen, and builders. His was not going to be a shoddy project but something that reflected the majesty of God.

Too often, our churches reflect our true thinking about the Lord. They are shoddy, dirty, worn down, and falling apart. Some churches seem more like museums to mediocrity than houses to reflect our devotion to a matchless God. I once was called to be the pastor of a church that had seen better days. The congregation was sort of shell-shocked as the community around them changed. They thought that everyone, including God, had bypassed them. As a result, the building became more and more decrepit. The shingles were sliding off the roof, the paint was peeling, and the yard looked like a pasture. It all reflected the sense of despair that the people felt.

We began to work on the building to say to the community, "We are alive, and we serve a great God!" I have never worked so hard at any place in my life! I wore out my gas-powered grass trimmer and nearly wore out my back. I cut down small trees with my chain saw and led the church to paint, repair, throw out junk, and reroof the building. Yes, it was difficult, but the community began to get the message that we were alive and wanted to serve God with a clean, well-kept building.

Our outer circumstances often reflect our inward condition. Carelessness regarding our houses of worship reveals carelessness in our hearts. Solomon's care in building the temple shows us a heart devoted to God. May we have the same type of heart.

Lord, I will do my part in keeping Your house a place where You would be pleased to meet us in worship. In Christ, Amen.

GOD CAN USE ANYONE

2 Chronicles 36:15–23

One of the surprises in Scripture is that God chose to use some unexpected people to carry out His plan. One such person was Cyrus, king of Persia. He defeated the Babylonians in battle in 539 B.C. Once he was firmly in control, Cyrus issued a decree that anyone who wanted to go back home could do so and build a temple in Jerusalem. They would actually be rebuilding the old temple.

The writer of Chronicles says that while the people were captive in Babylon, "The land enjoyed its sabbath rests; all the time of its desolation it rested" (v. 21). What seemed a disaster for the people was a time of rest and restoration for the land. Our "down times" can be just that—times of restoration and reorientation. Maybe you have been fired from a job or had a breakup in a relationship. Those times do not have to be wasted.

God used a seeming tragedy to bring good for the soil and, ultimately, for the people of Israel. God raised Cyrus to power and used him to free the people to go home. Cyrus used these words in his proclamation: "The LORD, the God of heaven, has given me all the kingdoms of the earth and he has appointed me to build a temple for him at Jerusalem in Judah. Anyone of his people among you—may the LORD his God be with him, and let him go up" (v. 23).

Whatever your circumstances today, God can use you and bring good out of your situation. When life seems to be caving in on you, that is a good time to put your trust in God and ask Him to work it out for good. You might want to read Romans 8:28 in this regard.

Lord, You know exactly what I am going through.
Use me in this situation and bring ultimate good
from it. Give me strength and patience to endure
everything. In Jesus' name, Amen.

HOW IS YOUR FAITH?

Ezra 1:1–5

There's a new religion in Britain. So many people have now claimed to be a part of this "faith" that it was included as a choice in the 2002 census. It's not Baptist, Assembly of God, Catholic, or anything in between.

Instead, more than ten thousand Britons have stated that "Jedi" is their religion! Thousands of people have embraced as their true faith the made-up philosophy of George Lucas from his *Star Wars* films. Most of us know only the phrase "May the force be with you." But it will now be an official choice for all Britons who fill out their census form and have to choose a religion.[1]

What will be your faith? Will you hold to the beliefs of the Bible? These were the questions the Israelites had to answer during their years of exile in Babylon. Surrounded on all sides by pagans who were also their masters, the tribes of Israel felt tremendous pressure to throw off their old beliefs and embrace the "many-gods/anything-goes" attitudes of their victors.

Many Israelites lost their faith in the years spent far from Jerusalem, but a remnant stayed true to Jehovah. They trusted in God in spite of difficult circumstances, and the Lord rewarded their faithfulness. The day came when God moved in the heart of Cyrus, king of Persia. The king released the people and allowed them to return to Jerusalem and rebuild the temple.

When that time came, the faithful remnant was ready.

If you're like most of us, you hear some unusual religious discussions in the workplace, at the gym, or around your neighborhood. Everyone seems to have his own idea of what is right and how one gets to heaven—if he even believes in heaven. A Christian who stands for his faith will receive tremendous pressure to give up and give in.

What are you doing with your faith? Are you standing firm? Remember: it's more important to be faithful than it is to "fit in."

1. Excite.com/news, 8 October 2001.

Ensure that you're a part of the group that's decided to be faithful to God, no matter where you are and no matter who's around you.

One day, the King of Kings will say, "It's time to come home!" You want to be sure that you're part of the group that He invites to be with Him forever.

Dear Lord, help me to stand firm for You today.
May my choices about what I should say and
how I should act honor You. And if today is my
last day of life, may it be a day that points others
to the Savior. In Jesus' name, Amen.

APRIL 2

OVERCOMING FEAR
Ezra 3:1–6

The water looked as if it lay ten thousand feet below me. My heart hammered away in my chest with the force of a jackhammer. I wondered one last time if perhaps I'd made a mistake. After all, stepping off into space with nothing more than a cord for support—plummeting head-first toward the ground at insane speeds—wasn't what I normally did with my time.

Bungee jumping. Its prospect terrified me—and exhilarated me. After one more check of my sanity, I dove off into space—and loved every minute of it. When I find someone who's experienced the same thing, we immediately begin reliving those wonderful, frightening times.

Read again these words from verse 3 of today's passage: "Despite their fear of the peoples around them, they built the altar on its foundation and sacrificed burnt offerings on it to the LORD, both the morning and evening sacrifices."

The Israelites had returned to Jerusalem. Weak, with unsympathetic enemies all around them, they ignored their fears and honored God. They knew that they might be attacked because of their worship of the one, true God. But honoring Jehovah had become more important to them than giving in to their fears.

Think with me for a moment. We're reading about this event

thousands of years later because someone wanted to write down what happened to commemorate it. In other words, they were afraid but exhilarated because they refused to let their fears control them. Perhaps for years afterward, fathers and mothers who were there for the rebuilding of the temple sat around the table with their families at night and retold the story of worshiping God in the midst of hostility. And as the children listened, important lessons were passed from one generation to another.

As you overcome your fears and allow God to have first place in your life and priorities, other people will notice. As you stand for Christ, no matter what the cost, your family members will see and understand that a right relationship with God is worth fighting your fears.

Yes, stepping out into life, trusting only Jesus, might seem frightening, but it will also be the most thrilling thing you've ever experienced. Try it, and you'll be talking about it for the rest of your life.

Father, I want to trust in You alone. Help me to give You my fears and my inconsistencies. May I be a positive witness to those watching me today. In Jesus' name, Amen.

APRIL 3

WHEN FOUNDATIONS ARE DESTROYED

Ezra 3:10–13

"Blackness on blackness." Has your life ever felt like that? Have you ever had your foundations destroyed? Because of a young man by the name of Chris Haskins, many University of Wisconsin students have begun asking themselves these questions.

Haskins, a senior at UW, allegedly drove his vehicle while drunk on the evening of September 16 several years ago. His pickup veered across the road into the path of a sport utility vehicle carrying eight UW track and cross-country athletes. All eight were killed. Police said Haskins's blood alcohol level was 0.16 percent, well above Wyoming's legal limit of 0.10. Haskins decided to plead guilty after the details of his blood alcohol test were made public to the court.

The deaths of the eight student athletes stunned the UW campus. Already reeling from the attacks on the World Trade Center less than a week earlier, many people agreed with one student who likened it to "blackness on blackness."[1] If these allegations are true, in one moment a young man destroyed the foundation of his life and the lives of eight others.

Building foundations or destroying them—which are you doing with your life choices?

Today's passage shows us a bittersweet moment in the lives of the children of Israel. As the foundation for the new temple was being laid, both weeping and cries of joy rose up before God. The tears came from the people who were old enough to remember the former temple's grandeur. They wept for the majesty destroyed by their own disobedience. The cries of joy were from those people who realized that the foundation of the new temple represented their hope and trust in a God who would never fail them.

In your own life, perhaps you have shed tears of sorrow for foundations destroyed. If so, learn from your mistakes, confess your sins to God, and then allow Him to begin building a new foundation that represents a future dedicated to the Lord and bright with promise.

Dear God, I thank You that you still love me in spite of my sometimes poor choices. Although I've done wrong in the past, I want to turn from those mistakes and ask Your forgiveness. Please rebuild my life in a way that will please You and draw others to You. In Jesus' name, Amen.

1. Nytimes.com, Breaking News, 7 February 2002.

THE PAYOFF
Ezra 6:14–18

The payoff: it's what life is all about.

My oldest daughter sat beside me in the car. The backseat and the trunk bulged alarmingly with all of her worldly possessions. We were on the way to college. Leaving home, beginning her adult future, no curfew, no parents looking over her shoulder. I wondered what important words of wisdom I could give her at this moment that would make a difference. Had Susan and I done a good enough job parenting her? Had the lessons about living for Christ made an impression?

Amy began reminiscing about her friends from high school. She spoke of several problems they'd encountered with parents who had made unwise choices. Then, casually, she reached over and patted my knee. "Dad," she said, "I'm glad you're a godly man. I want that in whatever husband God chooses for me."

The payoff! All of those years grappling with a supremely gifted, supremely stubborn teenager suddenly became worthwhile. The times we went against the swift current of some parents' choices showed that following God's teachings would bring blessings.

In today's passage of Scripture, the children of Israel reaped the results of being faithful to God although they were surrounded by godlessness and hostility. Their payoff: the temple, completely finished, stood before them as a glorious witness to Jehovah. As they worshiped and celebrated, they had to have joy in their hearts for all that God had done for them.

Take a moment to look at the direction of your life. Check out your priorities. If you're married, examine the quality of your relationship with your wife and children. Is all of this leading to a wonderful payoff from God? In other words, are you on the right path?

Remain faithful to the commands of Christ day in and day out. Don't get discouraged or give up, even if you're the only family in the area living for Christ. Remember: a payoff is coming, a time of celebrating and rejoicing. Until then, stay on the path, point the way for others, and trust in God to bring you joy.

Heavenly Father, help me to remember that others
are watching me. May I not give up or lead
others astray. I trust in You to help me make
correct decisions and prepare my family for a
godly payoff one day. Until then, help me to
remain faithful. In Jesus' name, Amen.

APRIL 5

MAKING A DIFFERENCE
Nehemiah 1

The mayor had just left my house. Clad in galoshes and rain gear, and accompanied by the National Guard, she had used my phone to find out where the flood in our city threatened to wreak its worst damage. Unfortunately, we seemed to be at the epicenter of the rising waters! No cars could enter or leave our area. Angry currents swirled around stalled vehicles in the now-invisible streets.

My neighbor lived at the corner of an intersection. As I glanced out my window, I could see him laying sandbags in front of his door, piling them higher and higher. I sighed, then stepped out into the chest-high water and fought the current across a distance of a few hundred feet. "How can I help?" I shouted.

"Could you come into the backyard for a minute?" he asked. "I've got an idea that might reduce the water level around the house." Dale pointed to the wooden fence encircling the yard. "If we can pull a few boards out, it might provide a big enough area for the water to escape and the pressure to lessen."

Together, we worked against the weight of rushing water and stubborn boards. Many minutes and two boards later, however, we found success. The height of the water went down considerably within ten minutes of removing the boards. Dale's house remained safe and dry.

The right person in the right place at the right time doing the right thing can make a world of difference—in a world that needs to be made different.

Nehemiah was such a man. The remnant of Israel had returned to Jerusalem to rebuild the temple. Their problems, however, seemed insurmountable. They became frustrated, then demoralized. The work on the city wall stalled, then stopped. They felt powerless against the flood of hostility and godlessness from the enemies surrounding them.

As we will see in the coming days, Nehemiah came to Jerusalem's rescue. His willingness to put his life on the line for God inspired the people to construct the wall and finish the temple. That prophet made a difference.

What are you doing to make a difference in this world?

Someone, somewhere, needs your help. A situation exists that needs your input to be completed successfully. A world needs to be changed, souls need to be brought to Christ, Christians need to be encouraged. In short, godly men are still needed to make a difference.

The right man in the right place at the right time doing the right thing can make a world of difference. And God wants that man to be *you!*

Dear Lord, help me to focus on the needs of others today. May I not be so selfish that I miss opportunities to serve You and help others. Help me to make a difference in the lives of those around me. In Jesus' name, Amen.

APRIL 6

REBUILDING THE RUINS
Nehemiah 2:11–18

I stumbled over the rubble, watching my steps as I navigated a crumbled section of a wall. Ruins surrounded me. Instead of the sound of jackhammers and dump trucks, however, the only thing that could be heard were the oohs and aahs of fellow travelers.

My tour group consisted mainly of people like me, an American who had seldom seen anything more than two hundred years old. Now, faced with the excavated remains of Herod's palace and examining the building where Paul found himself imprisoned before going to Rome, we tried to comprehend the structure as it existed two thousand years ago. Israel, with its living history, was staking its claims on our imagination.

Have you ever noticed that ruins are beautiful only when they're old?

A recently burned house destroys the atmosphere of a neighborhood. The weedy, vacant lot is nothing but an eyesore. That abandoned shopping center is both pathetic and sinister.

Are you facing some kind of ruin in your own life? Whether a career, a marriage, or a reputation, if it's newly ruined, it's not pretty to behold. Vacant lots and vacant lives accomplish little. Ruined businesses and ruined reputations hurt others.

You can do three things with ruins: look at them, ignore them, or rebuild them. Today, we see that Nehemiah examined the ruins of Jerusalem's walls. He saw how vast the damage was, but he did not flinch from the task ahead. Nehemiah decided that it was time to rebuild.

What about you? Maybe you've ignored or looked at the ruins in your life long enough. Today, God wants you to begin rebuilding, allowing Him to be the Master Architect and giving Him the glory for a renewed mind, marriage, and character. Allow the Lord to be in charge, and your future can be even greater than your past.

Now, get to work!

Heavenly Father, I no longer want to look at the ruins of my life. Please help me to give You my failures and trust You to help me rebuild what's been lost. May Your will guide my life from this moment. In Jesus' name, Amen.

APRIL 7

PRAYER'S POWERFUL PARTNER
Nehemiah 4:1–9

Two men, a small boat, and a big storm—the situation didn't look good. Even worse, the boat sprang a leak! One man said, "Let's pray that God will get us safely to shore."

The second man said, "I have a better idea: you pray while I row!"

To tell you the truth, that's not bad theology. Nehemiah employed it while rebuilding Jerusalem's walls. When Israel's enemies saw the defense of Jerusalem going up, they threatened to attack. Verses 8–9 tell us, "They all plotted together to come and fight against Jerusalem and stir up trouble against it. But we prayed to our God and posted a guard day and night to meet this threat."

Pray to God *and* post a guard. In other words, trust in God for guidance and strength, but also use the gifts He's given you to overcome daily temptations and difficult situations.

If you're a man who is confident of his ability to get things done, maybe you need to be praying more for God's guidance. On the other hand, if you simply pray when in trouble but then sit back and do nothing, it might be time for you to begin accomplishing something, using your God-given intelligence and energy.

In your life, pray to God *and* post a guard. It's a great combination that the Lord will use to help you and others experience the abundant life that He promises to believers.

*Dear God, I want balance in my life. Please
guide me in coming to You first with my problems
and desires. But help me to apply Your wisdom
and my strength—guided by Your hand—to
everything I face. In Jesus' name, Amen.*

APRIL 8

WEAPONS INVENTORY
Nehemiah 4:10–21

We don't know the man's name, so let's call him "Mr. Smith." This man wanted to pray—a seemingly innocent desire. Smith wanted to pray before his flight took off from Los Angeles to Dallas. Again, in today's world, it sounds like a good thing for a passenger to do. At that point, however, Smith's judgment seemed to go awry.

In her welcoming speech, the stewardess told the passengers to stay in their seats with their seat belts fastened. Instead, Smith jumped up, grabbed the microphone from the stewardess's hands and decided to lead the whole plane in a prayer! Passengers became nervous by Smith's lunging for the mike. The pilots, notified of the incident, decided not to take off while Smith was still on the plane. The result: the flight was delayed while authorities threw Smith off the flight, refunded him his money, and decided not to press charges.[1]

Sometimes we can do the right thing in the wrong way. It's one reason God gives us so many Scripture passages concerning how to get along with our neighbors and with fellow family and church members. If we don't follow these practical guidelines, we can become guilty of turning people off and ineffectively presenting the gospel. Ignoring God's principles for getting along with others reveals our weak state. It keeps us unprepared for witnessing opportunities.

The people of Nehemiah's day maintained a high level of preparedness and vigilance. They worked to rebuild the walls of Jerusalem, but they also kept their swords beside them, ready to repel any attack from their enemies. In other words, these believers used everything at their disposal to accomplish their task for God. As a result, these faithful servants were successful in reestablishing their city.

Let's take a weapons' inventory:

1. How are your people skills? Do you actively care about others' needs?
2. How is your vocabulary? Is profanity a part of your everyday life, or do you ensure that you honor God with your mouth?
3. How strong is your relationship with your neighbors? Do you go out of your way to be a good Christian influence in front of them?

Caring concern, a godly vocabulary, and a consistent witness before a watching world are all weapons that believers can and must use if we are to accomplish God's task of winning our world to Christ.

---

1. Excite.com/news, 8 October 2001.

Let's keep building the kingdom . . . and stay armed and prepared.

Heavenly Father, I want to be the best witness possible for You. Please help me control my speech and my actions today. Let me be an effective witness for You. In Jesus' name, Amen.

BUSINESS ETHICS
Nehemiah 5:5–13

If you're a businessman, ponder this: how you treat your employees often says more about you than anything you do or say in your church. Treating others in the way you wish to be treated is not only the Golden Rule but also the best way to witness of Christ's love.

In the past, I've known certain business leaders who claimed leadership roles in their churches and denominations. A close examination of their business practices, however, revealed troubling ethics, hot tempers, or dubious relationships with their employees. *In every case*, these men eventually imploded, self-destructing and ruining their reputations.

We must remember that our living for Christ can know no barriers. If the life we live on Sunday is not the same one we live Monday through Saturday, then one of them is a lie! If the vocabulary we employ on the shop floor is not the same one we use with our fellow church members, we become guilty of hypocrisy. If our morality changes to fit the current crowd, we're immoral.

Nehemiah faced these same problems in the ruined city of Jerusalem. The old sins of selfishness and hatred of God's authority that had destroyed Jerusalem the first time now reared their ugly heads again. Unless they could be dealt with quickly and effectively, these subtle enemies would again wreak damage among the fragile remnant that was struggling to rebuild.

A lack of unity among the workers was already being felt. Those with money were not helping those who had little. Instead, they were charging excessive interest to their own people, not only handicapping the ability of the people to earn a living but also slowing the work on the city's walls. After all, if a man has to choose between foraging for food to feed his family and working to rebuild a wall, he will have to choose the former.

Please don't miss this. The nobles' selfishness and greed were more effective in hurting the rebuilding of the city's walls than were the enemies outside Jerusalem. A lack of consistency in loving our fellowman in a Christlike manner can have similar results in our local church fellowship.

It's time we men stood up for Jesus at home, at church, at work, and in our recreation time. May others see our love of Christ in the way we relate to them on an everyday basis.

Dear Lord, You know my heart. You know where I lack faith and where I need strength. Help me to be faithful to You in every situation in which I find myself today. May others see Christ in the way I relate to them. In Jesus' name, Amen.

APRIL 10

OVERCOMING TEMPTATION
Nehemiah 6:1–9

When are you most vulnerable to temptation? For many of us, it's right after we've accomplished something great for God. While we're in the middle of the project, all of our attention is on finishing well for the Lord. But after it's over, we might relax and let down our defenses. Satan can use that time of relaxation to attack us if we're not careful.

Remember Elijah? The prophet fought successfully against an evil king and queen. He defeated 450 false prophets of Baal in an act of supreme faith before a watching crowd. But when it was all over, when he relaxed, his troubles began. It ended with the prophet in a cave, begging God to let him die because Elijah had lost hope.

Nehemiah faced the same danger. The former ruin of a wall now stood strong and complete, a testimony to Nehemiah's faith and God's power. At that point, it would have been easy for the prophet to let down his guard a bit. If he had done so, however, Nehemiah—and Jerusalem—would have been destroyed because at that precise moment Israel's enemies decided to attack one last time. Because Nehemiah remained vigilant, however, he saw through the enemies' schemes and stayed on course for God.

As I write these words, my church is in the middle of a relocation program. Excitement is running high as we prepare to move to a great location. Beautiful plans inspire the congregation to give sacrificially. Already, however, I am talking carefully with key staff and lay leaders about how we can avoid an emotional, spiritual, and physical letdown after we move in. We want to stay prepared and effective for Christ.

What is your current "readiness" state? Are you staying on task for God, or have you relaxed just a bit? Remember: if it happened to Elijah, it can happen to you and me. Let's follow the example of Nehemiah and stand ready to serve God at every stage of our lives.

Dear God, keep me ever vigilant for You. I don't want to let down or give up. May Your Spirit keep me close to You during every part of this day. In Jesus' name, Amen.

APRIL 11

LIFE-CHANGING MOMENTS
Nehemiah 8:5–12

What's the best news you've ever received? "Honey, the doctor says we're going to have a baby." "Congratulations, the tests came back negative." "We made a mistake here at the IRS. Instead of your owing more on taxes, we've discovered you're due a substantial refund!"

Phrases, a few words strung together just right, have the power to change your life. Welcome words can engender strong emotions. I well remember the moment my future changed forever because of four words. They came in response to my question, "Will you marry me?" My future wife said, "Yes. I'd love to." Shazzam! I can still feel the goose bumps.

Today's passage deals with one of those life-changing moments. Ezra had found the book of the Law. The people had not heard God's Word read in decades. Some of the younger Israelites had never heard the complete Law! Much of what God had said no longer remained in the people's consciousness. The first part of chapter 8 tells us that Ezra began reading to the people at day-break—and he read until noon! As the powerful words of God fell upon the people's ears, they responded by weeping deeply. Promises given by God remained unclaimed because of the people's ignorance. Commands from Jehovah were not obeyed, not through willful disobedience but because the Israelites were unaware of what the Bible stated. The priests responded to the people by telling them to dry their eyes and, instead, rejoice because of what they were hearing.

Most of us are in a situation just the opposite from those Israelites of long ago. They had almost no Bible, but we have several Bibles in our houses, cars, and at work. But do we take advantage of the wonderful privilege we have? We need to read God's Good News for all of us regularly. If you're out of the habit of reading the Bible, one good place to begin is right here. Don't just read the devotionals. Be sure to look up and read the Scripture passages too, and meditate on them daily. They have the power to change your life forever. And that's definitely good news!

Heavenly Father, I want a true hunger for the Bible. Grow in me the desire to read it every day. Help Your words to sink deep within my life and my soul. May they take root and change me to be more like Your character. In Jesus' name, Amen.

APRIL 12

SHARING GOD'S GRACE
Nehemiah 8:13–18

About one month before my eighteenth birthday, I heard some information that rocked my teenage world. I'm not going to quote the exact words. Instead, I'll try to repeat what my brain heard on that fateful night: "By grace you are saved, through faith. Not by works, so that no one can boast." The news that it is impossible to get to heaven through your own good accomplishments hit me hard—because that's what I had been counting on for eternal life. In the moments following, I heard, and finally understood, the message of forgiveness and salvation. Bowing my head, I asked Christ to forgive me of my sins and take control of my life. I trusted in His grace alone to bring me safely to heaven.

What a life change!

In verse 17 of today's passage, we learn an astounding piece of news: "The whole company that had returned from exile built booths and lived in them. From the days of Joshua son of Nun until that day, the Israelites had not celebrated it like this. And their joy was very great." This means, according to my Bible dictionary, that for the first time in nearly a thousand years, the people of Israel celebrated God's goodness and power in the manner the Lord had commanded Moses and his followers. Imagine how many generations lived and died without ever knowing of God's commands and promises—generations that missed out on the power and joy of God's Word. Now, however, the Law once again made its influence felt in the lives of the Israelites, and they rejoiced.

What a life change!

Who among your friends and acquaintances does not know how to get to heaven? How many of them have never heard the life-giving message of salvation? Maybe it's time you begin asking God for opportunities to introduce these people to Jesus Christ. If you're not careful, the weeks, months, years, and decades can pass without your mentioning to your friends the good news of Jesus. Imagine what would happen in their lives if you could lead them to Christ today!

What a life change—for them and for you.

Dear Lord, You know my heart and my fears. You also know who among my friends and acquaintances need Jesus as their Savior. Please begin to help me look for opportunities to share Christ with them. May I make this a priority every day of my life, beginning today. In Jesus' name, Amen.

CONFESSION TIME
Nehemiah 9:1–8, 32–38

When I was growing up, basketball was my life. I could never claim to be great, only good enough to be chosen fairly early when teams were being made up. The main thing was that I loved it, lived for it, played it, and watched it on television, following my beloved Boston Celtics from one world championship to another.

As a young teenager, I faced a problem. It was a Saturday, and I had taken some money out of my dad's coat earlier that morning before leaving to play basketball. My reasoning: I needed something to drink when I got hot and winded (never mind the free water fountain—that never entered my mind). God must have a sense of humor. Now, taking a break, I turned my newly purchased soft drink up to take my first sip, and who should step into the gym but my dad!

"I thought you didn't have any money, son."

I can still remember thinking, *Brain, work fast!* If I confessed to taking the money, I knew that Dad would ground me from basketball forever. I couldn't do without my favorite thing in life. On the other hand, neither could I stand to lie to my father.

So, taking a deep breath, I admitted to Dad that I'd stolen the money. Interestingly, I've forgotten the punishment he gave me. But I do remember the feeling of relief washing over me as I confessed to my father that I'd sinned against him. And I remember his arms around me, forgiving me and telling me not ever to do it again.

Confession really is good for the soul. But you have to confess to the right person.

When was the last time you confessed your sins to God? When was the last time you ensured that you were right with those closest to you? Saying "I'm wrong" won't kill you or stop the world from turning, but it can give you a right relationship with God and with your family and friends.

If you're still reluctant, think of this equation: confession plus cleansing plus contentment equals clear relationships.

*Dear God, I want to be right with You and with
my family and friends. Please show me anything
in my life for which I need to ask forgiveness.
Give me the courage to confess this to You. And if
I've hurt anyone else, please help me to confess it
to them and make things right. In Jesus' name,
Amen.*

TERMITES AND TEMPTATIONS
Nehemiah 13:4–9

"Mark, you'd better come look at this." Joe, a neighbor of mine, directed me toward a stack of logs on my patio. I could see nothing out of the ordinary about the wood.

"Look closer," Joe insisted. He pointed out some small creatures that I thought were ants.

"What's the problem?" I asked. "After all, they're outside, not in the house. Surely they can't hurt much of anything."

Joe smiled gently at me, the way one would smile at a poor, stupid neighbor who understood nothing. "Those aren't ants; they're termites! Leave the wood and them close enough to your house, and they'll weaken floors and walls."

Guess what I did? You're right. I moved the wood and got rid of the termites immediately. It would be crazy to let an enemy have complete access to my house so they could destroy it.

In Nehemiah 13, however, that is exactly what we see happening. Remember Tobiah? He was one of Israel's chief enemies when they were trying to rebuild the wall of Jerusalem. Nehemiah returned to the city and discovered that the priest had given Tobiah his own room—in the temple! Nehemiah immediately threw Tobiah out and cleansed the room of all evil influence.

Perhaps it's time for you to take a careful look at your own temple—your body. Examine the thoughts of your mind, the habits of your body, the priorities in your daily activities. Do you see any enemies of God in any of these areas? If so, give them to God and let Him throw them out and cleanse you completely.

Termites and temptations: both can destroy foundations and homes. You can watch your house. Let God watch your life and keep you safe from enemies.

> *Heavenly Father, may I let none of Your enemies*
> *have a place in my life. Today, cleanse me and*
> *help me to live only for You. May I be careful*
> *what I allow into my life through my ears and*
> *eyes. I want You to have first place today and*
> *every day. In Jesus' name, Amen.*

APRIL 15

TAXES AND TITHES
Nehemiah 13:10–14

April 15 is certainly an appropriate day to talk about money, taxes, and monetary obligations. Which type of tax filer are you? Some of you complete your returns as soon as possible after January 1. Others of you are like me—you'll pull up to the mailbox just before midnight tonight and barely beat the postman as he picks up the last batch of mail for the day. Still others of you are desperately trying to file an extension right now!

Regardless of how you file taxes, one thing is certain: you either pay the taxes or you're punished with penalties and interest, jail time, or both.

When it comes to your money and God, however, no legal authority is looking over your shoulder. If you don't tithe, no one is going to haul you off to jail or put your name in the news to shame you. That's why it's so important for you to remember that God is quietly watching you every moment. He expects 10 percent of your money—your tithe—regularly. He has promised to reward you if you give back to Him what the Scripture says is rightfully His.

The problem is that money is a touchy subject with many of us. We have a tendency to think of all that we earn as being ours to do with as we wish. Any suggestion that we should give a significant portion of those earnings to someone else causes us to bristle.

I once saw a cartoon of a man being baptized. As the pastor

immersed him in the baptismal waters, the man stuck his arm straight up above the surface, holding his wallet and keeping it from being baptized! In other words, he was saying, "I'll give myself to Jesus—but not my money!"

Does the Lord have all of you? Are you bringing to Him and to His storehouse—the church—everything that He demands? Are you giving Him the 10 percent that He expects? If not, you're actually cheating yourself of a closer relationship with God and His rich blessings. Decide today to let God be the Lord of everything—even your possessions and earnings.

Father, may my heart and my checkbook be entirely Yours. Help me to give to You with a grateful heart. Multiply my offerings to support missionaries, build churches, and glorify Your name throughout the world. In Jesus' name, Amen.

APRIL 16

HOW TO HAVE A GOOD MARRIAGE
Esther 1:1–20

Let me say it right up front. My telephone skills aren't the greatest in the world. My lack of patience sometimes shows in this area. I just want to hear the essence of the message and then get off the phone as soon as possible. My wife, on the other hand, is probably like yours. Her idea of conversing on the phone is much different than mine. She and her sister, for example, can take thirty minutes to tell a story that I could relate in a fraction of that time.

This difference led to one of our all-time big fights, and it was all my fault. The phone rang in my office one morning. I had a meeting with my staff coming up in a few minutes, pink phone messages awaiting my response covered my desk, and two people stood right outside the door waiting to see me.

I answered the phone and heard my wife's cheery voice say, "Hi, honey!"

Now, I lead marriage seminars across the nation. My first book was on marriage. But at that moment, I blundered about as badly as a husband can. I said, "What do you need?"

Susan's voice got noticeably chillier. But did I learn my lesson? Did I pick up on what was happening? No. All I could see was a schedule needing to be kept.

"I have some good news to tell you," she went on. After a few more sentences, I interrupted her.

"Susan, just get to the bottom line, please. I'm in a hurry."

BOOM! Man, did I blow it!

"If you don't care any more for what's happening in my life than that, I'll just hang up now." A few sobs followed, then, *Click.* Now my schedule was really messed up! I called her back, and after another thirty minutes managed to make things better—a little.

In today's Scripture reading, we see that even kings and emperors have marriage problems. How we handle those problems determines if we will—or will not—have a good marriage. A lot of rules and principles will help us have a better relationship with our spouses. But Paul gave us the best one of all in Ephesians 5:25: "Husbands, love your wives, just as Christ loved the church and gave himself up for her."

In other words, give up your rights, live for her benefit, and you'll have a great marriage. Trust me, I've been there. A marriage firmly on track has a far higher priority than a daily schedule with everything checked off. And in the process, you'll also discover peace and contentment.

Dear God, help me make my wife the most important person in my life. May I be the godly husband You've called me to be, and may my actions and attitudes be a witness to others of how You can create a deep, happy marriage. In Jesus' name, Amen.

FINDING GOD'S WILL

Esther 2:2–17

"Pastor, I'm in a quandary. I don't know which direction to go with my life. What should I do?"

The young man sat across from me, brow furrowed in concentration. Beside him, his wife echoed the same words of confusion. They wanted to know God's will for their lives but weren't sure how to find it.

An hour later, I stopped in at a local bookstore to browse and drink some coffee. A young woman who works in the bookstore began telling me the problems facing her. She revealed one of them when she asked, "What am I supposed to do with my life?"

I told all three searchers the same thing: look at your talents. God doesn't bless you in certain areas without expecting you to use those gifts for Him. For example, intelligence, in and of itself, can be a remarkable gift. But I've seen many men and women wasting their intelligence because of wrong life choices.

God gifted a young woman named Esther with great beauty. Although we might not think of beauty as a gift that is usable for God, it turns out that the Lord employed that gift to place a peasant woman in one of the highest positions in the land. And, make no mistake: God placed her there for a reason.

A time came in Esther's life when God called upon her to save an entire people by using her beauty. She could have refused to acknowledge her gift. She could have denied her responsibility to God because of the danger involved. Instead, we read about Esther today because she took seriously her relationship with God and used her gifts wisely.

What are your talents? And what are you doing with them?

If you're not sure in what direction you should use your gifts, I encourage you to look at the different ministries in your local church. Every member should be a minister, and there very well may be an area of the church where you can plug in your unique abilities.

If you can't find an immediate outlet for your talents, don't despair. Ensure that you have given God the ownership of your goals, relationships, and time. At the proper moment, the Lord will show you a need that your gifts can fill—for His glory.

Like Esther, you might find that God has decided to use your talents in ways that you never could have imagined. Remain vigilant, submissive to God, and ready to serve.

Father, I want You to use the talents that You've given me for Your glory. Please show me the best way to give back in service to You those gifts. May my life make a difference for Your kingdom. In Jesus' name, Amen.

APRIL 18

IS ANYONE IN CONTROL?

Esther 2:19–23

The unnamed Canadian described the whole experience as terrible. The forty-year-old man left a convenience store late at night and saw two men approaching him. One of them mugged the Canadian and stole his money. When the case finally came to trial, instead of receiving what most of us would have thought was justice, things only turned worse for the victim.

The judge in the case pointed out that the area of Winnipeg in which the man was walking was known for roughness. Then the judge called the victim stupid for failing to be more careful. Finally, he let the attacker go free! The newspaper reporting the case quoted the judge as calling the victim a "stupid civilian, who admits that he was stupid."

The victim told the newspaper that he was insulted by the judge's remarks. The prosecutor's office is considering an appeal.[1]

Let's face it, injustice rules over much that goes on in this world. We shake our heads at stories like this and wonder if anyone is paying attention. We ask one another, "Is anyone in control?"

Make no mistake. God is not only in control but also is keeping

---

1. Excite.com/news, 21 July 2000.

a record of everything—every word, every act, every deed. And He'll be bringing true, lasting justice one day.

Look at Mordecai's deed in today's Bible passage. As we read the story of Esther over the next several days, it will seem as if an entire people will be wiped out. Good will lose; evil will win. Injustice will triumph once again. But because we already know the end of the story, we are assured that these seemingly horrific situations were, in reality, only temporary setbacks. God was using them to work a miracle in the life of His people.

This miracle started with Mordecai saving the king's life. The last verse in the chapter says, "All this was recorded in the book of the annals in the presence of the king." In other words, everything was recorded for later use. Near the end of Esther, the king will read of Mordecai's actions and realize that he is a true friend of the king.

What is being written about you in God's great record of life? How are you responding to the opportunities that God gives you daily? Your faithfulness in living for God, no matter what, will one day be rewarded. The Lord can use the seemingly difficult situations that you see around you to mature you and touch the lives of others.

God forgets nothing. He records everything. Let those thoughts give you strength to live for Him today.

Heavenly Father, I want my actions and thoughts to honor You. As I go through this day, help me to realize that You see and remember everything. May that realization give me strength to trust in You no matter what happens. Thank You for loving me and for taking care of me every day. In Jesus' name, Amen.

APRIL 19

Pride and Punishment
Esther 3:1–10

Doug Couvertier surely was a unique candidate for political office. After all, how many other candidates do you know who spend their own time and money begging people *not* to vote for them? At first, everything seemed to be going well for Couvertier's candidacy. Running for a position on the local city council, he seemed to be a shoo-in. Then disaster struck. Couvertier discovered that the Miami-Dade County charter requires government employees to resign from their jobs if they are elected to public office. Couvertier, a fire chief, was only three years from retirement, and he didn't want to lose that pension!

By the time Couvertier discovered the true nature of the situation, it was too late for his name to be removed from the ballot. The only thing to do was to push hard in every way to get the vote out—*against himself!* That's how Doug Couvertier found himself going door to door from dawn until dusk. He's a man with a mission—to lose.[1]

Imagine trying intentionally to lose! But before you shake your head too much in amusement, realize that many men are doing exactly that. Their attitudes and life choices are ensuring that they will one day lose in the game of life.

If you want to find a way to lose in life, look no farther than today's Scripture passage. Although he did not realize it, Haman was begging for his life to be ruined.

The world would disagree with me. At this point in Haman's life, he would have disagreed as well. After all, the king had elevated him to a position over everyone else in the kingdom. People were bowing down when he passed them. All of the world seemed to be his, except for one man—Mordecai. Because Mordecai was a Jew, he did not bow to anyone but God.

Instead of accepting this fact and going on about his business, Haman let pride get the better of him. His ego was so inflated that he demanded that all Jews be exterminated because of one man's refusal to bow! The noose, however, was tightening around Haman's neck, although he did not realize it. Pride would eventually kill him.

Remember Lucifer? He became Satan and was cast out of heaven, the enemy of God and a future citizen of hell forever. What happened to Lucifer? Pride.

---

1. Excite.com/news, 21 July 2000.

Haman, Lucifer, and—should we add your name to this list? How do you respond to slights and insults? What happens if someone doesn't treat you exactly right? Proverbs 12:16 says, "A fool shows his annoyance at once, but a prudent man overlooks an insult."

You have the choice of being a Haman or a Mordecai, a fool or a prudent man. By your actions and attitudes today, which will you choose to be? Putting pride aside and becoming a servant of Christ will allow God to bless you in both your relationships and your life choices.

Dear God, I confess that pride sometimes gets the better of me. But I want to be a wise man, not a fool. Help me to put aside pride today and let Your love and compassion be a part of my life. In Jesus' name, Amen.

APRIL 20

WHEN YOUR LIFE CAVES IN
Esther 3:12—4:4

"Mark, your wife has advanced ovarian cancer. There is almost no hope for her survival." With those words, my whole life changed. The doctor, a friend of mine, hated to tell me what he'd found during the operation. Friends crowded around me to give comfort. Later, when Susan came out of recovery, we huddled together to talk about the future. Our eight-year-old daughter needed reassurance and security.

What do you do when your life caves in? How do you handle it?

As a pastor for nearly thirty years, I have seen people at their best and at their worst. I have watched men and women struggle to deal with crushing difficulties. And in helping them at critical moments in their lives, I have discovered several truths about people and trials.

- Trials make people either bitter or better, but no one stays the same.
- Trials tend to reveal the weak areas in a person's life.

In today's passage, Mordecai learned that he and all of his people were to be destroyed in a few months. The situation looked hopeless. What Mordecai did and didn't do at this point is significant. He *did* mourn, and he did so publicly. But he *didn't* lose his faith in God; neither did he blame God or curse Him for the imminent threat.

Are you going through a tough time right now? Whether it's physical, marital, emotional, or job related, I encourage you not to lose faith. Instead, get even closer to the Lord and Savior who died for you and who loves you deeply. It might not make the trials go away, but trusting completely in God will strengthen the weak areas in your life. And as you walk through dark valleys, you'll know that you're not alone. Christ will be with you every step of the way, guiding your path and helping you to grow strong in Him.

Lord, I sometimes feel so weak and helpless.
During these difficult times, help me not to lose
my faith in You. I want to be a witness for You,
showing that Christ truly is sufficient, no matter
what a person is going through. Please give me
Your peace and Your strength today. In Jesus'
name, Amen.

APRIL 21

YOUR PLACE IN THIS WORLD
Esther 4:5–14

Calvin Wilson, twenty-seven, disappeared in 1985 in Natchez, Mississippi. His family reported him missing, but investigations turned up nothing. Fast forward to 2001. The Riverboat Gift Shop, housed in an historic antebellum home, decided to renovate the interior. When masons began working on the chimney, they discovered Wilson's fully clothed remains.

In 1985, the then-young man evidently had tried to burglarize the shop. Wilson fell head-first down the chimney and got stuck. Police believe that the fall injured him, preventing his calling for help. For sixteen years, Wilson's poor judgment kept him hidden away from a searching world.[1]

In our Bible passage for today, we see Esther being tested. Mordecai reminded the queen that she very well might have been placed in the kingdom for just such a moment. Would her judgment save her people or help lead them to their destruction?

Poor judgment, as we've just seen, can kill you. Failing to fulfill your life's mission can hurt many more people than just you. After all, you are not here on earth by accident. God placed you here, and He has a plan for your life. Are you willing to do whatever is necessary to please God and to make a difference for Him?

It might well be that God has brought you into the kingdom for just such a time as this.

> *Heavenly Father, I want to make a difference in this world. I want to accomplish Your will for my life. May I not shirk my duty through apathy or cowardice. Please help me to stand for You to-day—and every day. In Jesus' name, Amen.*

APRIL 22

WHEN THE GOING GETS TOUGH
Esther 4:15–17

"If I perish, I perish" (v. 16). With those words, Esther ensured that her life story would live for thousands of years after her. She had no idea that more than twenty-one centuries later people around the world would still read of her sacrifice and be blessed.

"If I perish, I perish." Literally hundreds of thousands of believers have said these or similar words throughout history. Being faithful to Jesus Christ was more important to them than continuing in their mortal bodies.

Christians in Rome refused to offer a bit of incense to a statue of Caesar and worship him. They paid with their blood, being torn to

---

1. Nytimes.com, 24 January 2001.

bits by wild animals in Rome's infamous Arena Games. They were put on poles, covered with pitch, and set aflame to provide illumination for Caesar's parties.

In every country and among every people, atrocities have been committed against the people of God. Those persecutions continue today. Torture and death for yourself is bad enough, but many martyrs also died knowing that their spouses and children also would be killed. Yet, the kingdom of God has blossomed, growing in the blood-soaked soil of such sacrifices.

"If I perish, I perish." You might not be faced with physical torture for your faith, but are you willing to stand firm in the face of peer pressure? When society turns a hostile eye on your actions for Christ, do you back off? In short, when the going gets tough, do you keep going? As the author of Hebrews says, "Therefore, since we are surrounded by such a great cloud of witnesses, let us throw off everything that hinders and the sin that so easily entangles, and let us run with perseverance the race marked out for us" (Heb. 12:1).

"If I perish, I perish." Commit to God that your desire is to be faithful to Him today and every day—all of the way to death.

Dear God, my desire is to honor You with my life and, if necessary, my death. May I be willing to say, "If I perish, I perish." Please allow nothing in my life to hinder my standing firm for You today. In Jesus' name, Amen.

ESCAPING SIN'S TRAP
Esther 5

When we were in fifth grade, my best friend Bobby and I decided to try something that we'd seen on a television show. We set a box out in the backyard, propped it up with a stick tied to a string, and put birdseed on the ground under the box. Then we hid in the bushes to see what would happen.

Surprise, surprise! Almost immediately, a bird flew down and began pecking at the seed. I pulled the string, the box clunked down, and we had a trapped bird! Then reality set in for both of us. We looked at each other and said, "What do we do now?" Neither Bobby nor I had really expected the trap to work.

Unfortunately—and I mean that sincerely—I volunteered to check out the box.

When I tilted the box up to get the bird, the bird "got" me instead. It flew up, shrieking, in my face. Its wings beat at me; it pecked my cheek; and, worst of all, it released what seemed to be a ton of what I'll politely call "bird residue" all over my head, face, and clothes. It didn't help that Bobby was rolling around on the ground in a laughing fit. I walked away from that experience wondering just who had trapped whom.

Sin often uses the same trap on us. We think we're in control of a habit, a relationship, a thought process. Then, too late, we discover that sin has trapped us, and we can't get out without our lives—and the lives of those we love—being hurt severely.

Did you just read today's devotional passage? If not, I encourage you to stop right here and open your Bible to Esther. Sin's trap was about to fall upon Haman—*and he was completely unaware of it.* Haman thought that he was the one in control. Pride and greed combined to lull him into believing that the gallows he was constructing would destroy his enemy. Instead, we'll see in the coming days Haman's swift entrapment by sin and his complete downfall.

Don't miss this. Haman thought that he was on top of everything—his job, his position in society, his reputation. In reality, he stood on the edge of a steep precipice, ready to fall off and lose everything.

Learn from a fifth-grader, from Haman, and from sin's trap. Don't let anything into your life that is displeasing to God, no matter how small you think it is—especially if you believe that you can control it. That's the first step to being caught in the box labeled "sin."

Heavenly Father, please examine my life and show
me if anything is there that displeases You. No
matter how small or how deeply entrenched it is, I
want to give it to You today. Please forgive me,

cleanse me, and help me to allow You complete access to every area of my life forever. In Jesus' name, Amen.

APRIL 24

THE CONTENTS OF YOUR LIFE
Esther 6

Police raided the church in Togo, not sure of what they would find. They had received complaints against the Church of the Lord for the Adoption. Whispered fears had made their way throughout the community where the church was located.

When police burst in, they found three ceramic pots, one by the entrance and two near the altar. All three were crammed full of "fetishes," objects that had no place in a true church. The police found vulture eggs, hyena paws, a panther's pelt—and human remains. Worshipers had complained that the pastor was using satanic practices in the services. Because of the human remains, police arrested the pastor and his accomplice—a witch doctor.[1]

Haman was like that ungodly church. His life is "crammed full" of attitudes and values that can never help a person. They lay quietly deep inside him, working their cancerous evil. Now, we see their effect as it began to come to the surface. The poison of an ungodly mind, if left unchecked, will always lead to death. And, at the end, that poison often works swiftly. Look at the speed with which Haman's downfall occurred.

Now, let's turn to your own life. If you're like most men, your schedule is pretty hectic. You could even say it's "crammed full" of appointments, mind-bending pressure, numbing responsibilities. What part of that mix is godly? What part brings you peace? Perhaps you need to purge some of what drives you on daily. If the Bible disapproves of something, you too should disapprove of it. If God has branded something in your life sinful, realize that it is already working to destroy you. Give it up today, and let God put you back on the road to peace.

---

1. Excite.com, 4 October 2001.

Dear God, You know how busy I sometimes find myself. Help me to stop right now and allow You to remove all ungodly thoughts and habits from my life. I desire to live completely for You today. May my heart and mind be reserved for You above anything and anyone else. In Jesus' name, Amen.

APRIL 25

REMAIN FAITHFUL
Esther 7

For many of us, the sound of the ice cream man as his truck drives down our street brings back pleasant memories of sun-lit summer afternoons and cool dairy treats. Some children in Albany, New York, however, have entirely different memories—and those memories can give them nightmares.

The whole situation came to light when the mother of a twelve-year-old boy happened to be outside when an ice cream truck driven by Raymond Delgado came down her street. She watched in horror as the truck swerved deliberately toward her son. When the boy jumped onto the sidewalk to escape, the truck crossed the opposite lane, hopped the curb, and began driving on the sidewalk toward her terrified son.

At the last minute, the truck stopped. When the mother rushed forward to protect her boy, the driver said that he was simply kidding with the child. Then he said that he "played" with kids like that all the time! The mother, naturally, failed to see the humor and contacted the police. Mr. Delgado was sentenced to six months in jail for the felony of reckless endangerment.[1]

Can you identify with that twelve-year-old boy? Do you sometimes feel as if something in life is pursuing you, trying to run you down, and you can't see a way to escape it? Esther and Mordecai probably felt just like that. For months, they had lived with the

---

1. Nytimes.com, 4 October 2001.

knowledge that they and their people were going to be slaughtered throughout the land, and they seemed unable to do anything about it.

Please don't miss this. Even when they couldn't see it, God's hand was working in the background, unfolding a plan that would punish Haman, rescue Esther and her people, and honor Mordecai by making him one of the most powerful people in all of the kingdom.

Do you remember the story of Joseph in Genesis? Both he and Mordecai became the second-most important individuals in powerful nations. But those positions came about only after extreme suffering by each of them. Because Joseph and Mordecai were willing to weather the storms without losing their faith in God, He rewarded them and their people.

Whatever you're facing in your life right now, I know that God can and will give you the strength to get through it. Take a careful look at the situation. Do you have any way to escape being in it? For example, if what is happening to you is a result of wrong relationships or wrong habits, give them up and allow God to begin bringing peace to your life. If, however, you can see no way out, I encourage you to trust in the Lord no matter what happens. God might have a plan to use you mightily, and this situation could be part of it. Remain faithful, and He will use it for His glory and for your edification.

Heavenly Father, You know what I'm facing right now. I ask you to give me strength during this trial. May I honor You, no matter what happens. If it's Your will, take this difficulty away from me. If not, however, please show Your strength in me during these events. Today, I ask for Your guidance. In Jesus' name, Amen.

YOUR FAMILY AND PRAYER
Job 1:1–5

The headline in *The Cincinnati Enquirer* read, "PARENTS AREN'T ALWAYS TO BLAME." The editorial spoke of the deaths of Cincinnati Police Officer Kevin Crayon and a twelve-year-old boy, Courtney Mathis. Courtney evidently took a relative's car from his parents' house late one night. The twelve-year-old went for a joy ride that ended tragically for both him and a policeman. Now the city of Cincinnati is asking, "Who is responsible?"

In April 1999, the city council made permanent a parental responsibility law. The law makes it illegal for parents to "fail to supervise" a child under eighteen. Violating the law is an "unclassified misdemeanor." In other words, parents can be fined but not put in jail.

But is it the parents' fault if a child with no prior trouble with the law sneaks out of the house after everyone is in bed? Exactly where do a mother's and father's responsibilities end? The city is still grappling with these issues. Meanwhile, heartbroken parents and a policeman's grieving family try to get on with their lives.[1]

Where do the lines of responsibility end for a parent? I'm sure of at least one thing: it is God's will that we parents pray regularly for our children. As we begin the book of Job today, we see this righteous man consistently lifting up his sons and daughters to God. From the verses that follow, we see that this practice, along with others, was pleasing to God.

This passage made an impression on me quite a few years ago. I've developed a habit of interceding for my children and wife several times a day. For example, after I've dropped my child off at school, I don't turn on the radio or listen to a CD until I've prayed for every member of my family. Believe me, it's a good way to start the work day.

If this hasn't yet become a regular part of your life, I encourage you to add to your daily schedule praying for your family. God

---

1. Enquirer.com, 27 September 2001.

will be pleased, your life will be stronger, and your family will be blessed.

Dear Lord, I lift up every member of my family today. Please take care of them and guide them into the center of Your will. And help me to be a Christian example to them. In Jesus' name, Amen.

USING DIFFICULT TIMES FOR GOD
Job 1:6–22

When we quote favorite passages of Scripture, I assume that none of us quotes these particular verses! After all, there was a godly man, a faithful husband, a good father. And what did God say to Satan? Take all that he has, if you want to!

In the space of a moment, everything in Job's life, with the exception of his wife, was taken from him. All of the children were killed. His wealth was stolen. Job had gone from being one of the wealthiest men in the world to a bankrupt, grieving father who would soon also lose his health. It doesn't get much worse than that.

Why would God allow such evil to happen to one of His faithful children? He wanted to use Job's experience to teach millions and millions of believers some important facts about the Christian life. First, we learn that bad things happen to good people. Instead of saying, "Why me, Lord?" when problems occur, we should look at Job and say, "What are you trying to do through me, Lord?"

Second, we learn it is possible to keep your faith in God even in crushing circumstances. Look again at verse 20: "At this, Job got up and tore his robe and shaved his head. Then he fell to the ground in worship." Job never quit trusting in God!

Interestingly enough, some Christians act as if the book of Job weren't in the Bible at all. If something bad happens to either themselves or one of their friends, they immediately say that it must be because of some sin in the victim's life. Others will swear that it's because the believer didn't have enough faith. Then some people decide that God isn't a loving God because He allowed the problem to occur, and they lose their faith.

We must always remember that God's trials serve a purpose that might have nothing to do with us! God allowed Job's problems so that He could help us during our trials. Of course, Job never knew any of this—and we might never know why we are going through tough times. But we must remain faithful, as Job did. In doing so, we very well might have the opportunity to touch many lives for Jesus Christ.

Heavenly Father, I don't know why You're allowing some of the difficult times I'm facing to occur. However, help me not to lose my faith or my witness to others during these times. Give me Your strength today—and every day. In Jesus' name, Amen.

APRIL 28

FINDING THE SAFE PATH

Job 2:1–10

The article was brief in content and length. The headline, however, intrigued readers: "Wednesday set aside as safe-walking day." The body of the article gave information concerning a day that had been set aside for the parents of Halle Hewetson Elementary School students. On that day, parents were encouraged to walk their children to and from school, teaching them the safest route.[1]

What is the safest route for you through this world? We have so many possible roads to take. Beautiful, seductive distractions tempt you to travel their paths. Power, wealth, success, lust, people's approval—which ones are pulling you away?

Job's every route through this world seemed to be blocked by

---

1. Lasvegassun.com/sunbin/stories/archives, 27 September 2001.

failure. Family? All destroyed. Marriage? His wife was urging him to curse God and die! Friends? They were trying to convince Job that he was wrong. Health? Completely broken. Business? Penniless and bankrupt. In other words, by every standard by which we measure success, Job failed.

And yet, Job was a success in God's eyes. Why? Because Job simply continued to keep ever before him his allegiance to God. He would not cave in to temporary setbacks. God, not the advice of society, commanded his allegiance. And this kept an incredible man on the right path through life.

Learn Job's lesson. Be willing to say, "Though [God] slay me, yet will I trust Him" (Job 13:15 NKJV). It will transform your life—and keep you on the right path.

Father, I never want to get off the path of Your will. Help me to trust in You and stay close to You all through this day. No matter what might happen, may I trust in You. In Jesus' name, Amen.

APRIL 29

GODLY ADVICE
Job 42:7–9

Let's talk for a moment about advice. Not the advice that you receive from others, but the "help" you try to give your friends. How good is it? How wise are your words?

Thomas Morris Jr. called 911 shortly after the anthrax scare several years ago. That phone call is infamous because of its chilling content and terrifying because of the false assurances that the operator gave to Morris.

Morris told 911 operators that he worked in the Brentwood mail processing facility and had been close to a powder-containing envelope. His superiors had reassured him that the envelope did not contain anthrax, but now Morris had become suspicious.

He was, in fact, dying of anthrax poisoning as he spoke those words during the 911 call. Sadly, just three days before his death,

Morris went to a doctor, who said he probably had a virus, not anthrax, and prescribed Tylenol.[1]

Think of bad advice as giving Tylenol to a dying man who should have had life-saving antibiotics. In today's Scripture, we see Job's friends receiving punishment from God. Their crime: they gave sincere, heart-felt advice that was completely wrong and against God's will! Had Job listened to his "friends," he would have missed God's blessings.

Don't be a person who dispenses wrong advice. Ensure that what you tell your friends is based solidly on the Bible. If it's not, put it far from your mouth and from the ears of others!

Dear God, may I soak myself in the Scripture so that I give only advice that pleases You and helps others. Let Your Word, not society's current morals, guide what I say to others. In Jesus' name, Amen.

APRIL 30

STANDING FAITHFUL IN TOUGH TIMES
Job 42:10–17

"My life is over. I'm ruined."

Those words came from my mouth about fifteen years ago. I sat in my office and wondered what to do next. A situation not of my making threatened to destroy me. I'd been as godly as I knew how. I'd prayed in faith for God to take away the problem. However, it seemed as if the heavens had turned to brass. Not only was God not taking away the problem but also it was getting worse!

That's when I lost my faith. I remember going home and telling my wife that I couldn't preach or pastor anymore. I'd always told people that God would take care of them, but I saw no evidence of it in my own life. Over the next several weeks and months, I somehow stumbled through my preaching duties, but my heart wasn't in it.

Then, one day, idly flipping through the Bible while sitting in

---

1. Nytimes.com, 7 November 2001.

my office, I began reading Job. My eyes fell on the passage we read several days ago. With everything gone, Job had said, "Though he slay me, yet will I trust Him" (Job 13:15 NKJV). Those words pierced my heart, and I found myself falling on my knees and calling out to God. I told him, "Lord, even if You take everything away, I'll never quit loving, trusting, serving, and believing in you."

I'd love to tell you that the heavens opened, my situation improved, and my problem went away. But that's not what happened. What did happen, however, is that I crossed a significant barrier in my life. I had made the decision to serve God no matter what. I believe that God was maturing me, helping me prepare for the future when my wife would face a life-threatening illness. And, as in Job's case, the Lord eventually restored everything in my life. Don't misunderstand me—it didn't happen overnight. I went through about ten years of difficulty after that significant day. However, my heart was healed, my ministry grew amazingly, and my peace with God remained wonderful.

God restored Job because he was faithful to his Lord. If you remain faithful, God will also restore you. He might not give you what you *want*, but the Lord will give you what you *need* for peace and strength. Trust in Him—today and forever—no matter what the temporary circumstances might be.

Father, sometimes I feel so weak. Today, I want to lean on You and feel Your strength and comfort. I want to be able to say what Job said. Help me to trust in You all of the way to death. And in the process, may I learn more of You and stand for You. In Jesus' name, Amen.

MAY 1

THE DIFFERENCE BETWEEN DAY AND NIGHT
Psalm 1

If I offered you a method for making a million dollars, and it was a certain process, would you listen? What if I offered you the ability to live your life in a wise, godly manner? Would you listen?

Sorry, but I do not have the million-dollar deal figured out, but I do know where to find the process for living.

That process is found in Psalm 1. It contrasts the difference between the man who wants to live in a godly manner and the one who does not. The contrast is between day and night. One man follows the way of God and is blessed. What is his process? First, he makes his own decisions about what he is going to do. He avoids evil company and refuses to associate with people who are cynical about everything. We often have to work with such people, of course, but we do not need to spend our "off" time with them.

The godly man looks to the true source of wisdom and strength—God Himself. He drinks in godliness as a tree drinks in the water running along its roots. Because of that action and attitude, the man yields fruit. He prospers.

On the other hand, the man who lives as if God were irrelevant is like chaff. He is blown away and has no lasting impact on life. Evil is its own worst enemy and is self-destructive. As the psalmist puts it, "The way of the wicked will perish" (v. 6). Oh, that might not happen right away. In fact, some of the world's biggest scoundrels seem to have it all. But appearances are deceptive. What they build will not last.

God keeps the way of His people: "For the LORD watches over the way of the righteous" (v. 6). These two ways of living could not be more diverse. One way is day; the other way is night. Where do you live?

I always want to be in Your light, Father. I have stumbled in the dark too long. Help me achieve what I most need. In Jesus' name, Amen.

MAY 2

A WAKEUP FOR THE WORN-OUT
Psalm 6

What man cannot identify with the third verse of this psalm: "My soul is in anguish. How long, O LORD, how long?" I have known plenty of times like that and suspect that you have too. We cry out to God that we have reached the end of our rope. We wonder aloud how long our situation might last. Does God know or even care?

This plaintive cry is as old as humanity but as modern as today's headlines. Suffering seems to send us into isolation. We feel alone because our closest friends seem to keep their distance. We might wonder if God Himself has turned His back on us. Grief wears us out and saps our strength and courage. Verse 6 says, "I am worn out from groaning."

The wakeup for us in such situations is that God *does* know and care. He "accepts my prayer" (v. 9). That is not a magic formula that instantly changes my outward circumstances. I think it does mean that my inward attitude can alter toward knowing that I am not alone. Verse 10 is the articulation of the psalmist's inner turmoil. He hopes that his enemies will be put to shame. Ultimately, all ungodliness will be routed. Meanwhile, we have to put up with a lot of grief.

Are you worn out? Do you need a pick-me-up? It does not come primarily from a bottle or a pill. Sometimes we need help from medication, and I am not knocking those helps. I simply mean that in the long run we are sustained by our faith in God. We go through some incredible experiences but are not crushed.

Thank You, Lord, that You are with us and sustain us in every circumstance. We understand that everything that happens to us is not of Your will. Even so, You are with us in all circumstances, and we give You our gratitude. Through Christ, Amen.

What Is Man?
Psalm 8

This is the question of the ages: What is man? Some people say that we are just biological accidents. We live for a flicker of a moment on a tiny rock spinning around a sun that is dying in a universe that is expanding on its way to destruction and collapse. Other people say that man is whatever he chooses to make of himself. Still others say that the question itself is meaningless and that we should simply do the best we can.

When the psalmist asked, "What is man?" he added an important qualifier on it—"that you are mindful of him?" (v. 4). That part of the question takes life out of the idea that man is a cosmic accident. We are persons in relationship to the Person, that is, we are not orphans; we have a Father.

One writer said that every man is a "folder of unfinished business." I really like that description. Does that describe your life? It does mine. I have unfinished business with my family and with my career. I am not finished yet and have plenty of more work to do in knowing God and being transformed into the likeness of Christ.

This, to me, is as real as anything in life. I am known by God. He is "mindful" of me. That means so much. In Psalm 8, this realization leads directly to worship: "O LORD, our Lord, how majestic is your name in all the earth!" (v. 1). To know that we matter, that we have purpose, that we are related and united—all of that leads us to know that we love God as He loves us.

This does not solve all of our immediate problems, of course, but it does give us an eternal perspective by which to live. We are here for a purpose, and we are related to God. Knowing this, we can really live.

Father in heaven, You really know us and care about us. This fact amazes us and sets our hearts for worship. Thank You for noticing us. In Jesus' name, Amen.

MAY 4

FOLLOWING THE SHEPHERD
Psalm 23

There is a huge difference between a shepherd and a sheepherder. A sheepherder is merely a hireling, a guy who does not care for the animals under his control. He goes about his work but does not get personally involved. If they live, fine; if they die, fine. Who cares?

A shepherd, on the other hand, actually knows his sheep by name. He loves them and will do anything, including going above and beyond the call of duty, to care for them. In biblical times, a shepherd was given a sacred trust to care for the animals. No real shepherd would have neglected his duty because life and death depended on it.

Psalm 23 likens God to a shepherd. He leads His flock to safe, green pastures where the food is good and the water is fresh. He goes with them through the tumultuous experiences of life, including the "valley of the shadow of death." Fear will not overcome them because they are not alone. God, the great Lord of the universe, is actually right in the crisis with them.

The Great Shepherd also prepares what His people need most in both this life and the life to come. He sets the table for us. We are His invited guests. His table is not dressed sparsely but is a lavish spread. Everything we need or want is there. And then, when life on earth is done, we will join our Shepherd for eternity, where the trials of life will be no more: "I will dwell in the house of the LORD forever" (v. 6).

Do you know this Shepherd personally? If not, this would be a great time to give yourself to Him and to decide to follow Him every day. He is a trustworthy guide all of the way.

> *Lord, You are not only the shepherd but also my shepherd. Help me follow You in obedience and faith. Set the table for me. I'll be there soon. In Christ, Amen.*

WAITING
Psalm 40:1–5

I admit it: I hate to wait. Standing in long lines drives me crazy. Wasting my time waiting for something to happen is not my idea of a great day or a great life. But sometimes you cannot do anything else. The doctor says, "You need surgery. We'll schedule you for next week." The days between the diagnosis and the surgery seem to crawl by while you want to scream, "Let's get this show on the road—now!"

Psalm 40 pictures a man who has had to learn to wait. He is caught up in circumstances beyond his control. Sounds familiar, doesn't it? In the midst of that crisis, he learns patience. Biblical patience is not sitting idly by while things happen around you. It is the ability to keep your focus in the midst of the trouble. Look at what the writer learned and shares with us.

God really does know what is happening to us. I love that phrase in verse 1, "he turned to me." Our cries to God do not bounce off the ceiling but go directly to Him. Next, "He lifted me out of the slimy pit" (v. 2). Our crises seem to be pits that we cannot crawl out of on our own. Following that, "He set my feet on a rock" (v. 2). Stability! A foundation! Solid ground at last!

Then, "He put a new song in my mouth" (v. 3). Problems change us. We take on a different attitude, and that changes our inner life. We begin singing a new song, a tune of grace and mercy. That, in turn, will help others notice the difference and wonder about the change in us.

Finally, we are led to a deeper level of trust. We understand more about God and how He deals with us. We emerge from a time of waiting more secure, deeper, and stronger. That, then, is worth waiting for.

> *Lord, You know that I don't like waiting. But I look at those around me who must do that—the prisoner, the person in the hospital, the woman with a bad marriage, the child who is abandoned. Help us all to wait in You as we move to resolve our dilemmas. In Jesus' name, Amen.*

DESIRING GOD
Psalm 42

Good questions often bring good answers. This psalm ends with a good question: "Why are you downcast, O my soul? Why so disturbed within me?" (v. 11). I have asked this question, and I imagine that you have too. Everyone has seasons when everything seems to go wrong and life tilts on its axis. We wonder which way is up.

Follow the thinking of the man who wrote this psalm. He begins by observing that, just as a deer pants for the life-giving water of a stream, so his own soul desires God. He desires God so much that he feels that desire as a thirst. People taunt him. They ask in mock seriousness, "If you're so good, then why doesn't your God rescue you?" I have been cut to the heart by such questions. Have you? The writer speaks of what he used to do. But his life has changed and he feels cut off from his community. Anyone who has ever been fired or laid off knows that feeling.

His thinking proceeds as he asks God, "Why have you forgotten me?" (v. 9). To be cut off from the community is bad enough, but has God Himself also turned His back? Verse 10 states the result in graphic terms: "My bones suffer mortal agony." He feels this distress all of the way down to his bones. I have been awake at 2:00 A.M. in great mental and emotional distress that felt physical. My innermost being was shaken. Yes, it felt as if my very bones were disturbed.

But the last verse, which repeats verse 5, puts life into perspective. The only thing that helps is to look to the correct source of help: "Put your hope in God, for I will yet praise him, my Savior and my God." That makes all of the difference in the world. We are not delivered from our problems automatically, but we are assured that God is with us, even when we do not feel Him. When we desire God as much as a desert animal desires water, He is there.

I am thirsty for You, Lord. I feel parched, dried out, used up. Come and be my companion on this journey. I cannot make it on my own. Through Jesus, Amen.

LOOKING FOR RESTORATION
Psalm 51

A man said in a recent conversation, "If I could just go back and undo what I did, that would change the course of my whole life." What had he done that was so drastic? He had committed adultery. He was a long-married community leader who had sown seeds of destruction by his action. I was never certain, however, if he regretted his action or only getting caught.

Psalm 51 was written by King David after his affair with Bathsheba. From its entire tone, you can tell that David knew that his sin was not just a trifle. It was an affront to God Himself. David began with a prayer for mercy. That is always a good place to start. Do you think that God knows what a mess we make of our lives at times? I think so.

David then acknowledged that his action was against not only the woman and her family but also God! That is serious business. Furthermore, he knew that he swam in the sea of common humanity that is corrupted from the beginning (v. 5). Restoration continued through a process of inward cleansing and a renewed spirit. David wrote, "Restore to me the joy of your salvation and grant me a willing spirit, to sustain me" (v. 12).

Repentance is turning from one path to another path. It is the realization that you are going the wrong way. To stop and change directions is difficult, but the result is worth the effort. "The sacrifices of God are a broken spirit; a broken and contrite heart, O God, you will not despise" (v. 17).

Is anything in your life telling you that you need to change directions? Restoration is as painful as surgery, but when a cancer is growing inside, what other option do you have?

Lord, I need the joy of my salvation renewed.
Spin me around so that I walk the right path.
Help me with my attitudes and actions. Through
Christ, Amen.

JUSTICE IS IN SHORT SUPPLY
Psalm 58

The headlines tell of another public official who accepted a bribe to pervert justice. He was discovered, but who knows how much damage he caused before being discovered? An FBI agent was found to be selling national secrets to another government. A pastor embezzled money from his church and then lied to try to get out of his predicament.

These modern injustices are nothing new. The psalmist knew them as well as you and I do. The complaint is against injustice, corruption, and wickedness. He took all of this very seriously. He thought that injustice hurt the entire society, not just a few individuals.

When former president Bill Clinton was facing impeachment, many people said of his sin, "Aw, leave the man alone. He didn't do anything that's so bad. So he had a fling with an intern. Big deal." Yes, it was a big deal. What was Clinton teaching young people? That marriage vows do not count? That wielding power over employees is acceptable? That justice should wink at certain behavior by powerful people?

Psalm 58 uses strong language about people who corrupt justice. They are filled with "venom" (v. 4), they are like "a slug melting away as it moves along" (v. 8), and "the wicked will be swept away" (v. 9). This is serious stuff! If we are tempted to think that truth and justice are irrelevant, think again. There is a difference between right and wrong. The psalm ends with this affirmation: "Surely the righteous still are rewarded; surely there is a God who judges the earth" (v. 11).

Are you weary of trying to do the right thing? Are you tempted to let up and take questionable shortcuts? If so, remember the perspective of this psalm. God *does* know and care that men do right.

Father, I'm tired. You know what I face at work and at home. Pressure to follow injustice is everywhere. Give me strength to do it right, no matter what. In Jesus' name, Amen.

DOWN BUT NOT OUT
Psalm 102

We all know what it feels like to be awake at midnight because anxiety will not let us sleep. We might toss that up to the pressures of modern society, but the dilemma is as old as the Bible. Look closely at today's psalm. The writer found himself pleading to the Lord because of his feelings. Consider what he felt.

He felt abandoned and lonely; therefore, he asked God, "Do not hide your face from me" (v. 2). I have been there, and you have too. We feel marginalized by our problems. The psalmist felt physical distress: "My bones burn like glowing embers" (v. 3). Many scientific studies have demonstrated the debilitating effects of stress. Our bodies respond to its harmful effects.

Grief closed in upon the writer. He felt it so intently that his normal activities ceased: "I forget to eat my food" (v. 4). Most of us respond to great stress in one of two ways. We either eat too little or too much. Maintaining balance in troubled times is difficult. Sleep disturbance is one of the most common effects of anxiety. The psalmist wrote, "I lie awake" (v. 7). When my wife and I were facing a time of great tension in a former church, our sleep patterns were affected greatly. I might fall asleep but awaken in two hours. I might be up at 1 A.M. only to see Carla coming into the den because she, too, was awake.

Bitterness is common for many people. We want to lash out at people whom we think are responsible for our trouble. "For I eat ashes as my food and mingle my drink with tears" (v. 9). Despair, the final giving up of any hope, can creep in on us too. "My days are like the evening shadow; I wither away like grass" (v. 11).

But that is not the last word. Hope is the final word. In speaking of God, the psalmist wrote, "He will respond to the prayer of the destitute; he will not despise their plea" (v. 17). God knows! He cares! He responds! If you are down, remember this—you are not out.

Help me, O Lord, to seek Your face and draw
from Your strength. In the end, it is all that I
have left. In Christ, Amen.

A STRONG FINISH

Psalm 150

Walk into the average church today and notice the men. What do they look like? Do they look happy to be there, engaged in the experience, excited at the possibilities of encountering God in worship? That is possible, but I would imagine that they look more like people standing in a line at the bank—bored, wishing that they were somewhere else, ready to get home for lunch and the game on TV. Why is worship so hard for us guys? Can we learn anything from the biblical pattern?

The book of Psalms starts out by describing a blessed man and ends up blessing God. The last psalm closes the ancient Hebrew hymn book (that is what the book was) by exploring the various ways by which the people of God could express their praise and worship. Their worship experience was just that—experience. They did not go to the place of worship, fold their arms, and get that look on their faces that says, "Go ahead. Bless me. I dare you." Instead, they became part of the experience itself. They thought of God wherever God was—in the sanctuary, in the heavens. They thanked Him for being God to them and for making Himself known.

They did not think that God likes only silence and drab colors. They made some noise for Him! They played the trumpet and strummed the harp and the lyre. They banged the tambourine and blew the flute. Even the crash of cymbals beat out the rhythms of worship.

When I was a teenager and beginning to get involved in church life, a debate arose over whether people should play the guitar in church. Like that was some big debate! In the words of an old song by Tom T. Hall, "It could be that the good Lord likes a little picking too." Worship, when given to God with sincerity and love, is acceptable. It is no mistake that the last word in Psalms is "Praise the LORD" (v. 6).

Lord, I'm often too stuffy when I approach You.
Remind me that I cannot impress You by stilted

*language or overly formal rituals. What You
want is me—all of me. I offer myself in Christ's
name, Amen.*

FOLLOW DIRECTIONS
Proverbs 1:1–19

The reality seems to have become almost a cliché—men hate to follow directions. That might be true for some men but not for all men. Many of us spend large amounts of time looking for directions that we can follow safely. Oh, signposts are all around us. They tug at us until we almost feel that we are in an undertow at the beach. They say, "Follow this path," "Come with us," and "We will show you the way." Unfortunately, many of our would-be guides seem to know less about the journey than we do. I heard a financial manager making a presentation to a group, trying to get us to invest in his material. I realized that I knew more about insurance and investing than did that financial counselor.

Where do we find certain guidance? The book of Proverbs is just such a guide. It begins by stating that the purpose of the collection of proverbs and wise sayings is "for attaining wisdom and discipline; for understanding words of insight" (v. 2). Consider the other words of a directed life found in the first few verses—prudence, discretion, guidance, knowledge. That is a powerful list. Wisdom is summed up in verse 7: "The fear of the LORD is the beginning of knowledge, but fools despise wisdom and discipline."

I have seen this truth borne out many times. People who are willing to learn from others and not "reinvent the wheel" in every area of life prosper. The man who always brags about doing life "my way" ends up being a poor role model. I do not mean that we cannot be unique. Far from it; we are all individuals. But God has given certain directions for life that we ignore to our peril. They are applicable to everyone, not just a few people.

Can you follow directions?

Lord, help me learn to follow Your way and not

always strike off on my own. When I learn to follow You, I know that ultimately I learn life's best lessons. Through the One who always followed that way, Jesus our Lord, Amen.

A GOOD IMPULSE GONE BAD
Proverbs 6:20–35

God created us with a powerful impulse to keep the species going. Someone has called this the "urge to merge." This desire is not something foreign to us. Instead, it is part of who we are as human beings. Sexuality is a built-in quality, not an "aftermarket add-on." From the earliest biblical passages, we are told to be careful with this part of life. It is not, as some people today claim, just a natural instinct with no social consequences.

The writer of Proverbs says that a wise young person learns that everything has consequences, especially adultery. Verses 27–28 put this truth into graphic terms: "Can a man scoop fire into his lap without his clothes being burned? Can a man walk on hot coals without his feet being scorched?" The answer to these rhetorical questions is obvious. In the same way, says the writer, "So is he who sleeps with another man's wife; no one who touches her will go unpunished" (v. 29).

Are there no consequences for adultery? Verse 32 puts it this way: "But a man who commits adultery lacks judgment; whoever does so destroys himself." I have seen this result too many times. Occasionally, a wife is the guilty party, but mostly it is the husband. He gets too friendly with another woman and ends up going farther than they intended. I think of a man who left his family for another woman only to end up destroying that relationship too. Proverbs 7:22 says that such a man is "like an ox going to the slaughter, like a deer stepping into a noose." The picture is of an unthinking, uncaring individual who acts as if wedding vows do not really matter.

If you are heading down this path, do a U-turn quickly!

Lord, You have implanted in me a strong physical need. But help me not to let it become my master. If I have failed, forgive me and restore me. In Jesus' name, Amen.

A CALL YOU NEED TO TAKE
Proverbs 8:1–23

God has issued a call to all men that we should not miss. That call is to pay attention to His wisdom and to profit from it. What is wisdom in the biblical sense? It is discernment and understanding. It is not only the ability to know right from wrong but also the capacity to move toward the higher things of life.

I know men who will nearly kill themselves in pleasures and pastimes but would keel over dead if you asked them to read a book or take a class. But think about how much there is to learn in life. We need to know about finances, family life, career issues, and civic matters—and that is just for starters. Wisdom calls us to be alive between our ears. That is difficult to do, of course. Life moves quickly, and we are always running to keep up. That is why this ally called wisdom is special.

The writer of Proverbs says that wisdom offers something more valuable than gems and precious metals. "Choose my instruction instead of silver, knowledge rather than choice gold, for wisdom is more precious than rubies, and nothing you desire can compare with her" (vv. 10–11). Why do we spend our lives digging for gold rather than pursuing wisdom?

Many of us would rather spend a day working in the yard than an hour studying to improve our understanding of God's Word. Think about it this way. When was the last time you read a nonfiction book besides this one? I do not mean that reading books is the height of wisdom, but it is symptomatic of our mind-set. We might think of reading a book as being like a root canal. But God says that wisdom is appointed from eternity. Therefore, no expenditure of effort to get it is too much.

*Lord, give me wisdom so that I can understand
You better and know what my life is for. In
Christ, Amen.*

MAY 14

MAKING DAD PROUD

Proverbs 10:1—9

My father was a man of few words, but I always knew that he
was proud of me. He was forty when I was born, so I never knew
him in his prime. Even in his mid-to-late adult years, dad was tough.
I can never remember him saying that he loved me. He simply did
not talk like that, but he showed it. Because of that, I wanted to
make him proud.

Imagine my surprise when I came across Proverbs 10:1: "A wise
son brings joy to his father, but a foolish son grief to his mother." I
did not always bring joy to Dad, of course. I was a typical strong-
willed kid who did his own thing. There were probably many days
when my father wanted to sell me to the Gypsies. Overall, though,
I respected him and felt his strength transfer to me when we spent
time together. I once took him to the seminary at which I was working toward my doctorate. Although he had only a seventh-grade
education, he seemed to understand what a doctorate meant. He
was proud of my achievement.

Although he has been gone for years, I still find myself thinking
of him, and I still want to make him proud. We never outgrow our
need for a father. Some of you reading this book think that you
never measured up to your father's expectations of you. He was
harsh, and you never knew quite where you stood with him. Many
men feel that way. The Good News of the gospel is that we have a
heavenly Father who looks upon us with pleasure. We can make
Him proud, too.

What does God want from us? Simply to be ourselves with all
of our strength, potential, and power. Make Him proud.

*Heavenly Father, You are proud of me, aren't
You? I belong to You and love You. Help me to*

know myself as Your son.
In Jesus' name, Amen.

A FIERCE DESIRE

Proverbs 13:4

In his book *Wild at Heart,* John Eldredge reminds us that the first man, Adam, was like his Maker. "Adam bears the likeness of God in his fierce, wild, and passionate heart." I love that phrase, *wild and passionate heart.* Sometimes I am that way, but not always. In fact, I am that way too seldom! How about you? Do you feel powerful and even a little dangerous? Or do you feel tamed, domesticated, and weak?

Do I mean that we men should get crazy on occasion? No, I mean more than that we should have an emotional meltdown at every football game. Today's proverb reminds us that our desires lead us forward. When we want something passionately, we stand a chance of achieving it. Otherwise, we are like a "sluggard"—lazy, passive, taking up space.

What are you passionate about? What stirs your blood? What can get you off your couch to do something? God inspired the writer of Proverbs to write, "The sluggard craves and gets nothing" (v. 4). This guy is so lazy that he doesn't even want anything! No wonder he doesn't get much. The other side of that coin is equally true: "But the desires of the diligent are fully satisfied" (v. 4). That means that results are fueled by desire. We need to want something enough to make it happen. Stretch yourself. Push beyond the limit. Someone put it this way: "Reach for the sky because if you should happen to miss, you'll still be among the stars."

What are you hungry for? Get out of the cave, kill something, and drag it home for dinner.

Lord, stir my passion about life. Help me really
live and be awake to this wonderful life that you
have given me. In the name of the Man who was
passionate about everything—Jesus. Amen.

CONTROL YOUR TEMPER
Proverbs 14:15–18

I was in a drive-through one morning trying to get a cup of coffee. A car was at the window, another behind him, and then me. The driver of the middle car got more and more impatient. He raced his engine several times, and finally rolled his window down and started screaming at the guy in front of him. "Hey, buddy, what are you ordering—chicken?"

He kept up this tirade for a while until the fellow at the window drove off. Then Mr. Patient squeeled his tires as he raced off without his order. It was a pathetic scene, although I laughed at him. But, I must admit, I felt a kinship with him. I am not very patient either.

In today's reading, we learn that "a quick-tempered man does foolish things, and a crafty man is hated" (v. 17). The "crafty" man here is a devious conniving fellow. Okay, tell the truth. What idiotic things have you done in haste or anger? Kicked the dog? Yelled at your wife? Drove your fist through a wall?

On the whole, a man who learns to control his temper and his actions will be better off than the one who flies off the handle every time he gets irritated. This does not mean that we have to be wimps. Far from it. We need great strength to control ourselves. What possible good do we accomplish when we act like spoiled brats?

Let your prayer time today be an opportunity to take stock of your attitudes. Ask God for strength to check your temper and keep you steady.

Help me, Father, to live on an even keel and not lash out at people just because I am upset. Thank You for being with me today. Through Christ, Amen.

A REAL TEST OF FAITH

Proverbs 17:1

When push comes to shove, what do you really believe about the way God rules the world? Do you believe that He really tilts the world toward righteousness, or do the spoils really go to the ruthless?

Consider today's reading carefully: "Better a dry crust with peace and quiet than a house full of feasting, with strife." This does not sound very modern or even very American. After all, we are supposed to get everything we can grab, right? But what if our endless pursuit of stuff is destroying our relationships and sucking the life out of our spirits? Probably most men have dreamed of giving up their stressful jobs and going off to live on a small island.

We normally do not have the option of running away, so we are challenged to structure our lives with care. We can intentionally choose the way of peace rather than the way of wealth. Ask yourself what brings you the most joy—a loving family or a garage full of stuff.

Most of us can live very well with only half the junk we own. I use the word *junk* intentionally. My house is so full of stuff I do not need. Nothing there is anywhere near as important to me as the smile on my wife's face when we see each other in the evening and she says, "Hi, sweetheart."

Build a home of peace. Work to protect your family. Nothing is too hard. Whatever it takes, it is worth the effort.

Lord, I know that You are the Lord of peace. Help
me to do whatever I need to do to live in peace
and love with those closest to me. In the name of
the Prince of Peace, Amen.

MAY 18

MONSTER IN A BOTTLE

Proverbs 20:1

When I was about ten years old, my father came home one day acting crazy. It took me a few minutes to figure out what was happening with him. Then it finally dawned on me. Dad was drunk. That day was the first time that I had seen him drunk, but to my great sorrow, it was not the last.

Many, many days went by over the next few years in which I realized that my father was an alchoholic. That fact was a source of shame and embarrassment to me as a teenager. I came to despise my father because of his habit. Once, I was using our family's truck, so he did not have it available. As I was driving home, I saw Dad coming down the road on our old Farmall tractor. He was on his way to a bar for a drink. This monster had ahold of him in ways I still find hard to understand and deal with.

Dad later met Christ and was changed in many ways, including being set free from alcohol addiction. I am proud of that fact, but you can imagine that I have strong feelings about alcohol. On the whole, the Bible has a consistent message about alcohol—you can live without it! I know that this message goes against the grain of conventional thinking. From what you see in popular culture, you would think that nobody can enjoy himself unless he has a drink in his hand.

If alcohol is a problem for you, get help now. You can find freedom from addiction. Almost all communities have programs that can help. Look for one in the phone book and call them. Your family will thank you.

Lord, help me hear the biblical message about
abstaining from alcohol. If it's already a problem
for me, help me kick it. In Christ, Amen.

JUST ENOUGH

Proverbs 30:7–9

How much is enough for you? You might ask, "What do you mean? Enough of what?" I mean enough of anything—salary, pride, food in your kitchen, joy in your heart. Anything. But how much is enough?

This is not an idle question. The prayer of the writer of Proverbs is for two things: "Keep falsehood and lies far from me; give me neither poverty nor riches" (v. 8). Our financial condition is closely linked to truth or lies. You know plenty of men who will do or say anything for a dollar. Greed infects them like a virus and steals their integrity.

The writer wants neither poverty nor riches, and both have their own temptations. Not all rich people are godless. Not all poor people are noble. On the whole, we do better with enough but not too much or too little. Americans have trouble with this concept of enough. Part of the very fabric of our culture is bound up in the word *more*. We are pressured to get more money, more possessions, more power, more prestige. The word *prestige* comes from the Latin word meaning a juggler's tricks. It is an illusion. Why would we want to own something just to impress someone else? Is God impressed by our possessions or achievements?

Are you caught up in a rat race, trying to get more but having less time to enjoy what you already have? Remember, in the end, only a rat can win the rat race, but you are a man. God made you for a relationship with Him.

So how much is enough? We seem to spend much of our lives trying to answer that question. Let the search for an answer be part of your prayer today.

Lord, help me know that enough is enough. Keep
me from greed and covetousness. You are enough.
In Jesus' name, Amen.

MAY 20

THE PERFECT WOMAN
Proverbs 31:10–31

I am married to the perfect woman. Wait! Don't roll your eyes or throw this book away in disgust. Let me explain. Carla is the love of my life. She is my best friend, my lover, and my companion for life. She is intelligent, tough at times, and tender at other times. For me, she is the perfect woman, and I cannot imagine what my life would be like without her. When I read from Proverbs 31, I find a description of my mate.

Many of you will say, "Hey, I'm married to that woman!" Right. That is the point. Marriage is an opportunity to grow together so that we feel closer rather than alone. I read this passage from Proverbs at some funerals for women who embody it in the eyes of their family.

The woman of this passage is industrious. She helps provide for the family and does everything in her power to keep the family on course. She does not waste time or resources; neither does she complain about not having opportunities. She takes advantage of the opportunities she does have and makes the most of them.

No one is technically perfect, of course. But as we grow together, willingly give ourselves to our family, and hold nothing back, we get close enough. The end of Proverbs states, "Give her the reward she has earned" (v. 31). Men, love your wives. God gave them to you as His gift. They deserve the best.

Thank You, Lord, for the woman with whom I have chosen to share my life. She seems more like a gift from You than a choice by me. Thanks for the blessing. In Christ, Amen.

LIFE MATTERS

Ecclesiastes 1:1–11

What a depressing view of life! The writer reflects the idea thrown around by some people of his era: "Everything is meaningless." Nothing is new or novel. Life is just a wheel spinning, going around and around with no clear goal. We are here a little while and then we are gone. What is the point?

This view of life is very much with us today. Plenty of novel invention and incredible creativity are around, but people still ask, "Is there any meaning in life?" Many men today are busy, stressed out, stretched like a cheap rubberband, and generally worn to a frazzle.

Have you bought into this view of life? Is your life going nowhere? The ancient Greeks had a myth about Sysiphus. He had offended divine will and was condemned forever to push a huge stone up a hill. Just as he got it to the top, it always rolled back down. He would go get it and repeat the process over and over again. Does that sound like your work week? An old song by Hoyt Axton reminds us that "you work your fingers to the bone, what do you get? Bony fingers."

A deacon at a church I once served had a funny poem about missing people. It had to do with placing your arm in a bucket of water and removing it. The hole that is left in the water is the hole that you will leave when you go! When I was called to another church, I had him read that poem publicly.

The good news of the message of Jesus Christ is that life matters. We are not on an endless wheel. We belong to the Alpha and Omega, the beginning and the ending. Your life is a journey, an adventure. Enjoy the ride!

Help me, Father, to stop going through the motions and start living. It all matters. In Jesus' name, Amen.

GRAB THE REAL GUSTO

Ecclesiastes 2:1–11

An old beer commercial urged us to "grab all the gusto" we could. The message was that if we bought that particular brand of beer, life would be happier and filled with adventure. Most of the stuff sold today promises the same thing. Advertisers have tapped into the concept that many men live hollow lives.

Will an empty life be made tolerable by any brand of beer, or a particular car, or a house in the "right" neighborhood? The writer of Ecclesiastes seemed to have filled his life with everything that he could experience: "I denied myself nothing my eyes desired; I refused my heart no pleasure" (v. 10). But what was the result? "Yet when I surveyed all that my hands had done and what I had toiled to achieve, everything was meaningless, a chasing after the wind" (v. 11).

Many a man has found his life filled with expensive toys but empty of anything of value. What can fill our lives? A relationship with God that is real, honest, and open is a good beginning. It puts everything into perspective and helps us live with grace and gratitude.

Go ahead. Grab the real gusto. A name is attached to it: God, heavenly Father, Lord. Take your pick. All of them point out that some meaning and power is beyond us but that we are wanted and needed. Imagine that. God wants to build the world with your help. Life has meaning. You count. What we do contributes to the construction or destruction of the world. That is a heavy thought but one that gives us a clear picture of how God operates. He wants us to contribute to His work. Go for it.

Lord, fill my life with meaning and keep me from
chasing the things that do not matter. In the
name of the One who is supremely worthwhile,
Amen.

TIME
Ecclesiastes 3:1–8

The ancient Greeks used to portray time as a man with long hair in the front but bald in the back. The image was that you must catch him coming toward you because once he is past, you have nothing to grab onto. That old imagery is true, isn't it? Most men I know are amazed at how quickly time passes.

I was looking at a box of old photographs recently. They included pictures of our sons when they were in kindergarten through third grade. Carla and I laughed when we saw them, but I felt twinges of grief too. At that time, one son was applying to various medical schools while the other was finishing his master's thesis and preparing to move to Oxford, England, for a Ph.D. program. Time has passed so quickly. They will never be my little boys again.

The writer of Ecclesiastes knew this truth. Things move on. People change. Time is limited and, therefore, precious. "There is a time . . . for every activity under heaven." I was with a group of friends recently. We went through the doctoral program together and meet in a study group twice every year. The first letters of our names spell out the name of our study group: D'STERB. One of our group said, "I just can't believe that I'm the father of a daughter in college." I can believe it. I imagine that you can too.

I am always amazed at people who waste time and talk about how they are bored. With so much to do and learn and accomplish, how could we be bored? Time will get away from you before you know it. It is like money, so spend it wisely. Invest it for future returns.

*Lord, teach us to use our time wisely. It speeds by
so quickly. In Jesus' name, Amen.*

TWO ARE BETTER THAN ONE
Ecclesiastes 4:9–12

The biblical account of creation shows Adam looking around for a mate. He viewed the various animals but found nothing like himself. Then God created Eve, and Adam responded, "At last! Somebody like me." Okay, that is a loose paraphrase, but it makes the point. We are made for a mate and most of us feel incomplete without one.

In today's reading, the simple statement is that "two are better than one" (v. 9). The reference is about friendship and working partners, but it applies to marriage too. "If one falls down, his friend can help him up" (v. 10). This is the realization that we can draw from each other's strength. When I am up, I can lift my wife if she is down and vice versa. I have experienced this truth many times. I will run into something that seems insurmountable. At just the right time, Carla says in words or deeds, "Go ahead. You can do it!" I do the same for her. Is that your experience too?

The writer of Ecclesiastes states that "if two lie down together, they will keep warm. But how can one keep warm alone?" (v. 11). An electric blanket can help, but that is not what he is talking about. He is talking about sharing our life with a woman. That takes courage, patience, and strength. But we receive more than we give. Christian marriage is a relationship in which man and woman do better when a third person—Christ—is present. "A cord of three strands is not quickly broken."

Single men—whether never married, widowed, or divorced—are not cut off from the blessings of God. This passage is not meant to imply that. Singles can live fulfilled lives. But when two people decide to marry, a relationship develops that is different from anything else. In this case, one plus one equals three.

Lord, thank You for my wife, my partner, my strength. Thank You for giving me just what You knew I needed. I pray that others will have the same joy of lifelong partnership. In Christ, Amen.

DON'T TRY TO FOOL GOD
Ecclesiastes 5:1—7

Picture a man rushing into the house of God on a worship morning. He is out of breath because he is late as usual. He feels tense and annoyed because his kids have caused him to miss the start of worship. As the service develops, he remembers that the offering plate will be around in a few minutes, so he grabs his checkbook and dashes off a quick offering. He halfheartedly sings a hymn or two and listens to the sermon with one ear. His mind is elsewhere. After the service, he scrambles to get his family to the car so he can get to the restaurant before the church down the block lets out.

Do you think he got much from worship that day or contributed much to its success?

How different is the scene described in today's reading. It tells us to "guard your steps when you go to the house of God" (v. 1). Take care to go with reverence. Then, "listen rather than to offer the sacrifice of fools" (v. 1). Pay attention and intentionally get something from worship rather than just passively letting it go by. "Do not be quick with your mouth"; "let your words be few" (v. 2). Listen rather than talk. Let God do the speaking in worship. You can talk later.

The simple fact is that we cannot fool God. We either worship or play games. Our entire commitment is open to Him. Thus, this admonition: "When you make a vow to God, do not delay in fulfilling it. He has no pleasure in fools; fulfill your vow" (v. 4). How are you doing with your commitment to God? Do you need to make some midcourse adjustments? If so, what are those adjustments? Take a few minutes and write them here:

- _____

- _____

- _____

Lord, I am serious about my relationship with

You. I am not satisfied with playing games. You know my heart. Help me keep my vows to You and to be careful with everything related to You. In Jesus' name, Amen.

WHO IS IN CHARGE HERE?

Ecclesiastes 9:11–12

The news brings the same tiresome fare: crime, famine, murder, terrorism, and financial irresponsibility and mismanagement. It seems so predictable that it is almost trite. Not only world events but also personal issues seem to make us throw up our hands and ask, "Hey, what's going on here? Is anyone in charge of this messy world?" In the words of an old song, we might want to say, "Stop the World and Let Me Off."

The writer of Ecclesiastes was a keen observer of the human condition. He asked uncomfortable questions and pointed out that life is not as predicable as some people seem to think. Consider today's reading. He noticed that the good guy does not always win; neither does the scoundrel get immediate punishment. "The race is not to the swift or the battle to the strong." Not only that, "nor does food come to the wise or wealth to the brilliant" (v. 11). Isn't good supposed to be rewarded and evil punished? How can things be as they are?

We live in a complex world. Actions that are intended to have one result often have unexpected outcomes. We cannot plan everything perfectly. Two forces at work are listed in today's reading: "time and chance happen to them all" (v. 11). Time is relentless and pushes forward with a force that nothing on earth can halt. And chance—who ever thinks about chance happening? Some people think that every event in the world is controlled by God. I do not think that. I think that God has given us great freedoms to act for good or bad. We may choose to use our freedom for evil purposes, but God can and does bring good out of our messes.

Who is in control here? Overall, God is. Trust Him.

I do trust You, Father. In the midst of my prob-
lems and the crises of the world, let me see Your
hand. In Christ, Amen.

TRUST THE PROCESS
Ecclesiastes 11:1–6

Garrison Keillor has a song about waiting for your ship to come in. In his version, about the time it comes in, it capsizes! Have you felt that way about your ship? Today's reading is a commercial term. The man who casts his bread upon the water is the man who takes a risk. He is willing to send his goods across the ocean in the hope of making a profit. He trusts the process.

If you wait until every problem is solved, every danger is removed, and every inconvenience is dealt with, you will never get anywhere! As the writer of Ecclesiastes puts it, "Whoever watches the wind will not plant; whoever looks at the clouds will not reap" (v. 4). In other words, just do it!

Mark Twain once wrote, "We should be careful to get out of an experience only the wisdom that is in it—and stop there; lest we be like the cat that sits down on a hot stove lid. She will never sit down on a hot stove lid again, and that is well; but also she will never sit down on a cold one any more."[1]

That is good thinking. Have you been burned by life's events? Have you been knocked down? Have you cast your bread upon the water but all you have to show for it is soggy bread?

Life does not offer us a money-back guarantee. If you have been knocked down, get up again. A boxer was once asked how many times he had to get off the mat to win. He said, "Just one more time than my opponent." I have been kicked around some. I have been turned down more times than the bed covers. So what? I will keep coming back until I draw my last breath.

Do not ever give up and become passive to life. In the end, the

---

1. Mark Twain, "Pudd'nhead Wilson's New Calendar." In *Following the Equator* (Hartford, Conn.: American Publishing Co., 1897), 124.

process of life works. If you need to, hit it again. Somebody needs your bread.

Lord, I am tired. Weary. Discouraged. You know what I've been through. Give me grace and strength for one more try. In Jesus' name, Amen.

TIME ENOUGH TO REMEMBER
Ecclesiastes 12:1–7

Older people have trouble finding God. Statistics show this, but our experience proves it. How many older people do our churches baptize each year? Not very many. You would think they would search for God as they draw to the close of their lives, but that is not usually the case. People seem to get harder and more rigid in their latter years.

The writer of Ecclesiastes implores us, "Remember your Creator in the days of your youth" (v. 1). Why? Because time rolls on and we find our world changing radically: "before the days of trouble come and the years approach when you will say, 'I find no pleasure in them'" (v. 1). Society says, "Let the young people sow their wild oats. They'll come around after a while." But if you sow wild oats, you cannot expect to harvest wheat.

The younger years are a time of discovery. What could be more worthwhile than the discovery of a relationship with God? The trouble is that the years seem to add more and more baggage that weighs us down and twists us. I love to see young people, especially young men, passionately pursing God. The Lord makes Himself known to us through our faith. That relationship is given by His grace. But we get to know God and His ways better as we study and serve.

Where are you in life—early manhood, middle years, or senior status? I assume you are reading this book because, regardless of your age, you are still pursuing God. You are "remembering" Him, to use the language of Ecclesiastes. I salute your efforts and join you in them. We seem to be on our pilgrimage alone at times, but remember that many men around you are looking for the same thing—knowledge of our Creator. Blessings on your journey.

Lord, You know my stage of life. No matter what it might be, help me in my discovery of Your ways. Through Christ, Amen.

MAY 29

A MOST UNUSUAL BOOK
Song of Songs 1:1–7

Song of Songs is the most unusual book of the Bible. It seems so strange in contrast to the rest of Scripture. It does not say anything about religious rituals, institutions, or themes. It does not even mention the name of God! What is it all about?

This book is an unashamed look at the joy of human love, with all of the excitement of meeting someone of the opposite sex, pursuing a relationship, and being head-over-heels in love. Many a man has read this book and said, "Hey, I understand this." Of course you do. It is about people just like you and me.

Although we live in a sex-saturated society, I believe that we have not done a very good job of understanding our own sexuality. The sleaziness of X-rated movies and the proliferation of pornography only point out that we seem to be missing something in our relationships. What is it?

Song of Songs tells the story of a young couple whose relationship mirrors the relationship that God desires for His people. He wants a close, monogamous "marriage" with His people. It is to be exclusive and offer its deepest joys and pleasures to those who want them most. Marriage is a good analogy for salvation, and salvation is a good analogy for marriage. The straightforward erotic nature of some of this book grabs our attention. "Take me away with you—let us hurry! Let the king bring me into his chambers" (v. 4). You do not need a theologian to tell you what that means.

What if God wants us the way a young lover wants his beloved? Can you remember the sense of need, almost desperation, of your wedding day? Song of Songs uses that feeling to say, "This is what God feels for you. Can you turn Him away?"

Lord, You are the Divine Lover. You want me, and I want You. Help my relationship with You to be deep and satisfying as love brings us together. Through Christ, the eternal Lover, Amen.

MAY 30

A Most Unexpected Gift
Song of Songs 4:1–15

I think of my wife as a gift from God. That sounds okay so far, but what if I told you that I consider everything about her, including her body, as part of that gift? On our wedding night, Carla changed into an outfit that can be described only by the phrase "For your eyes only." Wow!

Read today's Scripture passage. It might shock you if you are unfamiliar with it. The two lovers see each other as the gift from God. Listen to the language that the man uses to describe his wife. "Your eyes . . . are doves" (v. 1). "Your hair is like a flock of goats" (v. 1). That was a good thing in his time, but don't try using that language today! "Your lips are like a scarlet ribbon" (v. 3). "Your neck is like the tower of David" (v. 4). "Your two breasts are like two fawns" (v. 5).

You get the picture. He is madly in love with her. He wants her and celebrates her beauty. It all boils down to the fact that he is infatuated with her: "You have stolen my heart, my sister, my bride; you have stolen my heart with one glance of your eyes, with one jewel of your necklace" (v. 9).

We men are sometimes put off by that sort of language, at least when we get a little older. But I remember feeling just like that about my wife in the early years. We have been married thirty years, and I love her more now than I did then. I used to write her love poems that would probably embarrass me now. I use different language now, but it is still reflective that I consider Carla a gift from God.

How about you? Are you thinking of your wife that way, or is every day a struggle? Your wife is a gift from God. Treat her as the precious person she is.

Lord, on my own I might not be much, but with my blessed wife, I am whole. Thanks for this indescribable gift. In Christ's name, Amen.

MAY 31

PASSION IN THE RIGHT PLACE
Song of Songs 7:1–9

Danger lurks around the corner for every man. It waits to pounce like a crouching lion. This danger tears more than flesh; it destroys the spirit as it focuses on the essence of our male identity. What is that danger? It is pornography.

Pornography means literally "flesh writings." Its sole intent is to arouse men, but it promises what it cannot deliver. It portrays alluring women who seem to exist just for our pleasure. Get real! It is all fantasy and can get its hooks into a man and enslave him. A friend of mine is hooked. He visits porn sites on the Internet and tells me that thousands of them are out there. I will take his word for it because I am afraid of it and will not go searching on my own.

Why is porn so powerful? I think it is because God has designed men with strong passion—emotionally, physically, and spiritually. When directed toward a wife, physical and emotional passion is right and beautiful. When directed toward the love and service of God, spiritual passion is great. But pervert any of that and direct it in the wrong direction, and it becomes a trap.

In today's reading, the man expresses his passion for his beloved. I cannot help but smile when I read this. He loves this woman with a passion that is pointing in the right direction. Reading his descriptions of her reminds me of my own early discovery of love and passion toward my wife. God made us this way so that we connect at a deep and abiding level. Men and women are made to commit to each other and live their lives in harmony and happiness.

Live with all of the passion in you. Just keep it in the right place.

*Lord, I want to be Your man more than anything
else in life. Keep me clean. Forgive me when I've
failed. Accept me for who I am. You know me
better than I know myself. Through Christ,
Amen.*

WHO IS YOUR MASTER?

Isaiah 1:1–18

Who is your master?

"Hold on!" you say. "We live in America, the land of the free and the home of the brave. I'm *no one's* slave!"

I'm not speaking of political freedom, however. I'm talking about that which drives you and controls most of your thoughts and desires—in other words, your master.

Years ago, I met a couple in Missouri whose marriage was in serious trouble. The man had a mistress. She wasn't a blond or a redhead. She didn't have a great figure; in fact, she was completely round! Her name was softball. The husband played it nearly every night of the year, traveling hundreds of miles to participate in tournaments. He won many trophies—but he lost his wife.

Recently, a pastor I know lost his church because of another type of ball. He played golf six days a week, sometimes managing to work in nine holes on Sunday afternoon!

Poker, football, golf, softball, ESPN, work, weightlifting—I've seen all of them contribute to the breakup of a marriage or a career. So, I ask you once more, who is your master?

As we begin the book of Isaiah, we see the prophet reminding the Israelites that they had forgotten that God is to be their Master. Because they had forgotten God and had chosen to follow another, Isaiah told them that they would be punished with defeat, destruction, and the loss of their land.

That does not have to be how the story is played out, however. God, through the prophet, held out a hand of forgiveness. If His people would repent and return to Him, they and their land would be healed. In other words, the right Master ensures that you will walk the right path. Living under God's discipline frees you to experience peace, joy, and an abundant life rich in the Lord's blessings.

Do you remember to whom you belong? Are you making God the Master of your life every day?

Lord, I truly want You to be my Lord. Please remind me daily that You are to be the One I serve. Keep me from sin and from poor choices that can pull me from Your presence. As best I can, I give You my full allegiance right now. In Jesus' name, Amen.

JUNE 2

YOUR LIFE AND GODLY FRUIT
Isaiah 5:1–4

Have you ever had a vegetable garden? Not long ago, I read an article in which the author had calculated how much time he spent working in his garden. Plowing, planting, fertilizing, weeding, picking the produce—it all added up to an incredible amount of man-hours. By the time he was finished, the author realized that he could have bought the most luxurious fruit and vegetables cheaper than what came out of his garden!

Why would someone spend that much time and effort with corn, peas, and tomatoes? Most of those who raise vegetables do so because they love that activity. The feel of the dirt on their hands and the pleasure of seeing the result of their labors keeps them coming back every spring.

Several years ago, I planted some tomatoes. I fought weeds, worms, and birds to protect my investment. Every day after work, I'd head out into the garden to check on my labor of love. Visions of plump, ripe tomatoes bursting with flavor floated through my thoughts.

Imagine, then, my surprise when I found corn growing on my tomato vines one afternoon! Small, stunted ears poked out from the places where juicy red fruit should have been. The corn had a sour taste and was worthless for food. I had to trash the whole garden.

Did that really happen, you ask? Of course not! You and I both know watermelons don't grow on apple trees and corn doesn't blossom from tomato vines. Although we know this principle of life, we sometimes ignore it when applied to our own souls.

God has spent much time planting and cultivating your life. He has done so because He loves you. Now, however, the Lord expects to see the right kind of fruit blossom as a result of His efforts. So let's take a tour through your life and inspect what is being produced from your use of God's gifts.

What does God see as He regards your life? Does He see a healthy, fruitful garden? Or does he see a plot full of weeds and debris? Are you giving the Lord a bountiful harvest of good works and souls won for Him? Or are you coming to God empty-handed?

When a farmer has a garden that doesn't produce, he often plows it under and begins again. After all, destroying something that produces nothing is the first step in bringing into existence something else that *will* be fruitful. If that's true, what should God do with your life? And if you see that your life is unproductive for God, what are you going to do about it today?

Heavenly Father, I want to be productive for You. Please purge from my life that which is displeasing to You. May the fruit of my life honor You and build the kingdom of God. Help me, today, to be "God's man" in every way. In Jesus' name, Amen.

JUNE 3

HEARING GOD'S CALL
Isaiah 6:1–8

Have you ever heard it?

I have. I heard it on a Monday morning while sitting in the church office in Simpson, Louisiana. The Sunday morning service the day before had included a list of missions facts in the bulletin designed to deepen our commitment to prayer for missionaries around the globe. I had no idea that God had prepared those missions facts for me.

That Monday morning, I was looking over the Sunday bulletin once again when my eyes fell on a particular sentence. Paraphrased, it said, "On any given Sunday, less than 1 percent of France's population can be found in any evangelical church. The need for workers is great."

That's when I heard it. The call—from God—to do something with my life. As Susan and I responded to the Lord's leading, we found ourselves living in France, learning the language and the culture, sharing Christ, and building a new church. We saw men, women, teenagers, and children come to know Jesus as their Lord and Savior. And it all started with "the call."

Have you heard it?

Isaiah had been a priest for some time when he encountered God while ministering in the temple. That encounter shook the prophet to his core, humbled him in the face of God's holiness, and gave him a vision of his people's spiritual need. In short, when Isaiah heard the call of God, it changed his life forever.

God calls each of His children to a specific task. And it is only in hearing God's call and discovering your appointed task that you'll begin to experience the abundant life that He's promised all believers. Call out to the Lord today; seek His face; read His Word. Do this consistently, and you'll begin to discern the call of God upon your life.

Have you heard it?

Heavenly Father, please speak to me and show me Your will for my life. I truly want You to have first claim upon me. May I be willing to do whatever You desire me to do, go wherever You want me to go, and share the gospel with those whom You place in my path. In Jesus' name, Amen.

DRIVING IN THE DARKNESS
Isaiah 9:1–3

For many years following World War II, the French maintained a driving habit necessitated by the infamous blackouts during enemy bombings. Drivers would turn their headlights off at night. During the war, it made them invisible to unfriendly airplanes. But in the decades that followed, the habit made for heart-stopping encounters at intersections.

As an American living—and driving—in France, I "foolishly" kept my headlights on when driving in the evening. It took only a few nights of horns honking and lights flashing, however, to convince me to turn off the headlights. And although I lived in France for quite a number of years, I never got used to driving in darkness. On quite a few occasions, only quick reflexes aided by the providence of God kept me and the car safe.

Driving in darkness. That phrase could well express the general state of many people in our world today. Isaiah used the phrase *walking in darkness* (v. 2), but with our fast-pace life, many of us seem to be speeding toward destruction as fast as we can. Hurtling down life's highway, unable to see what's ahead, we often hide our uneasiness by pursuing more pleasure, more possessions, more power.

The prophet Isaiah reminds us that God has seen our desperate situation and wants to help us. "The people walking in darkness have seen a great light" (v. 2). That light, of course, is Jesus Christ, God's Son. As we give Him control of our lives, we no longer have to worry about journeying through this world in the dark. First John 1:7 reminds us that when we have fellowship with Christ, we walk regularly in the light.

"Driving in the darkness." "Walking in the light." Which phrase describes your life? The first phrase guarantees a terrible wreck one day. The second phrase promises safe paths no matter what occurs in life.

Dear God, I want to walk with You throughout this day. Help me to follow Your path, relate to people with Your love, and use my time to do Your will. Place within me a deep desire to walk in the light and avoid spiritual darkness. In Jesus' name, Amen.

JUNE 5

USING YOUR STRENGTH FOR GOD
Isaiah 10:1–3

A friend of mine was describing how he had started getting in shape. He's designed his own strength program.

"I began with five-pound potato sacks, holding one in each hand. I held them straight out to either side, working each day until I could hold them like that for two minutes. Then I moved up to ten-pound potato sacks. Now," he continued, "I can hold two fifty-pound potato sacks straight out for two minutes!" Then he added, "In a few weeks, I'll be strong enough to put some potatoes in those sacks!"

How strong are you? After all, there are several types of strength. Some of you reading this are physically fit; others of you are strong in people skills; still others are powerful in the area of business and finance. God's Word gives an important principle to all strong individuals: you must not use your strength to exploit people. Even if the law is on your side, God says that you answer to a higher authority.

James 5:4–5 says, "Look! The wages you failed to pay the workmen who mowed your fields are crying out against you. The cries of the harvesters have reached the ears of the Lord Almighty. You have lived on earth in luxury and self-indulgence. You have fattened yourselves in the day of slaughter."

In other words, just because you're strong enough to make others bend to you, it doesn't mean that you have God's permission to use your strength in that way. The Lord will judge us on how we treat our employees, our coworkers, our bosses, and our families.

Today, decide to use your strength to help others, not hurt them. Commit to lifting the weak, not to putting them down.

Heavenly Father, please help me to see others as You see them. May I use the gifts that You've given me to help Your children, not fatten my own purse or build up my own ego. In Jesus' name, Amen.

JUNE 6

ULTIMATE JUSTICE
Isaiah 11:1–9

I had just pulled into the parking lot of a fast-food restaurant. As I prepared to get out, I saw a man, a woman, and a little boy exit the restaurant and go to the pickup truck next to me. The little boy struggled to get up into the truck and lost his footing. In trying to catch his balance, he dropped his food. That's when the man lost his temper.

"You stupid idiot!" he yelled (actually, he used some other words that I won't repeat). "You can't do anything right!" Then he slapped the boy several times and began kicking him.

That's when I came out of the car as fast I could. "Hey!" I yelled. "Stop it now." The man looked over at me and glared. But he did stop. The woman got into the truck and gathered the sobbing boy into her arms. Her husband (I presume) stomped around to the other side, slammed the door, and squealed out of his parking space. Then he put the truck into park so fast that it rocked back and forth a few times. Looking in his rearview mirror, he saw me writing down his license number. As he continued to watch, I pulled out my cell phone and began to make a call. The man took off at that point. But I continued my call to Child Protection, explaining the situation and giving them the tag number. They assured me that the agency would look into the family situation in the next several weeks.

I've often thought of that little boy. Did he receive help? Is he out of that abusive situation? You and I both know that there are a million other stories just like that one; in fact, some of them are far worse.

In today's passage, we read that one day Jesus Christ will come, judging everything and everyone evil. No cruel act will go unpunished. No harsh words will be overlooked. Knowing this, we should have two attitudes. First, our behavior toward everyone should be pleasing to Christ. Second, we can afford to be patient in the face of injustice. We know that this present world and situation are not at all the final word.

Take a moment to thank Jesus Christ for His gifts of salvation and grace. Ask Him to give you opportunities for sharing with others the precious gift of the gospel. Remember, Jesus is coming soon. You want to be ready to face His judgment, and you want to help others be ready, too.

Lord, may I remember that You are coming in judgment—maybe today. Help me to share Christ with others and to be patient in the middle of difficulties. Thank You for the salvation and grace You give me every day. In Jesus' name, Amen.

JUNE 7

FACING DOWN YOUR FEARS
Isaiah 12

I'm a wimp when it comes to the dentist. The word *macho* is nowhere in my vocabulary or personality when I walk into the dentist's office and settle myself into his chair. You've heard stories of guys telling the dentist, "No pain medication, Doc. Just go ahead and drill." That is *not* me! I ask for everything possible to keep me from feeling any nerve twinges.

I've faced down a drunk who was threatening to kill his family, offering myself as a substitute hostage (by the way, I won him to Christ, baptized him, and saw him become a member of the church!). I've sat with a potential suicide victim as he waved his gun around, saying he'd take me with him (we both survived). But when the dentist's drill starts toward my mouth, sweat breaks out.

Of what—or whom—are you afraid? Maybe you can face a hostile situation without fear, but wondering what will happen to your children as they grow older keeps you awake at night. Perhaps the state of your marriage paralyzes you emotionally and keeps you from trusting in God as you should.

Whatever your problem might be, I encourage you to memorize Isaiah 12:2, especially the first part of the verse: "Surely God is my salvation; I will trust and not be afraid." The Lord knows the situation you're facing right now. He promises to give you both the wisdom and the strength to make it through your trials. And in the middle of those trials, God also promises to give you His peace.

Don't fear the world. Trust in God.

Heavenly Father, You know what I fear. Help me to give You that fear today. May I rest in Your peace and strength, no matter what might occur throughout the next twenty-four hours. In Jesus' name, Amen.

JUNE 8

SHARING GOOD NEWS
Isaiah 24:1–6

Have you heard about the incurable optimist who fell off the top of a twenty-two-story building? As he passed the fourteenth floor, he said to an astonished observer, "Everything's all right so far!"

"The best is yet to come." With heaven awaiting the believer, that statement is certainly true. But it's also true that the worst is yet to come. Several books in the Bible, as well as today's passage, tell us of a worldwide swath of destruction that will precede the second coming of Christ. That destruction will touch both the Earth itself, and many of its inhabitants.

Perhaps we should ask ourselves why the Lord tells us of these coming calamities. As we discussed a few days ago, the knowledge of these events can serve as a warning to all of us concerning our faith and our behavior. But the wise Christian will also use it as an incentive to share Christ with as many people as possible and as often as possible. After all, we not only do not know when this event might occur but also are unsure of when death might intervene in the lives of those we know.

The optimist in the preceding story was right—for the moment. But we know that he was rushing toward the sudden end of his life. Your friends might feel good about themselves and the direction they're going in life. But do they really know what will happen at the end of their lives and this world? Are they prepared for that end?

God has called you to tell your friends and colleagues about the way to forgiveness of sins and the assurance of eternal life. They can escape the horrors of the coming judgment—but only if you share with them the Good News of the gospel. In doing so, you allow them to come to know Christ and then to say, "You're right; the best is yet to come!"

> *Dear God, You know the people with whom I need to talk about Christ. Help my lifestyle, my vocabulary, and my actions honor You, and make it easy and natural for me to witness. Give me wisdom and boldness today that I might take advantage of the opportunities to witness that You give me. In Jesus' name, Amen.*

JUNE 9

THE RIGHT PERSPECTIVE ON TROUBLES
Isaiah 25:6–8

The sharp snapping of canvas in the wind was the only sound to disturb the quietness of the rural setting. Dignified, spreading trees that reach majestic heights only through the passage of decades sheltered the men and women from the summer sun. Slowly, the burial party lowered the tiny casket into a newly dug grave. I struggled to find some words of comfort for the grieving parents who only days before had welcomed the birth of their first child.

Death. It robs us of relatives and friends. It intrudes into every family. It thrusts us into situations that we never wanted.

But death does not have the last word.

The words from God in today's passage remind us of a time

when death will be gone forever, swallowed up, destroyed by the power of the risen Savior, Jesus Christ. On that day, we will rejoice together in heaven. We will feast on the best that God Himself has to offer us!

Meanwhile, we must stay faithful, not losing our faith even when death rips loved ones from us at the worst of times. Death's time is short; the believer's time is for all eternity. Even as the tears flow for the one lost temporarily through accident or disease, a note of triumph can be heard. The parents of the baby knew it that day at the funeral. Their faith stood strong in the midst of sorrow. And yours can too.

Heavenly Father, thank You for giving me the assurance of eternal life. Thank You for conquering death once and for all. Help me to remain faithful to You even when sorrowful times come. In Jesus' name, Amen.

JUNE 10

A PASSION FOR GOD
Isaiah 26:9—13

My daughter, Amy, is fairly small. Alhough the oldest of three girls, she is dwarfed by her younger sisters. However, she can out eat them and everyone else I know when it comes to her favorite food—chocolate. I've watched her order chocolate ice cream with hot fudge on top. When others pass up dark, semisweet chocolate for lighter fare, she will sweep up the dense confection with a satisfied smile. One night at a restaurant with her husband, she ordered "Death by Chocolate," a dessert for two. When the waiter brought two spoons, she seemed genuinely puzzled. "Why would I need another spoon?" she wondered aloud while finishing off the dessert.

What is your passion? For some people, it's work. For others, it might be a sport or a hobby. Regardless of what it is, your passion has the power to elicit amazing dedication from you. Think what would happen if you had the same passion for God that you have for football, ESPN, music, or whatever it is that grabs your heart and soul.

In verse 9 of today's passage, we see one of the secrets of Isaiah's greatness. His passion was to know God more, to commune with Him as often as possible. Most of us don't remember who was the national champion in basketball or football five years ago. We don't remember the "Play of the Week" that made us gasp with delight three weeks back. But nearly three thousand years after Isaiah wrote his prophecy, it still has the power to speak to and inspire us.

It's okay to be passionate about different things in life. After all, that's how great deeds get accomplished. But ensure that "a passion for God" is at the top of the list of your daily goals. It will ensure that your life counts for something and makes a difference.

Dear God, I want my life to count for good in this world. Help me to be passionate about living for You, no matter what the cost. May others see You in my actions and attitudes. In Jesus' name, Amen.

JUNE 11

HEAVEN AND ENCOURAGEMENT
Isaiah 35:4–10

If you knew me well, you'd laugh at the next statement: I used to be in a singing group. We were fairly successful, recording six albums in seven years and staying as busy as we wanted touring. Only three of us were in the group, and we all sang. The reason I said that you'd laugh at this revelation is because my voice could best be described as a hoarse frog croaking in the night! I think the only reason I was in the group was because I helped start it, and I owned the guitar.

One day, however, all of this will change. In chapter 35 of Isaiah, we see God promising us that "the ransomed of the LORD will return. They will enter Zion with singing; everlasting joy will crown their heads. Gladness and joy will overtake them, and sorrow and sighing will flee away" (v. 10). On that day, I'll have a great voice!

And so will you. We'll sing for joy as all of our problems cease forever. Old football injuries, damaged emotions, strong temptations—they'll all be gone. In the presence of God, perfect bodies and perfect relationships will be the norm. How wonderful that day will be!

God places verses like these in the Bible to encourage us and to help us get a right frame of mind about our current situation. If it's good, don't get too attached to it! This world will not last. If you're going through tough times, don't get too discouraged. Those tough times will fade into nothingness when you're before God, forever singing His praises with the rest of the redeemed.

We might never meet each other during our time on earth, but I plan to meet you before God's throne. I'll be the one with the great voice!

Heavenly Father, help me to remember that this world is not my final home. May I always remember that heaven is my ultimate destination. Throughout this day, I want to honor You with a joyful spirit, knowing that one day I'll be with You forever. In Jesus' name, Amen.

JUNE 12

TRUST AND THE CREATOR
Isaiah 42:1–8

Looking straight up at the stars, I watched in amazement as we blasted off from Earth, rocketed past the moon, and began our journey through this solar system and deep into our galaxy, the Milky Way.

The narrator at the planetarium in the Smithsonian Air and Space Museum helped us understand the significance of the latest images taken by the Hubble telescope orbiting our planet. But as I watched the results of man's technological advancements, I couldn't help but think of Jesus Christ. He created all of this—and more. We will probably never explore even a small fraction of our own galaxy, much less the billions of galaxies that lie beyond our vision.

Yet, God spoke it all into existence, sees all of it in a glance, and knows how to keep it functioning smoothly.

This Creator is the One who humbly came to earth and sacrificed His life for you and me. In other words, we serve a great God! Our Savior is all-powerful!

In light of what I've just written, let me ask you a question. What in your life right now are you not entrusting to Jesus Christ? What worry is robbing you of your joy? Remember, the One who spoke the universe into existence is the same One who loves to hear your requests and your needs. Turn to Him with your problems and trust Him to help you today.

> *Dear Lord, please help me to remember Your awesome power and might. May I trust Your love and Your strength throughout this day. Thank You for saving me, for forgiving me of all of my sins, and for giving me an abundant life. May I live that testimony before others today. In Jesus' name, Amen.*

JUNE 13

LIFE CHANGE
Isaiah 53:1–6

How did it all get here? My weight, I mean. I never intended for it to happen. After all, I was on the tennis team in school. I played basketball, football, badminton, squash. How did this rubber tire get around my waist?

It happened little by little. I've grown older. I used to run up and down the basketball court. Now, I sit in front of a computer (as I'm doing now) and let my fingers run up and down the keyboard. Above all, my knees have paid a terrible price for the added weight. Too many trips to the Mexican restaurants and fast-food drive-thrus have taken a toll. So, I've tried to make a significant change in my lifestyle and habits. For example, before beginning to write this day's devotional, I worked out for about an hour. Fat-free Italian dressing has become my constant companion. Now I read labels before consuming something.

What about you? How did it happen to get into your life? I'm not talking about weight now; I'm talking about sin. If we're not careful, we can let what we call "little sins" accumulate in our lives. We don't think much about them. After all, when we look around at the lifestyles of others, we seem pretty good! But each of the sins in our lives made the sacrifice of Jesus Christ necessary. The sins that we tolerate helped nail Christ to the cross and deprived the heavenly Father of His Son.

Perhaps it's time for a change in habits. Let's take our sins seriously, admit that they're wrong, turn from committing them, and ask Christ to forgive us. We must lighten the spiritual load that is weighing down our souls. Let's exercise our faith every day through regular prayer and Bible reading. At the same time, we must watch what our soul takes in; good spiritual nourishment is important!

Doing all of this not only makes us feel better spiritually but also pleases God. Fit bodies are nice, but fit souls make a difference in the world and influence others to come to Christ. Let's begin getting fit!

Heavenly Father, help me not to tolerate any sin in my life, no matter how "small" I might think it is. Help me to become spiritually fit for You, beginning today. In Jesus' name, Amen.

JUNE 14

PARTIES OR PARACHUTES?
Isaiah 55:1–2, 6–7

The incidents of September 11, 2001, have changed us all. Not just Americans, but people throughout the whole world have been affected by those terrible events. Business executives and office workers in high-rise buildings now feel less secure. They wonder what they would do if their means of getting out of a skyscraper were suddenly cut off.

An Israeli company believes that it has the answer to such concerns. Apco Aviation has designed and produced a new product called the "Executivechute." The backpack-type parachute, which is now being marketed in the United States and Japan, has a $795 price tag and weighs four pounds. This parachute for office workers can be used from a minimum height of ten stories. According to the manufacturer, it will ensure a "reliable but hard landing" that could produce some minor injuries. "But we figure a twisted ankle is a small price to pay for life," a spokesman added.[1]

A lot of different ways exist to spend your money trying to have a good life and escape difficulties. You can spend it wisely or foolishly—it's up to you. You also have only a certain amount of time and energy. Again, how and on what you expend these valuable resources is entirely up to you.

You can spend your life on parties or parachutes. You can live for today or prepare for tomorrow.

God's Word encourages you to buy water that will cause you never to thirst again. Your parched life will be satisfied forever when you seek the Lord with all of your heart. Finding Him will ensure divine guidance through an unstable world.

If you've not yet done so, I encourage you to invest your life completely in Jesus Christ today.

Dear Lord, help me to expend my resources on that which will last for eternity. I don't want to waste what You've given me on habits and things that will not stand the test of time. Please guide my life according to Your will today. In Jesus' name, Amen.

JUNE 15

WHEN THE "WHY" CAN'T BE ANSWERED
Isaiah 55:8–12

"Daddy, where does air come from?" "Why can't we find the end of the rainbow?" "Where does the sun go every night?"

Every child goes through a "why" stage at some point in the

---

1. "Parachute for High-Rise Worriers," 8 November 2001, BBC News, news.bbc.co.uk/2/hi/americas/1645897.stm. Accessed 19 August 2003.

formative years. When my children were asking those questions, I was sometimes tempted to answer like the dad in the comic strip "Calvin and Hobbes." One night Calvin asked his father, "Where does wind come from?" His dad said, "Wind comes from trees sneezing." My kids would have understood a response like that better than the answers I gave them!

Not only children ask why things are as they are. Inquisitive people seem to be the ones who make the astounding scientific discoveries and come up with great new products. Finding out why and how things work can make for a rich, fulfilling life. There comes a point in life, however, when asking "why" can become a hindrance to your faith.

"Pastor, why did God let me get cancer?" "Why did my father die?" "Why did my marriage break up when I was trying so hard to live a Christian life?" Why, why, why?

In essence, God tells us in today's passage that we simply can't understand all of the events that He allows to happen in our lives. God has a plan, and He works to accomplish it in spite of the sin in this world and the freedom of humankind to reject Him. What God is doing is far above our ability to comprehend. We might as well decide to hold off asking "Why this tragedy?" until we get in the presence of the One who can answer such questions.

One day, in heaven, everything will become clear to us. Until that day, let's decide to have faith in God, no matter what might occur.

Dear God, I don't understand everything that's happened in my life. Help me, however, to avoid bitterness or lack of faith in You because of the tough times. Remind me that You are in control and that You love me. In Jesus' name, Amen.

JUNE 16

THE WATCHMAN
Isaiah 62:6–7

Is this any way to promote religion? Several years ago, Oslo, Norway, decided to let Muslims broadcast prayer calls for the first time in that Christian-dominated nation. Rather than every day, however, the city council ruled that a mosque would be allowed to use a loudspeaker to broadcast a prayer call into the streets for three minutes every Friday.

Unfortunately, this only made the atheists in Norway angry. They felt "oppressed" by the decision. So now "The Atheist Society" will also be allowed to use a megaphone to invite members to meetings, shouting from a rooftop once a week: "God does not exist."

From rooftops—as well as televisions, magazines, radios, and computer screens—all over the world, a variety of voices shout their false beliefs without embarrassment or shame. Where, in all of this, is the voice of the man who stands for Christ?

In today's Bible reading, we see God giving a command to the church. All over this world, we are to be communicating clearly and consistently the truth of Jesus Christ to a searching world. Others will proclaim their untruths, pointing multitudes to the wrong path. Now more than ever, the kingdom of God needs godly men to stand up to correct these ungodly voices. The Lord has called you to be a watchman and declare the truth.

Heavenly Father, I know that You have called me to do more than live a life that will meet my own needs. Please guide me into a lifestyle in which I will share the truth of Your love without embarrassment. Bring into my life those who need Christ, and give me the courage and wisdom to share with them the good news of Christ. In Jesus' name, Amen.

JUNE 17

HEROES AND WORSHIP
Isaiah 65:17—20

Taking my family on a tour through Washington, D.C., touched me emotionally many times. But one situation finally moved me to tears. Standing before the Marine War Memorial that commemorates the raising of the flag on Iwo Jima, I thought of the thousands of young lives given for the liberty of my country. Looking around, I could see nothing but simple, white gravestones for what seemed like miles, mute testimony to the cost of peace for America. Arlington National Cemetery holds the remains of heroes who were faithful to the end.

Another grave is geographically far away but nonetheless close to my heart. It contains nothing today because of a divine resurrection. But that empty tomb at one time held the body of the greatest hero of the greatest war ever fought. Jesus Christ engaged all of the forces of hell and gave His life that we might have peace. In dying, faithful to the end, He won life for us. The cost of our peace with God rested on Christ's shoulders—and He never flinched from His duty.

We are moving toward a wonderful future, a future made possible by Christ's sacrifice and victory. Let's take a moment to thank God for such wonderful love. And let's ask God to give us the same dedication to others that Christ had on the Cross for us.

Dear God, when I think about what Jesus did on the Cross for me, I stand overwhelmed and humbled by Your love. Thank You for not giving up on me. Thank You for the promise of a wonderful future bought by Christ on the Cross. Please help me to honor You by standing firm this day for Your truth. In Jesus' name, Amen.

JUNE 18

GOD'S PLAN FOR YOUR LIFE
Jeremiah 1:1–9

Walking through the Library of Congress during one of my visits to Washington, D.C., looking at original, key documents that outlined the formation of America, I noticed two things. First, I was reminded once more that the faith in God of our founders could be seen clearly. Unashamed to talk of God in the White House or Congress, the lawmakers who laid the foundation of the United States assumed a belief in God and the liberty to speak of it anywhere. Second, I realized how far our nation has fallen. Government, society, and the media are limiting more and more the right to speak of God and our faith in Jesus Christ. In doing so, they try to ignore our country's beginnings and strike out on a course that leaves God far away. The end result can be only disaster.

At the beginning of the book of Jeremiah, you can see God confirming a knowledge of and a purpose for the prophet before he was ever born. Perhaps God has not called you to be a prophet, but He certainly knew you before your birth. And the Lord has a unique plan for your life.

Have you sought out God's plan for you? Or have you lived for only your own pleasure, doing what you want and fulfilling your own needs? Our country is in desperate shape spiritually. We need men like you to discover their place in God's plan for this world and then go about the business of accomplishing it.

Together, working for God, we can change this world.

Dear Lord, help me not to succumb to selfish desires. I want to know Your purpose for my life. Thank You for knowing about me and caring for me before I was ever born. Help me always to remember that I have a divine calling upon my life, and give me the strength to fulfill it. In Jesus' name, Amen.

JUNE 19

THE DANGER OF A DOUBLE LIFE
Jeremiah 2:1–9

The man came to his pastor and said, "I'm worried. For the next two weeks, I'll be with some of the most ungodly people in our company. We will be together almost constantly during training sessions in Florida, and I'm afraid they'll harass me because of my faith. Please pray for me."

The pastor did pray for him, and off the man went.

Several weeks went by, and the pastor saw the man one Sunday at church. After the service, he asked the businessman how the two weeks went. "Just great!" the man replied. "Those guys never found out I was a Christian!"

Has there ever been a time when you loved the Lord more than you do now?

In today's Scripture passage, Jeremiah delivered God's scathing message to His people. God reminded the Israelites that He had delivered them from slavery in Egypt and worked mighty miracles in their midst. He commended them for loving God "in their youth." Now, however, the people had polluted their pure worship of God by also sacrificing to false gods. The Lord told His people that they would be judged because of their spiritual perversion.

I repeat, has there ever been a time when you loved the Lord more than you do now? The businessman in the preceding story saw no problem with living like the world and also coming to church to worship. But God says that we must follow only Him. Anything else is spiritual pollution.

As we will see in the book of Jeremiah, the prophet pleaded for his countrymen to turn back to God and be healed. If you've been living a double life, if you've allowed any sin to coexist with God in your life, listen to God's message. Return to a white-hot passion to live for your Savior. Give Him, once again, first place in your life.

Heavenly Father, I want You to be first in my life. I desire to have a strong love for You, a love that will neither die nor falter. Today, may You be at the center of everything I do. In Jesus' name, Amen.

JUNE 20

CLEAR MESSAGES
Jeremiah 6:16–19

Marilyn Wells relates the following experience.

At the end of a long day of driving, we encountered roadwork. We were unsure which lane to drive in, and the flagman was no help; his signal light went up, down, across and back again.

"What do you think he wants us to do?" my husband asked. We proceeded cautiously and finally drew abreast of the flagman—who, we realized, was frantically warding off mosquitoes!"[1]

Employers, what message about Christ are you sending to your employees through the way you treat them? Employees, what lessons about Christianity have your bosses learned through the way you work for them?

Some people decide that "the bottom line" is the be-all and end-all in life. For those people, nothing matters more than making the most money possible. Although every business should make a profit, at some point we must realize that relationships with our God and our fellow workers are even more important. In fact, God will bless your business in the best way if you live out a Christian life before people in the workplace. In the words of Jeremiah, "Stand at the crossroads and look; ask for the ancient paths, ask where the good way is, and walk in it, and you will find rest for your souls" (v. 16).

Dear Lord, I want to be a good witness at work today. Help me to work to the best of my ability. And help me to treat others with dignity, showing them the love of Christ. In Jesus' name, Amen.

JUNE 21

CHRISTIANS AND THE WORKPLACE
Jeremiah 7:1–7

Let's continue the discussion that we began yesterday about Christians in the workplace.

"If that's the way Christians treat one another, I want no part of it!"

---

1. Marilyn Wells, *Reader's Digest*, June 2001, 131.

I heard that statement in a store not long ago. It came from someone who had seen two Christians verbally spar with each other over minor differences between their denominations. Although those two people didn't realize it, they were giving a horrible witness for Christ's love to the unbelievers who were watching day in and day out.

Do you work with other Christians? Please understand that you and the other believers in your workplace are on the same team! Even if you belong to different churches and denominations and don't agree on everything, you have the same Savior, Jesus Christ. As believers, unite to pray for your lost coworkers. Band together to share Christ with others. Don't let small variations between churches keep you from teaming against Satan where you work. As God says to His people in today's passage, "Change your ways and your actions and deal with each other justly" (v. 5).

Dear God, while I'm on the job today, help me above all to get along with other Christians. May we bond together as a team that can honor You and witness for You. May our love for one another be a true testimony to my coworkers. In Jesus' name, Amen.

JUNE 22

AVOIDING SEXUAL HARASSMENT
Jeremiah 14:10–21

This is the third day of our discussion about living out our Christian faith in the workplace.

The following illustration comes from a book titled *Best of the World's Worst*. Under the heading of "The Worst Case of Sexism" is the following incredible custom.

"When the young women of the Emerillon Tribe of French Guyana reach marrying age, they must prove that they are worthy of matrimony by spending five days and nights in a hammock, without food, fending off armies of giant, biting ants."

And how, you ask, do the ants know to attack the young women?

"The ants are led to the hammock by a trail of honey poured by the Emerillon medicine man!"[1]

How do you treat those of the opposite sex in your workplace?

Sadly, some men and women deal with the opposite gender in a derogatory manner. Others make inappropriate sexual remarks and then hide behind the statement, "I was only joking. Don't you have a sense of humor?"

God has commanded you, as a Christian, to treat in a godly manner everyone with whom you work, realizing that they are created in the image of God. The person working beside you is someone for whom Christ died. Relate to him or her in honor and holiness. It very well could be that your godliness and loving holiness will begin to rub off on others, which will lead to a better atmosphere for everyone.

> *Lord, please help me to treat the women in my workplace with Christian love and dignity. Today, help me to guard my eyes, thoughts, and speech. May I do nothing that would dishonor You or embarrass them. In Jesus' name, Amen.*

JUNE 23

FINDING THE RIGHT FOUNDATION
Jeremiah 20:1–9

The Leaning Tower of Pisa is famous only because of its poor foundation. We now know that the entire Piazza dei Miracoli (fancy Italian for the square in which the tower stands!) is sinking. But the spot under the tower itself seems particularly unstable.

What makes the tower such an interesting story is that during the first stages of its construction, the builders could already see the tower beginning to lean—but they continued building anyway. But here's the truly amazing part. When the tower was finished, already leaning so far over that it posed a danger to those underneath, the people of the city decided to put in seven heavy bells

---

1. Stan Lee, *Best of the World's Worst* (General Pub Group, 1994).

(the largest weighed nearly three and one-half tons)! They figured that putting the bells on the other side of the tower would act as a counterbalance. Instead, it simply added to the weight of an already unstable building.

For the last several days, we've discussed how to get along with others in the workplace. My point in mentioning the Leaning Tower of Pisa is that you should ensure that you have a good spiritual and moral foundation on which to build people skills and coping strategies. If you're not totally committed to Christ—if you're not trying to love others with the love of Christ—then your foundation is weak. Simply adding new behavioral patterns to a poor foundation will only make it worse.

So for today, instead of focusing on the problems of your co-workers, take a few moments to focus on yourself. Ask God to show you any cracks in your foundation. Ask the Lord to forgive you of any sins, cleanse you, and prepare you to be the best co-worker you can be.

Heavenly Father, please show me any cracks in my spiritual foundation. Help me to let You be the only basis for my life, and may my faith in You be evident to everyone in the workplace. In Jesus' name, Amen.

JUNE 24

THE RIGHT GUIDE
Jeremiah 31:1–5

In a "Peanuts" cartoon, Charlie Brown notices that the fronts of Linus's shoes are freshly shined, but the backs are scuffed. He points out this fact to Linus. Linus then tells Charlie Brown that he meant to shine them that way.

"I care about what people think of me when I enter a room," he explains. "I don't care what they think when I leave."

I hope that Charlie Brown wasn't using Linus as a social guide!

Speaking of guides, who is your guide through life? Who is the example you want to follow? The Bible says that Christ's love should be your standard. For example, how much should you give to God? Christ, your example, gave all of His life as a sacrifice for you. How much should you love others? Christ's love forgives and offers grace.

As we contemplate the wonderful words of God in today's passage—"I have loved you with an everlasting love; I have drawn you with loving-kindness" (v. 3)—each of us should renew our allegiance to God. We should ask God to make us willing to give Him as much as we can—and give it with a grateful heart to be a fragrant sacrifice for our Lord.

Heavenly Father, I am overwhelmed when I think of Your love for me. Thank You for the constant, never-ending grace that You offer to me. May I give back to You today in the same way that You give to me. I offer You the gift of my love and my life, wholly dedicated to You. In Jesus' name, Amen.

JUNE 25

THE KEY TO RECEIVING GOD'S HELP
Jeremiah 33:1–3

"If you don't ask, they'll never buy."

It was years ago, but the words of my sales manager still ring in my ears. I had decided to try working an extra job to get caught up on my bills. The sales position would be given to only one or two of the ten applicants. We all went out on calls for the next week, determined to do our best and win the permanent position. Even before the end of the week, however, several people dropped out.

When the manager asked how much they'd sold, two individuals admitted that they'd sold nothing. In fact, they had assumed that no one would buy their product, so they hadn't asked for an order!

"If you don't ask, they'll never buy."

I remembered those words and asked everyone I could for an order! At the end of the week, the sales manager offered me a permanent position. I had asked, and my customers had responded positively.

As you read today's Scripture passage, apply God's Words to yourself. You might feel like Jeremiah, rejected by others, put in prison, all alone. But God wants you to know that He loves you and wants to come to you and help you with your problems.

But first you have to ask for help!

If you don't ask, you very well may not receive. On the other hand, if you call upon God today, you will discover His mighty power beginning to strengthen and encourage you, no matter what your situation.

Heavenly Father, thank You for loving me. Thank You for allowing me to call upon You right now. Please bring Your mighty power to work in my life and my situation today. I trust in You to make a real difference, and I pledge to give You the glory. In Jesus' name, Amen.

JUNE 26

THE DANGER OF FALSE PRIDE
Jeremiah 38:17–39:8

Today's passage is longer than usual, but it is worth reading.

Often, when we see an event happen, we are not around to see "the rest of the story." The true outcome of the event might not surface for decades. In chapters 38–39 of Jeremiah, we see the true end of ignoring God's warnings. The king could have had his family spared and his health undamaged. Instead, we see God's prophecy coming true. The last thing King Zedekiah saw before having his eyes put out was his sons slaughtered in front of him.

Oh, the terrible price of pride!

King Zedekiah didn't want to be seen listening to Jeremiah, God's prophet. He didn't want to have to swallow his pride and admit that his advisors were wrong. So he ignored the prophet's instructions and brought a devastating judgment upon his city, his family, and himself.

Proverbs 21:2, "All a man's ways seem right to him, but the LORD weighs the heart." Are you listening to God or to the world? Are you receiving living instructions from the Bible or from current culture? Is pride keeping you from admitting to others that you are a follower of Christ? If you want to be on the right path and have a life of peace, follow God's will—and nothing else.

Dear Lord, I don't want pride to keep me from following Your instructions. Help me to listen to You through regular prayer and reading of Your Word. Guide my feet today, oh God. In Jesus' name, Amen.

JUNE 27

TEACHING THOSE WHO WATCH
Jeremiah 42:7–17

Sunday school was about over when little Johnny raised his hand. "Mrs. Johnson, there's something I can't figure out."

"What's the problem, Johnny?" the teacher asked.

"Well, according to the Bible, the children of Israel crossed the Red Sea. Is that right?"

"Yes, Johnny," the teacher responded, glad to see that the boy had been listening to the lesson.

"And the children of Israel beat up the Philistines and the Egyptians and a bunch of other folks, right?"

"Again, Johnny, you're right."

"And the children of Israel marched around the city of Jericho until the walls fell down?"

"Johnny, you've learned your lessons well."

"Okay," the boy said, "here's my problem. If the children of Israel did all that, what were the grownups doing?"

What are grownups doing in your church?

Jeremiah told all of the grownups who were left in the land that they had better make every effort to be found in a right relationship with the Lord. They should not turn to Egypt or any other secular power for help. Their trust should be in God and in God alone. The grownups had already seen the effects on the king's children through his lack of faithfulness to the Lord. Now they had a chance to live for God, trust in Him, and live in peace with each other in the land.

No matter what church you attend, God's instructions are the same: the grownups had better ensure that they are giving the children and teenagers a good example to follow by acting in love toward others in the church and being faithful to the Lord.

What is your life teaching those who watch your actions, habits, and relationships?

Father, help me to remember that others are watching what I do and how I react to situations. May I trust in You, even in difficult times. May I treat others with Your love. And may those who are coming behind me learn a godly lesson by how I live today. In Jesus' name, Amen.

JUNE 28

YOUR LIFE'S MESSAGE
Jeremiah 51:58–64

We Americans love bumper stickers! They can express how we feel about a variety of issues: "Don't blame me; I voted for _____" (insert the name of your choice). We also use them to give advice: "If you can read this, you're too close." One of my favorite bumper stickers is this one: "I hate bumper stickers!"

What kind of message does your life communicate? At the end of Jeremiah's life, we see him standing faithful.

For most of his ministry, Jeremiah found himself in the minority. Going against the flow, branded a traitor to king and country, imprisoned and threatened with death, this man of God never wavered. People knew what he stood for and whom he served. Jeremiah's life carried a clear message for all of the world to see.

What kind of message does your life communicate? Are you standing faithful for God at this phase of your life? Are your actions and relationships giving glory to the Lord? In other words, are you projecting the message of Christ for all of the world to see?

When you have spoken your last words, ensure that you've lived your life such that no one will wonder about your eternal destination or your commitment to God. Live clearly and consistently for your Master, Jesus Christ.

Dear Lord, today I want to live for You in such a clear way that everyone around me will know that I stand for You. And at the end of my earthly life, I still want to be found faithful. Between today and then, help me to give myself completely to You every day. In Jesus' name, Amen.

JUNE 29

PHYSICALLY INEPT AND SPIRITUALLY BANKRUPT
Lamentations 3:21–25

In his book *A Life on the Road,* Charles Kuralt shares some expressions that he picked up in the hill country:

- She's as ugly as homemade soap.
- He's too blind to see through a barbed-wire fence.
- He's such a liar he has to get somebody else to call his hogs.
- She was born tired and raised lazy.
- He ain't worth the salt that goes into his bread.

Today's passage of Scripture talks of a people who probably felt like all of the above descriptions. The children of Israel had been unfaithful to God. As a result, the Lord used the nation of Babylon to judge them through defeat and captivity in a foreign land. A pitiful remnant stayed in Jerusalem, left there because of age or illness.

Physically inept and spiritually bankrupt. Have you ever felt like that? If so, please understand that it is at exactly this point that

God reaches tenderly toward His people and offers them another chance and a hand of love.

Whatever your situation as you read these words, know that God still loves you. He wants to help you and will forgive any sins that you've committed. Admit them, turn away from the lifestyle that produced them, and receive complete cleansing and forgiveness. The way out is the way up. God can take the way you are right now and completely change you. Come to Him today.

Dear God, sometimes I see what a mess I've made of my life. I don't want to continue to live like this. Please take away my sins and help me change my lifestyle. Wash me, cleanse me, and make me fit to serve You once again. In Jesus' name, Amen.

JUNE 30

TURNING YOUR LIFE AROUND
Lamentations 5:16–22

It happened in India. A young man, desperate for money because of a gambling habit, decided to rob a passerby. He waited until darkness descended on the city, then situated himself in a narrow alley. A shadow crossed his path, and he snaked out his arm to pull in the victim. Several blows to the head felled the "mark," and the young man quickly took the victim's wallet and fled.

On the other side of the city, the thief opened the wallet and found a lot of precious cash and a surprise—the ID card of his father-in-law! Meanwhile, the father-in-law had regained consciousness and told his story to the police. The result: the young man lost his wife, his reputation, and his freedom—he was sentenced to jail time for his crime.

Robbing a family member is bad. Robbing a church is probably worse. But robbing God? Can you imagine robbing your heavenly Father? Can you see yourself stealing from the One who gave His only Son to die on the Cross for your sins?

Jeremiah closed Lamentations with an acknowledgment that Israel had stolen from God and deserved every punishment that God had brought to bear upon them. Yet, he also asked the Lord for forgiveness and restoration. He hoped that God had not utterly abandoned His people.

We know that God has not abandoned His people. The books of Ezra and Nehemiah tell us that God worked a miracle to bring Israel out of Babylon and back to Jerusalem. We know that the Lord led His people to rebuild the city of David and the temple. God judged His people so that they might repent and be saved.

Perhaps you feel as if you've robbed God. Blessed with some wonderful physical or intellectual gifts, you might have squandered them through selfish living. Perhaps you now realize how wrong you've been, and you wonder if God can still possibly love you and use you in His service.

If I've just described you, then take heart! The Lord wants to reclaim you and renew you. If you turn to Him, He will work a miracle in your life and fit you for service in His kingdom. Turn to Him and live.

Dear Lord, You have given me life. Please forgive me for stealing from You by living for myself and my own agendas. Take my life and use me for Yourself completely. I want to be Your child and Your servant. In Jesus' name, Amen.

JULY 1

LIVING BY GOD'S DESIGN
Daniel 1:1–2

Is your life on cruise control, or is it going someplace on purpose? Are you living or just surviving? Are you alive, or do you go through the day like a zombie? These are difficult questions, but they are not idle. The fact is that life can be lived by design and on purpose, or it can trip to the default mode and just get by.

In today's reading, the king of Babylon captured Jerusalem and deported its citizens. The Jews, of course, saw it as a time of national disaster. How could such a thing happen? Were they not supposed to be God's people of the covenant? Was such an event even remotely in God's plan for them?

Daniel says that God used the king of Babylon for His own purposes. "And the Lord delivered Jehoiakim king of Judah into his hand" (v. 2). The biblical perspective is that God's people live with an awareness that God notices everything in life. Nothing is totally away from His overall control. That is quite a statement. Did God really deliver His people into the hands of the Babylonian leader? Yes.

God does not plot evil against us, of course. He does not cause every event because He clearly has given us free wills. But God moves events toward His aims and uses the circumstances of life as His raw material for building. Now what does all of this have to do with us? You and I face circumstances today that make us wonder, *Are things out of God's overall control? Has the Lord gone to sleep and forgotten about us?* No, the Lord has not forgotten us. He is still in control. What might seem like disaster can end up being a building block for the next stage of life. Our need now is to trust God.

Father, I do trust You although things happen around me that baffle me. I cannot understand everything about You or even about my own life. But this I know—You are the Lord, and I belong to You. Help me to live on purpose. Through Christ, Amen.

JULY 2

STAYING PURE IN A DIRTY WORLD
Daniel 1:3–8

Okay, I will admit it: the very idea of staying morally pure in a world like ours seems absurd, even laughable. How could we pull off such a feat? Is it possible? After all, everywhere we turn we are not just exposed to but absolutely bombarded with trash, junk, and filth. Walk into a family grocery store and scan the shelves in the checkout line. You will see more cleavage there than on many television shows.

But also think about the business atmosphere in which you work. Is it hospitable to growth and development, or is it cut-throat and hostile? Trying to stay morally and spiritually clean in such an environment can be tough. Some churches have gotten into that pattern, too. Instead of being a greenhouse for growing disciples, they have become freezers for preserving specimens.

Young Daniel and his friends found themselves in an environment they did not choose. They were offered the choicest meats and wine from the king's table but chose not to defile themselves with it. We do not know what the exact food was, but the point is that the young men did not see themselves as part of the prevailing culture. They intentionally acted differently from people around them. That is difficult. How many times have you gone to a company party and felt the pressure to drink as much as everyone else? What is the prevailing attitude in your company about sex? Is there a clear line between right and wrong, or does your firm deal in the gray area? You get the point. We often work for companies that are in the business of making money any way they can. Morality and compassion are left for some other organization.

Lord, You know the pressure I work under. There are suggestions to cut corners, shade the truth, use inferior materials, or tell half-truths. Help me in this world to love You enough to keep myself as pure as possible. Through Jesus, my Lord, Amen.

JULY 3

LOVING GOD WITH YOUR BRAIN
Daniel 1:15–21

Think about your mind for a minute. You might be tempted to say, "Hey, I can't because I've lost mine." No you haven't. It's still there. Some men have jobs that seem to numb their minds while the body goes along on autopilot. Churches have done a fair job of telling men to love God with their bodies and their hearts. But what about our brains? Can we love God with our minds?

I have had to have several MRI tests on my head because of an accident I had several years ago. I have seen images of my own brain. Also, I once visited the gross anatomy lab of a medical school and saw sections of human brains that the students were studying. The brain is the physical organ that contains the mind.

God gave us brains for a reason—to use them! I have been privileged to be around some great minds. I think of a scholar who wrote and edited some of the most influential books of the twentieth century. I think of an evangelist who has traveled the world drawing millions to Christ. There was a musician whose recordings have sold in the millions. But there is also an "average" guy who has a lot of creativity to make life better for his family and other people he knows. He uses his brain to love God.

In today's reading, Daniel did just that. He acquired knowledge and understanding. He studied and applied himself. Because he used his mind in the service of God, he was able to influence countless people through the king. Now that is using your brains!

How is your mind? Is it like a car, finely tuned and running on the right fuel? Or is it mushy, sluggish, and fed on a mental junk food diet?

Lord, I want to love You with all of my being, including my mind. Help me serve You and others with my brains. Through Jesus, who used His wonderful mind, Amen.

JULY 4

FROM CONFUSION TO CLARITY
Daniel 2:1–23

We live in a day of great confusion and bondage. People are searching everywhere for liberty and clarity, but they often find only darkness and chains. Open your morning newspaper. It contains claims, counterclaims, and just plain weird stuff. The mantra of the day seems to be "Let me do whatever I want and believe anything. So what if it's wrong?"

The fourth of July is a good time to think about freedom. In today's reading, Daniel had learned that the king of Babylon had ordered all of the wise men, including Daniel, to be executed. The king was frustrated because the wise men could not interpret one of his dreams. The king's counselors objected to the edict, saying, "No one can reveal it to the king except the gods, and they do not live among men" (v. 11). But Daniel had another perspective. He praised God for wisdom: "He reveals deep and hidden things; he knows what lies in darkness, and light dwells in him" (v. 22).

That perspective makes all of the difference in the world. Daniel told the king, "No wise man, enchanter, magician or diviner can explain to the king the mystery he has asked about, but there is a God in heaven who reveals mysteries" (vv. 27–28). Yes! The world cannot deliver, but God can. God offers freedom from confusion and darkness.

How are you doing in your life's walk with this God? Do you think of Him as a Guide and Companion along life's dark path? Faith is like taking your life into you own hands to, in turn, place your life into the hands of a heavenly Father. It involves a choice to turn to Him. This choice cannot be forced.

Father, would You enter my life to bring clarity out of confusion, light from darkness? I know I need you. Be my Lord, through Christ, Amen.

JULY 5

AMAZED BY GOD
Daniel 2:46–49

We often fear what we do not know. That also goes for people we do not know. When I was in seminary, I had wanted to take a class with a certain internationally known professor. I knew his name and had read some of his books. But the semester I got there he announced that he was taking a position with another school in the same city. My first semester would be his last. His classes filled up quickly, and I could not get the class I wanted.

Later, I called him and invited myself to lunch with him. The day came, and I went to meet him. We had a nice meal and a stimulating conversation. Toward the end of our time, he leaned forward and asked, "Okay, what is your agenda?" He was a psychologist and assumed that I had some hidden agenda. I gestured to the table and said, "This is my agenda. I wanted to meet you, look you in the eye, and get to know you as a man, not a legend." He just laughed and relaxed. What I wanted was a person-to-person relationship.

Young Daniel found king Nebuchadnezzar prostrate at his feet. But being worshiped is not a healthful situation for any man. It does not lead to a person-to-person encounter. Only God is to be worshiped. The king had been amazed that Daniel was able to interpret his dream. He said, "Surely your God is the God of gods" (v. 47). Daniel let him know that all of the credit went to God and not him.

To be amazed by God is a healthful perspective. It leads us to acknowledge our dependence upon Him. Is God amazing to you?

Lord, You have amazed countless generations with Your work and wonder. Let me be part of that number who is wowed by knowing You. In Jesus' name, Amen.

JULY 6

STANDING UP TO AN IDOL
Daniel 3:1–6

I first came across this statement in college: "Power corrupts, and absolute power corrupts absolutely." Years passed before I began to understand what that meant. Most people simply are not equipped to handle great power. They are tempted to misuse it for their own grandeur rather than for the common good. Give a Hitler an army and he will begin a worldwide conflict. Give Saddam Hussein poison gas and he will spray it on his own people.

Kings and politicians have a way of feathering their own nests. King Nebuchadnezzar was no exception. He made a golden image of himself and sent out a decree that when certain music played everyone was to fall down and worship the idol. The consequences of not doing so were severe: "Whoever does not fall down and worship will immediately be thrown into a blazing furnace" (v. 6). The powers of the world play for keeps.

Our temptation is always to give in to such bullies. When we owe our possessions to the state, we have to dance to some awful tunes. The situation reminds me of a line from the old Merle Travis song, "I owe my soul to the company store." Sometimes the expectation is not so crass but is instead understated. I wrote these words around Christmas time. The message around me everywhere is that I must go buy something for everyone I love or I am a bad friend, parent, and spouse. Walking into a shopping mall against my will makes me feel as though I'm prostrating myself in front of a golden idol. Have you ever felt that way?

Christian men are called to identify the idols vying for our attention and to ensure that we treat them for what they are—man-made trifles that do not deserve worship. Next time you spot one, stand up to it.

Help me, Lord, to be both perceptive to the idols around me and brave enough not to bow. Give me strength in Jesus' name, Amen.

JULY 7

THE COURAGE TO STAND UP FOR PRINCIPLES
Daniel 3:7–15

The music played, and the people bowed. Everyone except the three young Jewish men named Shadrach, Meshach, and Abednego. They were Daniel's friends. When they heard the music that signaled the call to worship the king's idol, they ignored it. As the Scripture puts it, "[They] pay no attention to you, O king. They neither serve your gods nor worship the image of gold you have set up" (v. 12).

Power and principalities do not like to be ignored. The little tin gods of our world prance and strut and try to convince people that they are worth worshiping. But the follower of Christ has only one focus of worship—God Almighty. The man who is loyal to Christ is often treated the way the three young Jews were handled. The king himself summoned them and tried to explain the error of their ways. He gave the instructions again and then delivered the ultimatum: "But if you do not worship it, you will be thrown immediately into a blazing furnace" (v. 15). To top off the threat, the king insulted their faith: "Then what god will be able to rescue you from my hand?" (v. 15). Yes, what god indeed?

Are you facing pressure on your job to worship things other than the Lord? Are the powers that exist in your world squeezing you and trying to bend you? Resisting is tough. When you resist, you feel as though you're the guest of honor at a barbecue—and you're the main meal! Let your prayer today be for the strength to stand for your principles.

Help me, Lord, to be the man I want to be. I'm squeezed on every side to give in and go along. But You have called me to something else. Strengthen me, Lord, strengthen me. In Christ, Amen.

JULY 8

THE POWER OF PROMISE
Daniel 3:16–17

Have you ever been faced with a decision that made you feel that you were "damned if you did and damned if you didn't"? The three Hebrew young men in today's reading faced a nearly unbelievable choice. The results were certain and clear cut. Worship the king's idol or die. No appeal or reprieve would be granted. They would die a fiery death because they refused to worship the idol of the Babylonian king. They were told to give in to societal pressure or give up their lives. That often seems to be the choice today, too. Give in. Go along. Don't make waves. Take shortcuts to success. Do that—or watch your dreams of success burn away like leaves in a furnace.

But you have to hand it to those Hebrew boys: they stood toe to toe with the king, looked him in the eye, and said "No." The king had taunted them about their faith. He asked who could save them if he decided to toss them into the fire. Not even their God could do so, he said. Their answer must have taken him by surprise: "O Nebuchadnezzar, we do not need to defend ourselves before you in this matter" (v. 16). Why? They had already made up their minds. Faithfulness sets a course of action before a detour pops up. No matter what they faced, they knew what they would do.

The power of promise helps us control the future. For example, when I promised my wife at our wedding that I would be faithful to her, that promise set the course of my life. No matter what I faced in the future, I already knew what I would do. I did not need to ask myself what the best course of action was because I already knew it.

Promise God your faithfulness. You will be amazed at the difference that makes in your life.

Lord, I do promise myself to You. Give me the grace to stay true to that promise. Let it guide my decisions every day. In Christ, Amen.

JULY 9

THE GREAT "IF"
Daniel 3:17–18

I admit it: I like movies and stories with happy endings. Who can avoid feeling warm all over the moment George Bailey gets his life back in the movie *It's a Wonderful Life*? But life often does not end like that; it seems more like *Nightmare on Elm Street*. Everything goes wrong. Nothing seems neat, simple, and easy. Evil smirks at its seeming triumph. What are the faithful to do?

The three young Hebrew men standing before the king of Babylon knew that they faced a terrible dilemma. They would be forced to bow before an idol of the king or be cremated while still alive! In the midst of that spiritual battle, their reply is instructive: "If we are thrown into the blazing furnace, the God we serve is able to save us from it, and he will rescue us from your hand, O king" (v. 17). That sounds great—a note of triumph and a witness to the power of God. We Christians today too often stop right there and speak and live as if we were exempt from the bruises and smashups of life. We are not, of course, but I rarely hear people talk about what it means if God has plans for rescue in other ways.

The men facing the furnace did not presume upon God. He certainly could rescue them if He chose. But carefully consider the rest of what the men said: "But even if he does not, we want you to know, O king, that we will not serve your gods or worship the image of gold you have set up." That one tiny word—*if*—carries incredible power. If God chooses to rescue us, great; but if not, that is great too. We will remain loyal to Him.

Now *that* is faith! When everything goes our way, faith seems easy. But what happens when you face the furnace? Even if that is your course, do not give in to anything or anyone other than God.

More than anything in the world, Lord, I want
to be faithful to You. Through Jesus, our Lord,
Amen.

LIKE A SON OF GOD
Daniel 3:19–25

From the first day we open our lives to the living reality of Christ, we feel as if He is alive within us. He is present with us, like a friend, only closer. The apostle Paul would say in one of his letters in the New Testament, "To me, to live is Christ" (Phil. 1:21). Christ is everything—life itself.

That the followers of Jesus have loved today's Scripture reading is no real mystery. The king of Babylon had been told by three young Hebrews that they would not bow before him and worship his idol. His fury blazed like the furnace he had prepared for anyone who dared to disobey him. Babylon was not known for its freedom of worship.

The three men—Shadrach, Meshach, and Abednego—were tied up and delivered to the furnace. But the king did not get the satisfaction he anticipated. In fact, what he saw disturbed him greatly:

"Look! I see four men walking around in the fire, unbound and unharmed, and the fourth looks like a son of the gods" (v. 25). The pagan, pluralistic mind of King Nebuchadnezzar could not make sense of what he saw. How could three human beings remain unharmed by such a blaze? And who was that fourth figure?

I understand his confusion. Have you ever looked upon a miracle but could not comprehend it? We pray for God's presence with us, and when He answers our prayer we stand dumbfounded and ask, "What is this?"

The Son of God is with us in ways of which we are not always aware. Do you feel as though you were in the furnace now? Remember, you are not there alone.

Gracious Father, You are here with me, no matter what. You know what I'm going through. Help me to know Your presence. Through Your Son's name, Amen.

JULY 11

DEAD MEN WALKING
Daniel 3:26–30

A fireman I know once got trapped in a burning house. He had gotten disoriented in a hallway when fire broke out at both ends of the hall. He believed that he was going to die that day. With smoke and flame all around him, he simply did not know which way to go. All he knew was that he did not have much time. At what seemed to be the last second, the smoke cleared a bit, and he saw sunlight coming into a window at one end of the hall. He ran to it, broke it out with an ax, and climbed to safety. His fellow firemen treated him as if he had returned from the dead.

Someone who has tasted death has a way of grabbing our attention. No wonder, then, that King Nebuchadnezzar was so amazed when the three young Hebrew men emerged alive from the furnace. Everyone in the palace knew what had happened. This was not some fluke in which the men managed to find a way out of danger on their own. Only God could have brought them out. The

Scripture says that it was as if they had never gone into the fire at all: "there was no smell of fire on them" (v. 27).

The king was moved to praise the one true God who had saved the men from the furnace. He even decreed that no one could even so much as speak against their God. The saving power of God is not to be trifled with. The Lord saved the three young men to demonstrate His power to Babylon. Knowing God is serious business, and we come to know Him when we see what He has done in others' lives.

Do you know the God who has brought the dead to life? Is your own life a testimony to His saving power?

Lord, I was as good as dead until You got hold of me. Thanks for delivering me from my own form of a furnace. In Jesus' name, Amen.

JULY 12

BE CAREFUL WHAT YOU ASK FOR
Daniel 4:19–37

Have you ever asked for something and then felt sorry when you got what you wanted? This happens with not only possessions but also attitudes. A man might be extremely successful in business and strive for more and more only to find out that what he ends up with is trash.

Take, for example, King Nebuchadnezzar in the book of Daniel. He had a dream and wanted an interpretation. He saw a tree that withered down to a stump. A young Hebrew captive, Daniel, was brought to him to tell him what it meant. In his own eyes the king had become strong and wealthy, but he never gave God any credit for his fortune. His arrogance led him astray. The dream meant that he would lose his sanity and live like an animal until he acknowledged the Lord.

Many a man, especially in midlife, has felt his life whittled down to a stump. He worked hard, played by the rules, and ended up in his middle years with a life that was not what he intended. How about you? Did you get what you asked for, or did you acquire something far different?

The point of today's reading is that we do better when we live with an awareness of our dependence upon God. That does not mean that we will not face challenges. People get laid off, careers are shot down by a flaming economy, families disintegrate despite our best efforts to the contrary. But when we arrogantly claim that we are self-made men, we end up like the ancient king—living on the level of an animal rather than raising our eyes to God. He has set us on a great adventure in life. We are made to count the stars, not bay at the moon.

Lord, I acknowledge You as my very life. You are everything to me. Accept my praise for Your grace toward me. In Christ, Amen.

JULY 13

THE HANDWRITING ON THE WALL
Daniel 5:1–16

We use the expression "the handwriting on the wall" to indicate something that is evident and usually harmful. The economy might signal a downturn that will affect our job. We say, "I saw the hand-writing on the wall and changed careers." The origin of that expression comes from today's reading.

King Nebuchadnezzar's son had taken over the kingdom. This young king, Belshazzar, threw a party for his friends and advisors. To impress them, he had the golden goblets that had been stolen from the temple in Jerusalem brought in. They drank from them and "praised the gods of gold and silver, of bronze, iron, wood and stone" (v. 4). While they were engaged in this primitive behavior, a human hand appeared to them and began to write on the wall. Hence, the expression "the handwriting on the wall."

Our contemporary culture revels in the "gods of gold and silver." Everything seems to revolve around a robust economy with plenty of cash to go around. There is nothing inherently evil about that. Everyone needs a job and the basics of life. But we go way beyond the necessities. We are turned into "consumers" rather than contributors. The rich are held up as being the most virtuous in society. After all, if they are rich are they not being blessed by God Himself?

Let me invite you to spend some time today considering what God might be saying to you personally and to humankind generally through His "handwriting on the wall." Are you living with circumstances that seem to shout, "Turn! Make some changes! You're going the wrong way!"? A friend of mine died a couple of years ago, but not before he had made some major changes in his life. He realized that some of the "gods" he had pursued in his younger days were idols that let him down.

You know me better than I know myself, Lord.
Show me Your handwriting, and give me strength
to change what needs changing. Through Christ,
Amen.

JULY 14

TESTED AND FOUND WANTING
Daniel 5:18–30

You and I are tested every day. I do not mean this in an exclusively theological sense. I simply mean that our choices and actions daily show of what we are made. If we go around with a chip on our shoulder all the time, we prove ourselves to be hostile and volatile. On the other hand, if we have peace within our heart, that will be displayed in our actions.

But the concept of testing is theological, too. Life itself is a testing ground in which we show our orientation to the will of God—or the lack of it. Ancient King Belshazzar, the young successor of the king who took Israel captive, arrogantly treated his success with pride. He saw the handwriting on the wall but could not read the message. His advisors could make no sense of it either, so they sent for one of the Hebrews—Daniel. The king asked Daniel to interpret the message on the wall. What he found out was not pleasant.

The inscription consisted of these words: *mene, mene, tekel,* and *parsin* (v. 25). What does that mean? "You have been tested and found wanting." Literally, the words mean "numbered," as in "you're days are numbered" and "weighed," as in "You have been weighed . . . and found wanting" (v. 27). The last of the words means "divided," as in "your kingdom [will be] divided and given to [others]" (v. 28).

I have never seen words like that on my wall. You probably haven't either. But the meaning is clear. God calls us to work in cooperation with Him. We need both humility and confidence. I have seen many men rise and fall. The ones who seem to have lasting power are the ones who realize that they are not the center of the universe. They know that God is.

Father, weigh my life in the loving scales of Your grace. Help me get rid of whatever does not belong there. Through my Lord Jesus, Amen.

JULY 15

HISTORY REPEATS ITSELF
Daniel 6:1–5

One of the most tragic things in life is to see the destructive patterns of one generation repeat itself in the next. For example, a man might have grown up in the home of an abusive father. He vows that he will never act like that, but in the years to come, he ends up being just like his father. Or a man puts up with alcohol or drug abuse at home only to become addicted himself later. This sort of vicious cycle repeats itself countless times in not only individual lives but also national lives.

We saw earlier how King Nebuchadnezzar had put three Hebrew men into a furnace because of their refusal to pray to the king's idol. They escaped unharmed, and you'd think that their story would be told for generations as a lesson against idolatry. But it seems that some lessons can be learned, but they cannot be taught. Some time after this event, a new king came to power—Darius, a Mede. One of the Jewish captives, Daniel, had risen to power in his court. Some of the other leaders were jealous of Daniel, so they devised a plot to get rid of him.

Their plot sounded just like the one sprung earlier on Shadrach,

Meshach, and Abednego. The men plotting against Daniel said, "We will never find any basis for charges against this man Daniel unless it has something to do with the law of his God" (v. 5). Had they learned nothing from the earlier debacle? Apparently not, because they hatched a plan to convince the king to issue a decree that would go against Daniel's religious duty.

Do you ever feel that life is a conspiracy against you, that nearly everything stands between you and God? Welcome to the world! The key is to find ways of being faithful to the Lord without letting earlier mistakes repeat themselves.

Lord, deliver me from the errors of my forebears and my children and grandchildren from my errors. You are larger than history, so I am not stuck in an endless cycle of rebellion. Give me liberty through Christ. Amen.

JULY 16

IN THE JAWS OF PERSECUTION
Daniel 6:6–16

What a terrible thing it is to be attacked because of godliness. You might face this dilemma regularly on your job. Because of your faith, some coworkers might call you "Holy Joe" or, worse, make you the butt of tasteless jokes because you try to live for God. I have worked at several places where fellow workers made fun of me because I was going into the ministry. Their abuse was aggravating to me, but it was not dangerous.

Some people live in situations where their faith puts them in physical danger. In some nations, Christianity is like a magnet attracting persecution. Gabriel, a native of Sudan, lived with that threat for years. I got to know him through one of my pastorates. Gabriel was reared Christian in a Muslim nation. His family faced enormous pressures because of their beliefs. He finally came to the United States as a refugee to escape persecution. But even here his refugee status was treated too lightly. He had great trouble getting permission to stay in this country, but he persisted until he did.

Daniel, the administrator in Darius's court, was singled out for attack by petty, jealous men. They convinced Darius to issue a decree that no one was to pray to any man or god except the king himself. The punishment for anyone breaking that decree was to be thrown into a den full of lions. Daniel paid no attention to the king's decree and continued to pray to God "just as he had done before" (v. 10). His actions were reported to Darius, who reluctantly ordered Daniel to be tossed to the lions. He even said to Daniel, "May your God, whom you serve continually, rescue you!" (v. 16). The king meant it.

Do you find yourself in the jaws of persecution now? Do not give up. God is still Lord and is trustworthy. Trust Him.

Lord, You see what I'm going through now. Help me to be strong in the midst of this pressure. In Jesus' name, Amen.

JULY 17

DELIVERANCE
Daniel 6:17–23

A man I know speaks of his life of deliverance. Like many men, he got caught up in a round of ever-increasing thrill seeking. One vice led to another in a downward spiral of depravity. Drugs, alcohol, prostitution—they were all part of his life. Then one day he had an encounter with Jesus Christ. After that, his life was not the same. He has a new focus in life. He knows who he is and where he is going. In his eyes, he has been delivered.

Well he should think that. Deliverance is exactly what happens in our lives when Christ enters. Do not think that you have nothing from which to be delivered just because you are not like that guy. I have never taken illegal drugs, been drunk, or visited a prostitute. But that does not make me a lily-white saint. Far from it! I know myself to be filled with every sort of desire and action that makes salvation necessary. After all, if I could save myself by being good, then Christ came for nothing.

Daniel, the young Hebrew in Babylonian captivity, honored God even in difficult circumstances. What he got for his troubles was a one-way trip to a den full of lions. King Darius ordered him thrown into the pit because Daniel would not cease to worship God. Actually, Darius did not want Daniel harmed and hoped that God would rescue him. The king spent a restless night and then went to the lions' lair first thing in the morning. He called out for Daniel, who answered, "My God sent his angel, and he shut the mouths of the lions" (v. 22).

Do you need deliverance in your life? The Scripture states clearly that the only real source of such deliverance is God. Would you trust yourself to Him today?

I trust myself to You, Lord. You know my circumstances. I might not be plucked from a lion's mouth, but I know that I won't be abandoned. In Christ, Amen.

A QUIET WITNESS
Daniel 6:24–28

M. B. was one of the steadiest men I have ever known. Day in and day out, he reminded me of the Energizer Bunny—he kept going and going and going. M. B. was a man of deep faith. He loved God with a passion, but it was a quiet commitment. For years, he visited a local prison and led a Bible study. He went on mission projects and contributed to countless lives through his writings. I think of M. B. as one of God's quiet witnesses.

I think of a biblical character who was a quiet witness, too. His name was Daniel. What was Daniel's great accomplishment? He survived! Sure, his devotion to God kept him from being dinner for a pride of lions, but something was communicated in his mere survival. King Darius was tricked into issuing a decree that landed Daniel in the lions' den. That action went against his real wishes, but he had to follow through with its conclusion. He had Daniel put into the pit and then spent a sleepless night fretting about it. When the king went out the next morning, he found Daniel safe.

Daniel could have gloated and strutted. Instead, he simply noted that he was safe because of God's protection. That simple testimony turned things around for many people. For those who had falsely accused Daniel of treason, it meant death. To his fellow Hebrews, it meant courage. To the king, it meant conversion; he issued this decree: "I issue a decree that in every part of my kingdom people must fear and reverence the God of Daniel. For he is the living God and he endures forever" (v. 26).

You and I might not write great books or speak to millions of people, but we can live a quiet, steady faith. Who knows who is watching?

Keep me steady, Father, walking straight ahead regardless of whether anyone seems to be looking. May my life be a witness of Your grace. In Christ, Amen.

JULY 19

An Indescribable Vision
Daniel 9:20–23

Someone has said that life is what happens while you are waiting to accomplish your plans. That is true. We make our plans and set off to accomplish them. Along the way, we get delayed, sidetracked, lost, turned around, and sometimes stopped in our tracks. All the while, life swirls around us.

The same is true with our spiritual lives. We read a book like this one in the hope that it will help us grow in our faith. We attend workshops and seminars to jumpstart our spirit. We pray and pour out our heart to God in the belief that He will hear us and grant our requests. All of this is right and proper, of course. We should pray, study, attend worship, and so on. But all the while we find that things happen while we attend to our religious duties, things that are not planned, coordinated, or even expected.

Daniel was praying when he was overcome by a vision of almost indescribable events. He wrote that "while I was still praying" the vision came. What do you think would happen if our prayer time was "interrupted" by a divine visit? I heard about a minister who went into the sanctuary and got down on his knees as he did every day. He said, "O God, hear my prayer. O God, hear my prayer." A voice came from heaven saying, "Yes, what is it?" They found the minister that evening. He had died of a heart attack!

The Scripture does not promise us a vision or a heady understanding every time we worship God. The evidence, though, is that we should give ourselves to the Lord in devotion. If He chooses to give some great vision, wonderful. If not, that is okay too, because we are still entering the presence of God.

Lord, keep me from being a mercenary in my devotion to You. I leave fully in Your hands all matters of how You reveal or conceal Yourself to me. Through Christ, Amen.

JULY 20

A SECURE FUTURE
Daniel 12:13

Fortunes are made and lost by people trying to guess the future. A commodities trader might bet a wad of cash on the price of pork bellies. An entrepreneur might take a huge chance on a start-up business. Each is betting that their take on the future will pay off in financial dividends. This happens in almost all areas of life.

Most things about the future are obscured from our vision and knowledge. For the most part, that is good. Would you really want to know everything that will happen to you? But there is one area about the future that is open to our knowledge. It is an open door into God's presence, and it has a sign above the door saying, in effect, "Welcome! Come this way."

The book of Daniel is filled with narratives of the Hebrews who were taken into captivity by the Babylonians. Three of them were tossed into a furnace but escaped alive. Another was put into a den of lions but came out unscratched. In all of this, the deciding factor was the presence of the living God of Israel. God, as opposed to the idols of the various nations, is alive and active in the lives of His people. At the end of this book, Daniel hears words that offer hope and promise: "As for you, go your way till the end. You will rest, and then at the end of the days you will rise to receive your allotted inheritance" (v. 13).

Think of that: the future of a person who lives with faith in God is secure. After a lifetime of trials and stress, we receive this greatest of good news. But this is more than "pie in the sky by and by." Knowing where we stand with God right now gives us a steadiness in life. Why would anyone bet his future on anything else?

For the future I have in You, O Lord, I am truly grateful. May I live worthy of it. Through Christ my Savior, Amen.

UNBELIEVABLE DIRECTIONS

Hosea 1:1–3

I know a missionary who went to a primarily Muslim country. She said that one of the biggest hurdles she had to jump was the assumption of her American friends that she would never make it as a missionary! To their minds, she was a "sweet southern belle" who, as a single woman, just could not adjust to the rigors of her mission field. She has proven them wrong for years.

God often calls people to do seemingly strange things. Think of asking middle-aged Moses to lead his people out of Egypt. What about telling Abraham to sacrifice his only son? People who want a tame, predictable, domesticated deity had better skip the God of the Bible. He moves history along in a direction that we can hardly imagine. He chooses people and situations that would never make it into a "how-to" manual on our idea of virtue.

In today's reading, God tells one of His prophets, Hosea, to marry a woman we would not imagine Him to pick out. "When the LORD began to speak through Hosea, the LORD said to him, 'Go, take to yourself an adulterous wife and children of unfaithfulness'" (v. 2). Wait a minute. What is that all about? The Lord told His prophet intentionally to marry an adulterous woman? What about the seventh commandment?

The book of Hosea is not a tale about the domestic woes of a man and his wayward wife. It is a book about God. Do you want to know what God must have felt when He considered His relationship to Israel? If so, read Hosea and you will see: "the land is guilty of the vilest adultery in departing from the LORD" (v. 2). The relationship between Hosea and his wife, Gomer, was as strained and strange as that between God and His people.

Are you living in unusual circumstances? God might be deepening His relationship to you.

Lord, there are things in my life that I would not choose on my own. But if they can be used for Your glory, then use them. In Jesus' name, Amen.

JULY 22

ANSWERING TO THE WRONG NAME
Hosea 1:4—11

Names have interested me for a long time. They once meant something that signified a characteristic or a profession. Redd might have indicated that the family had red hair. Black or White might have pointed to complexion. Smith was the blacksmith, Tanner was the person who tanned the hides of animals, and Cooper made barrels.

Names are important. Someone said, "It doesn't matter what name you call me. What matters is the name I answer to." That is a perceptive statement. What name do you answer to?

The prophet Hosea endured a stormy relationship with his wife by which God communicated His message to Israel. Hosea's first child was named *Jezreel*. That name reminded the people of the terrible consequences of disobeying the Lord (see 2 Kings 10 for the background). Hosea's second child was named *Lo-Ruhamah,* which means "not loved." He named his third child *Lo-Ammi,* which means "not my people." Imagine the effect of those names on the children as well as the nation!

I know many people who have names—real or imagined—that they answer to. Those names give them a sense of who they are, for good or bad. For example, I know a man who answers to the name "failure." I know a teenager who answers to "loser." A mother thinks she is named "dummy." A pastor is mistaken that his name is "unloved."

Do you have a name like that? Do you sometimes give in to the temptation to believe that you have a negatively descriptive name? If so, look at what God told the nation: "In the place where it was said to them, 'You are not my people,' they will be called 'sons of the living God'" (v. 10). He changed the name they answered to! They are God's people. So are you. That is who you really are.

Deliver me, Lord, from the self-pity that tempts me to answer to the wrong name. I know who I am—I am Yours. Help me to live like a child of God. In Jesus' name, Amen.

JULY 23

ONE OF LIFE'S HARDEST CHOICES

Hosea 3

One of the most devastating elements of a marriage in trouble is adultery. Any way you think about it, marital infidelity is poison to a relationship. Of all of the relationships in the world, marriage most needs trust.

We live in a culture that winks at infidelity. "Everybody does it," much of the media tell us. Adultery is made to seem normal, fun, glamorous, and even expected. As a pastor, I have had to help pick up the pieces of too many families that splintered over this issue. In one family, the husband left his wife and two children to take up with another woman who had been married and divorced several times. In another marriage, the wife left the husband because he had been injured in an accident and was no longer "fun."

Anyone who has ever worked with such families, or who has experienced it for himself, knows that putting the relationship right again is extremely difficult. For some people, it is too hard, so they give up, file for divorce, and live with the consequences.

God told the prophet Hosea to marry an unfaithful woman. Her actions, and in return, God's guidance, would serve as a living example of the Lord's faithfulness in the midst of humankind's unfaithfulness. In Hosea 3, God told Hosea to go to his wife, who had been out on the streets, and to "show your love to your wife again." Can you imagine how hard that was? Hosea had to swallow his pride and open his heart to his wife, who had taken advantage of him time after time. Most men might have said, "Good riddance." But remember, this is a story about God. It is a reminder of how He treats us. Aren't you glad He responds that way?

Lord, I have not always been faithful—to You or to my own ideals of conduct. Thank You for giving me another chance and for showing me Your love. Through Christ, Amen.

JULY 24

Too Stiff to Turn

Hosea 5:1–7

I can still see him in my mind's eye. Strutting around the meeting hall, he looked like a Bantam rooster. People would talk to him, but he would not look them in the eye. He looked around to see who was watching him. He was the leader of a well-known television ministry. His ego was inflated, and he seemed to lord his position over others. It made me sick at heart to see it happen. Not long afterward, he got into trouble of a sexual nature, and his ministry came crashing down.

I remember that experience because, although I was a young man at the time, it taught me a lesson that I carry with me today. God does not have any celebrities or stars in His service. Any time a person gets too big for his britches, the Lord will find a way to burst his bubble.

This happens with nations as well as with individuals. The prophet Hosea saw the attitudes of his countrymen and knew where it would lead. Part of the judgment of God was prophesied by Hosea: "Their deeds do not permit them to return to their God. A spirit of prostitution is in their heart; they do not acknowledge the LORD" (v. 4).

In their attitudes, the people were too stiff to turn. After all, when you are getting everything you want, why would you need God? Everything seemed to be going their way, and their desires were being satisfied. What could God have to do with them? That kind of thinking has brought down many a man, family, business, and even nation.

So how about you—how loose are you? Can you turn toward God?

You know my heart, Lord. At times, I am so busy running my life that You seem far away. Help me acknowledge You and live in Your grace. Loosen up my stiffness toward You. Through Christ, Amen.

JULY 25

LOVING OUR CHILDREN

Hosea 11:1–9

Someone once asked Ruth Bell Graham if she had ever considered divorce. She looked over at Billy and said, "No, but I've considered murder." You have to love her honesty. Most of us have been so frustrated with people—even the ones we love—that we have considered drastic action. You had might as well confess it. You have been there.

But the deeper reality is that we guys would fight a chain saw if it were necessary to protect our family. Our wives and children are the most important human relationships we have.

What do you believe God thinks of His human family? Is He perpetually angry with us for our rebellion, angry enough to lash out with diseases, accidents, and death? Somehow, many of us seem to believe that very thing. I had a bad accident a few years ago. Someone asked me if I thought God was mad at me.

Well, no, I never once thought that. I thought that I had been too careless.

The prophet Hosea provided a voice for God's communication about ancient Israel and for us today. God narrated His love for Israel and for their subsequent rebellion against Him. Many people think that the story ends there, but it does not. Listen to the tender pleading of the heavenly Father toward His people: "How can I give you up, Ephraim? How can I hand you over, Israel? How can I treat you like Admah? How can I make you like Zeboiim?" (v. 8). Like a father looking at his beloved child, God says, "My heart is changed within me; all my compassion is aroused" (v. 8).

Wow, did you notice that phrase? "All my compassion is aroused." God loves us more than we love our own children. In my case, that is a lot, and it probably is with you too.

God, my Father, Your love for me overwhelms me.
That You could care for me as You do is amazing.
I willingly respond in love for You. In Jesus'
name, Amen.

A New Day

Joel 1:1–12

Can you remember where you were on September 11, 2001? Most of us can remember our exact location and our actions when we learned of the attack on the World Trade Center, the Pentagon, and the crash in Pennsylvania. I was working in my church office when someone called to tell me what had happened. I turned on the television and was horrified at the sight.

Some events have a way of turning our seemingly safe worlds upside down. One minute things are going along in a routine way, then—bam!—we are never the same. You can think of several events like that in your life.

The book of Joel tells of a series of events that took ancient Israel by storm. The country was invaded by a merciless army, not of soldiers, but of locusts. Remember that in those days, before good storage methods, farmers' crops could be ruined by the weather or by insects. The locust invasion brought total destruction. The Lord asked the nation through Joel, "Has anything like this ever happened in your days or in the days of your forefathers?" (v. 2). How can things get so out of hand?

I know many people who remember Pearl Harbor and the events of December 7, 1941. They asked the same kind of question then. Every tragedy, especially on a national or global scale, brings about introspection. We wonder where God is and why this disaster has come upon us. Some people virtually give up all hope of coming through it. As the prophet put it, "Surely the joy of mankind is withered away" (v. 12).

The end of every chapter in life is the beginning of another. We experience tragedy or major setbacks and are tempted to say, "My life is over." But God might be saying, "My son, your life is just beginning in this new day." Do not surrender your hope. Locusts never have the last word.

I have known my share of trouble, Lord. You know what I've been through. But in it all You have been my guide and my strength. I trust You, no matter what. Through Christ, Amen.

JULY 27

Making Up for Lost Time
Joel 2:18–27

A man sat across from me one day, pouring out his life story. He had turned his back on the religious training of his youth and had gone into adulthood with great dreams of making a name for himself. He thought that all that talk about God and what He wanted from humankind did not apply to him. This man discovered over the years that his life was on a downward spiral. His drinking and overall irresponsible behavior nearly ruined his life. He wept bitter tears and shook with grief as he told me, "I've wasted my life. What can I do now?"

What a shame that some of us have to get to that point before we ask, "Am I on the right road? If not, where is the U-turn lane?" I have made some decisions that I now regret. I wish there were a way to turn back the clock and change those decisions. Can you imagine how our lives would be different if we could do that?

I thought about today's reading when my friend told me how he ruined his life. The swarms of locusts had devastated Israel. Famine and death would soon follow them like clouds swept in by a cold front. The word of the Lord through His prophet sounds unbelievable: "I will repay you for the years the locusts have eaten" (v. 25). What a concept—the promise that the lost years could somehow be redeemed. The time lost in dead-end pursuits and self-delusion could somehow in God's providence be filled, changed, and made useful.

My friend accepted the grace of God and His promise of salvation. The years that had been "eaten" were redeemed because this man now has a new understanding of himself. He is a child of God. Somehow, that makes all of the difference in the world.

Lord, we all have periods that seem wasted, gone forever, eaten away. But You promised to redeem them. I can't see how You could do that, but I trust You. Take my years and use them for Your glory. In Jesus' name, Amen.

JULY 28

TRYING TO LIVE ON PAST GLORIES
Amos 5:1—6

He used to be a sports star. In high school, everyone knew that his skill on the football field would take him far. He made it onto the college team and pressed on with an eye toward the NFL. The time came for the draft, and he was selected. But a bright future was cut short by a back injury that forced him into early retirement. Today he is an angry shell of a man. Everything good in his life seems to have been left on the field. The present is only a screen on which to play reruns of his "glory days."

You might not know this man, but you know others just like

him. In fact, you might be that man. These guys constantly look back over their shoulders at what they believe they lost along the way. All of the good stuff was "back there." Today is filled only with regret, bewilderment, and despair.

Does God have anything to say about such situations? The answer is "yes." The prophet Amos was the Lord's voice when he said to the people of Israel, "Seek me and live; do not seek Bethel, do not go to Gilgal, do not journey to Beersheba" (vv. 4–5). Bethel, Gilgal, and Beersheba were the sacred worship places in the nation's past, back in the "good old days." It seemed that back then people could go to one of those sites and find God.

But pay attention to what the Lord says: "Seek me and live." "Seek me," says the Lord. This is an invitation to a living relationship here and now. It is not a backward glance at some possible glory time. It is here and now, today and tomorrow, looking forward. Do you feel left behind, that all your good days are over? God invites you to seek Him today and live in a current relationship.

Lord, it's so tempting to look back at days gone by and wonder why we can't live them again. But help us to take stock of where we are in relationship to You today. Help us to see this day as a gift to be opened now. In Christ, Amen.

Easy Enough for a Child to Understand
Amos 5:21–24

We spend a lot of time and energy working on our religion. I mean that literally—we work on it. Often, it becomes a set of rules and regulations that are constantly being expanded, refined, encoded, and, finally, embalmed. Jesus was furious with people of His day who used religion as a club against people rather than as a stretcher for the injured.

That was nothing new in Jesus' day, though. It has been going on since humankind's earliest days. Religious practices that are meant as steps toward God end up being a spiritual Alcatraz that effectively walls us off from God. The very thing that is supposed to take us into the presence of the Lord of the universe forms a ball-and-chain shackle that stops our progress.

The prophet Amos took a hard look at his people and their condition. What he saw was not pretty. The people were going through all of the right motions and getting the religious rituals correct, but it was all empty show. It was as if they were putting on a play without noticing that the audience was no longer watching.

What were the people doing? They were observing feasts and gathering in assemblies. They were even giving the Lord great sacrificial gifts. What was God's response to their practices? Not what you would expect: "Away with the noise of your songs!" (v. 23). Full worship practices brought by empty people gained them nothing. God turned a deaf ear to such noise.

So what does the Lord want? "Let justice roll on like a river, righteousness like a never-failing stream!" (v. 24). This is so simple a child can understand it. God wants us to treat each other right! When we do that, we find our offerings acceptable and our songs pleasing to Him.

Lord, help me not to stumble over the simplicity of Your call. Help me treat my fellowman with justice. I know that You are pleased when I do right by him. In Jesus' name, Amen.

JULY 30

ALL PUFFED UP
Obadiah 1–4

The CEO of an important company spent more than a million dollars on his wife's birthday party. He wanted to show off and impress everyone with his wealth and influence. Otherwise, what would be the point of such extravagance? A few months later, the news media showed this man as he was led from his office in handcuffs after being arrested for fraud. Much of the money that he had been throwing around belonged to someone else.

Another man owned a small business but acted as if he were royalty. He treated his employees with an air of indifference. At best, they were a necessary evil. When the economy turned downward, his business got into trouble, and he blamed his employees. He cursed some and fired others. When his business went into bankruptcy, the owner put a .38 into his mouth and pulled the trigger.

The prophet Obadiah thundered against the pride of his nation. He knew that pride puffs people up with hot air. But every balloon is subject to being burst. Listen to his judgment: "The pride of your heart has deceived you, you who live in the clefts of the rocks and make your home on the heights, you who say to yourself, 'Who can bring me down to the ground?'" (v. 3).

They saw themselves as above others—literally living in the upper reaches of the area. But that was symbolic of how they felt. They were above common people in every way. That sort of thinking got them into trouble. When we see ourselves as living above everyone else, life has a way of showing us otherwise. A simple virus can put us in bed for a week and remind us of our mortality. A bad business decision can put us out of business and pounding the sidewalks looking for work.

What will pride do for us then?

Lord, keep me from being deceived by my pride. In truth, I know who I am. My gifts and abilities might make me stand out a little from my brothers, but I'm really just one of the guys. Thanks for keeping my feet on the ground. In Christ, Amen.

JULY 31

THE BOOMERANG OF ACTIONS
Obadiah 10–15

Life has a way of giving back to us what we give to others. I think of this as the boomerang of actions. What we throw out into the world has a habit of coming back to us. If we are angry, suspicious, and mistrusting of others, they will treat us the same way. If we are friendly, open, and honest, we receive the same. Oh, I know. Sometimes things do not work out that way. That is the exception and not the rule. For the most part, we get what we give.

A story is told of a stranger who walked into a village. He was met at the village gate by an old man who seemed to have a lot of time on his hands. The stranger asked, "What kinds of people are here? What are they like?" The old man said, "What kinds of people lived in the place you came from?" The traveler said, "The people where I came from were mean and unfriendly." The old man said, "You'll find the same kind of people here." The next day, another stranger came to the village. He saw the old man at the gate and asked the same question. The old man replied, "What kinds of people lived in the place you came from?" "Oh," said the stranger, "they were good people, friendly and kind to each other." "Well, you'll find the same kinds of people here," said the old man.

Obadiah the prophet took his people to task for turning their backs on each other. Their fellow Jews were plundered by foreigners, but Obadiah's people "stood aloof" (v. 11). They did not get involved. The boomerang of actions has always been true. What they gave out they later got back. Funny how it always happens like that.

Do you know someone who needs your help? Don't "stand aloof."

Lord, help me sow the seeds of love to reap a harvest of peace. In Jesus' name, Amen.

AUGUST 1

WHEN CHRISTIANS RUN FROM GOD
Jonah 1:1–12

Excitement filled seventeen-year-old Harold Chandler Jr. as he slipped away from the grounds of the Kentucky Baptist Home for Children. Running away promised to be an adventure he'd looked forward to for a long time.

Walking along the Cumberland River, his foot slipped. Harold fell off a cliff, tumbled wildly, then—darkness. Much later, he awoke to incredible pain and weakness. Two broken arms, a fractured hip, one lung punctured, and almost a gallon of blood lost kept him from moving to safety. All he had to protect himself from storms was a pillowcase. The next four days proved to be a nightmare of confusion and fear. "I said, 'Lord, if you let me make it through, I'll never run away again,'" Harold later recounted.

Two fishermen finally heard the boy crying for help from the edge of his rocky perch overlooking the river. "We couldn't believe it," one of them said. "Most of him looked blue or black, and he had blood all over." Today, Harold Chandler Jr. is happy to be back at home—alive and safe.

Have you been like Harold Chandler—or like Jonah? Are you running away from God's service? Perhaps you've used busyness or family involvement as an excuse for quite some time. Or it could be you've looked forward to being on your own, believing it promised much excitement and adventure.

Sooner or later, we all learn that life away from the presence of God is not really living. Perhaps today's passage has spoken to your heart and you're ready to "come home." If so, you'll find a heavenly Father waiting to embrace you with open arms. Come to Him, surrender to His love, and you'll discover, like Jonah, the complete forgiveness that God offers.

Heavenly Father, I don't want to run from You. I surrender to Your will for my life this day. May I stay squarely in the middle of Your presence at all times. In Jesus' name, Amen.

AUGUST 2

GOD'S GRACE AND OUR SINS
Jonah 1:15–2:10

Mrs. Soman, forty-three, wasn't feeling well. She went to her local hospital in Guyana to complain about chest pains. They felt a lot like the pains she'd complained of at the same hospital ten years earlier. When doctors began looking at some x-rays, they could hardly believe what they saw. Lodged in her chest was a pair of surgical scissors! For ten years, they had resided close to her heart, always potentially dangerous.

Records show Mrs. Soman had undergone a chest operation in the same hospital after complaining of the pains so long ago. "The system clearly broke down, because you do a count of instruments before and after surgery. Clearly, this was not done," said the president of the local medical association. A surgeon was scheduled to remove the scissors. This time, you can be sure they'll count all of the instruments before sewing her up!

Our unconfessed sins can cause us—and our loved ones—much pain. Leave them alone, and they'll do much damage to our spiritual heart. But when we come to Jesus Christ and admit our sins, asking for cleansing and forgiveness, then we find the Great Physician ready to operate and take out the harmful invader.

Jonah didn't deserve to have a second chance. After all, he was unrepentant when the great fish swallowed him and saved him from drowning. But God was offering grace to his prophet. Like Jonah, when you lose all hope, if you'll only look up to God, you'll find the "God of the Second Chance" ready to offer you grace and redemption, especially at the moment you don't deserve it!

Dear God, You see everything within me. Please show me anything harmful I'm keeping instead of giving to You. Help me to confess my sins and receive forgiveness through Your Son, Jesus Christ. Thank You for another chance. Thank You for Your grace. In Jesus' name, Amen.

AUGUST 3

THE POWER OF A CHANGED LIFE
Jonah 3

Perley King had a problem: he was out of Cheerios, his favorite cereal. So Perley did what any of us would have done. He got into the car and drove three miles to a food store to replenish his supply.

What's so newsworthy about someone going to the store for cereal? First, Perley left the house in the middle of the night when everyone else in the family was asleep. Second, he took someone else's car. Third, he didn't have a driver's license. Fourth, Perley couldn't get a driver's license no matter how well he drove—because he is only seven years old!

It seems that early one morning (April 1, which is certainly fitting for this story), Perley woke up before his parents. He found his sister's keys, got into the car and began using the skills he'd mastered on a computer driving game. When his parents found out about the early morning spin, the seven-year-old found himself in hot water. But there was also a positive side to this story.

General Mills is giving Perley and his parents a year's supply of Cheerios and a new bicycle. Why the new bicycle? Perley's parents want to ensure that their son never drives to the store again![1]

We can accomplish an awful lot through dogged determination. But nothing compares to the power of a great message coming from a changed life.

When a renewed Jonah walked into the city of Nineveh, his message of repentance fell upon that city with enormous force. Within three days of the prophet's arrival, even the king of Nineveh felt God's conviction upon his soul. The result of this changed man's message was to turn an entire city around for God!

What does God want to do with your life? What message does He want you to proclaim? Remember, your testimony of God's saving grace, coupled with the testimony of a changed attitude and different habits, can influence others to discover Christ as Savior.

Dear Lord, I want to be a changed man. May my life reflect to others what You've done in my heart and soul. Help me to be consistent in sharing with others what Jesus has done for me. In Jesus' name, Amen.

1. "Cheerio Run," 15 April 2000, in Furthermore: A Wired News Special Collection, www.wired.com/news/furthermore/0,2348,0-2000~4-20,00.html. Accessed 19 August 2003.

What Is Your "CQ"?

Jonah 4

"Pastor, we can't go see those people!"

A group of us had gathered at the church to visit guests who had recently attended our church. The man who spoke those words was a faithful Christian—but he had a problem.

"Why can't you visit this couple?" I asked. "Didn't Jesus die for them?"

"Well, pastor—" The man began struggling. "Yes, he did. But I don't think these people will fit in here."

I tried to be gentle. After all, getting the man mad would accomplish nothing. "But if we treat everyone with the love of Christ, shouldn't we be able to minister to this couple and make them a part of our local body of believers? And if we don't tell them about Christ, then who will?"

The man gave up. "You're right pastor. I've just got some prejudices I need to get rid of." He held out his hand for the card. "I'll be glad to talk to this couple."

Notice that I didn't tell you "what kind" of people we were talking about. They could have been any race, religion, or social level. The point is that we must care for *all* people because God cares for *everyone*.

What is your CQ—your Caring Quotient? Do you love and care for others as Jesus loves and cares for you?

Heavenly Father, I want to love everyone without prejudice. Although I might need sometimes to disapprove of a person's lifestyle and behavior, help me still to love the person. May I witness to and care for every single person You bring into my sphere of influence. In Jesus' name, Amen.

GOD'S JUDGMENT UPON MY LIFE
Micah 1:1–9

In my own personal devotions for this day, I read the following verse from Proverbs: "A man who remains stiff-necked after many rebukes will suddenly be destroyed—without remedy" (29:1).

There comes a time when a nation or an individual can run out of more opportunities to repent. God shows us grace—but He also expects us to respond with a changed life.

I've seen it happen time and time again in my ministry. A person who claims to be a Christian strays into moral failure. Godly friends try to intervene. Loving calls to come back into fellowship are ignored. Then, after months or years of unrepentant sinning, the person is suddenly struck down. Either through the loss of personal health, finances, or influence—maybe even the loss of life itself—judgment comes from God. Too late, the person realizes the error of his ways.

I don't ever want God to have to deal with me that way! I want to listen to God and allow Him to guide me daily.

What about you? Are you risking God's judgment because of your lifestyle? Are you putting your life in danger and your family in jeopardy because of poor habits and relationships? Let today's devotional be a wake-up call. Come to Christ and repent.

Dear God, I don't want You to have to bring sudden judgment upon me because I refuse to listen to You. Please show me anything in my life that shouldn't be there. Then, give me the courage and conviction to confess it to You and allow You to take it from my life. I want to live with You being first in my life from this day forward. In Jesus' name, Amen.

ABUSE OF POWER
Micah 2:1–4

I heard recently of a woman who left the United States to join in the reconstruction effort of a poverty-stricken, war-torn country. Before her departure, she piled all of her possessions into a storage facility for safekeeping, gave the storage company her credit card number so they could deduct the monthly payments, and set out on her journey.

After some time, she came home for vacation and was shocked to find her storage unit cleaned out and rented to someone else! Apparently there had been a problem with her card that had prevented the storage company from deducting the monthly payment. Due to the crippled infrastructure of the country she was in, she was unable to receive any mail or phone calls. So, although the company claimed to have given her ample warning, she was completely unaware that any problem existed until she arrived back in the States. The company claimed that selling her possessions was entirely within their rights, however the woman pointed out that they had violated a state law that required storage companies to notify other involved contacts before any stored property can be auctioned. The company had not notified any of the four relatives she had listed on her rental agreement.

A lawsuit followed. The woman pointed out that everything she owned was gone—she wanted a million dollars in return for that loss. They had sold photos of herself with the President, the Vice President, and other famous people; a signed edition of her favorite novel; all of her personal letters and poetry; the only existing copy of her master's thesis; and her grandmother's black velvet evening dress. All the things she most wanted to keep were gone.

In today's passage, Micah tells the powerful and wealthy that God's judgment will fall upon them because of the way they've abused those who are poorer and weaker than they. We would do well to listen to and apply this lesson to our own lives.

No matter what kind of salary we earn or what position we hold, someone is almost always poorer and weaker than we. How we treat them says much about our love of God. We can abuse others, or we can love others—but we can't do both. We can exploit others, or we can love God—but we can't do both.

Treat carefully and tenderly those under your control.

Heavenly Father, may I love others as You love me. May those with whom I interact see Jesus in me by the way I treat them. In Jesus' name, Amen.

AUGUST 7

BACK TO BASICS
Micah 3:5–8

Ah, the wonders of modern technology! Today, we are accustomed to seeing our mail loaded onto jets and flown around the world—sometimes overnight. We watch as shiny trucks bundle our mail into groups sorted by zip code then efficiently deliver them to homes all across our great nation.

Don't tell this to Charlie Chamberlain. Charlie is a mailman. More precisely, he is a U.S. Postal Service contractor. Charlie doesn't fly planes. He doesn't even drive a car or truck as he delivers the mail. Charlie uses a mule train and rides a horse! He carefully guides his mules, laden with letters and goods, down a trail in the Grand Canyon, delivering mail to the village of Supai on the Havasupai Indian Reservation.

Why would Charlie Chamberlain choose this mode of delivery? In reality, he has no choice. The village is accessible only by foot, horseback, or helicopter. Everything for the village—groceries, mail, dry goods—has to be brought in by Charlie and his mules. "It's amazing what people can do when they put their minds to it. They can pack things you never would have thought," he says. Chamberlain counts a disassembled washing machine among his most unusual deliveries.

Is there anything he can't deliver? "The chopper takes the ice cream. That's about the only thing we can't take," Chamberlain says, hopping onto his horse and heading dutifully down the trail for another seven-hour round trip to deliver the mail.[1]

When it's time to make a decision, to whom do you listen? Postman Charlie Chamberlain, faced with an incredibly difficult task of getting mail into the Grand Canyon, eschewed technology and complicated delivery plans and went back to basics: backpacks and mules.

In Micah's day, the children of Israel were listening to false prophets. The result was a nation and a people conquered and nearly destroyed because of sin.

Many people want to give you advice. As a Christian, you need to ensure that you're listening to godly advice, not popular but false prophets. Do what Charlie Chamberlain did: get back to the basics. Read the Bible, memorize Scripture, and apply God's Word to your heart and life. It will keep you on the right path and deliver you safely to your ultimate destination, heaven.

Dear God, help me to listen to You. Place within me a thirst for reading Your Word, and help me to apply it to my life. May I stay away from false prophets and follow only godly advice. In Jesus' name, Amen.

AUGUST 8

The Winning Side
Micah 4:1–7

In the first months of pastoring my current church, I got involved in a three-on-three basketball league. Played in our gym and made up of other church members, it was a good way for me to get to know the men of the church. There was just one problem: at the age of forty, I was a good bit slower than in my younger days.

The staff member in charge of putting the teams together, however, helped me quite a bit. On my team I found a gentle giant. Close to seven feet tall, a former college basketball player only a

---

1. "Mail by Mule," 9 October 2000, CNN.com, www.cnn.com/2000/US/10/09/mail.by.mule/. Accessed 19 August, 2003.

few years removed from competition, Greg had a great jump shot and rebounded ferociously. Guess which team won the championship!

When we received the trophy, I didn't for one minute think that I deserved it because of my prowess as a player. It just so happened that I was allowed to be a part of the winning team.

As we leave the book of Micah today, we see the prophet looking toward the end of time. He tells his people, and us, some wonderful news. We are on the winning team! God will defeat all evil and injustice. Peace will one day rule forever. However, it's important that we commit to staying with Jesus Christ every day. He and He alone has the power to make everything right.

As a team member, do as much as you can for Christ. But never forget that it is Christ who brings the victory. So, no matter what this day brings you, rejoice! You're on the winning team!

Heavenly Father, thank You for putting me on the winning team. As a believer, help me to do as much as possible for Your kingdom. And, help me to remember that You are stronger than anything I will face today. In Jesus' name, Amen.

AUGUST 9

RUN FOR COVER!
Nahum 1:1–7

The phone at the end of the hall in my college dorm finally became free. I stepped into the booth, closed the door, and turned my face toward the back for privacy.

When I left home at the age of seventeen, I was, for all intents and purposes, on my own from then on. Although I had a great upbringing and a solid, supportive family, I'm one of those people who likes to do things without having to count on a lot of other people. So I was sure that I could accomplish growing up at college without needing any advice from Mom or Dad back at home. Boy, was I wrong!

"Hello."

I heard my parents pick up the phone, and I began to cry. A romance in ruins had turned me into a young man much in need of comfort and advice. Fifteen minutes later, I emerged from the phone booth calmer and wiser. My last words to my parents were, "I'm sorry I've been gone for so long. I'll see you this weekend."

How long has it been since you've come to God, spent time with Him, and listened to Him? Stay away from His presence too long and your heart grows cold. You begin to lose your way.

If you've not done so, I encourage you to memorize Nahum 1:7 and apply it to your life. God is a great refuge. He will give you peace and strength today.

Dear Lord, thank You for allowing me to come to You today. Help me to stay close to You every day. Your advice and comfort are what I desire, above all. In Jesus' name, Amen.

FORGOTTEN GRACE
Nahum 2:8–13

Saturday afternoon, blue skies, nothing to do. Cruising past the church, dressed in a golf shirt, shorts, and sandals, I saw cars in the parking lot. *Hmm*, I thought. *I wonder which Bible study group is having a fellowship?*

A few minutes later, I reached home. My wife ran out to meet me, phone in her hand. "You've got a wedding to do right now!" she yelled. "Everyone's waiting for you!"

I broke the world record for getting into a tuxedo and out of golf clothes! Embarrassed, I walked into the church and admitted to the bride and groom that I'd forgotten the wedding!

Let me tell you something even more embarrassing. The city of Nineveh, to which Jonah had preached (see the devotional reading for August 3), had forgotten the grace that God had shown to them. Now the prophet Nahum told them that their forgetfulness would bring destruction upon the entire city.

Forgetting a wedding is bad; forgetting God's grace is a disaster.

How is your memory? Do you remember the day you came to Christ and He forgave you of all of your sins? Do you remember that first, wonderful taste of grace? Ensure that your thoughts, relationships, and actions reveal that you still remember God's work of grace in your life. Don't forget. Stay faithful.

> *Heavenly Father, I never want to forget what I was before You touched my life. I don't want to forget how You have come into my life and transformed me forever. May everything I think and do today tell others that I remember Your grace. In Jesus' name, Amen.*

AUGUST 11

A LOOK AT UNFAITHFULNESS
Nahum 3:1–7

Have you been unfaithful? In all probability, at some time in your life, you have.

Please understand, I'm not talking about unfaithfulness to your wife. It's the relationship with Jesus Christ that you have as a believer that concerns me right now.

If you've not yet read today's passage of Scripture, please do so before continuing any farther in this devotional.

Did you see verse 4? The mightiest power in her day, Nineveh was about to be destroyed by God's hand. The prophet told Nineveh that her lust and unfaithfulness led to her downfall. The lust was a wrong desire for power and military conquests of other nations.

In other words, lust and unfaithfulness are not limited to the sexual area. They can discolor *any* part of your life. Lust to be the best athlete in your favorite sport can ruin your marriage and damage your testimony. Lust to have the most money or prestige can drive you away from church and home for too many weeks. I could go on with more areas, but you get the picture.

What area of your life is the weakest? How is Satan tempting you to be unfaithful to God? This week, whether on the job, relaxing at home, or playing sports, remember the example of Nineveh—and avoid it at all costs.

Stay faithful—always.

Dear Lord, I want to be faithful to You every day of my life. Please hedge me about with Your protection. May my priorities, my habits, my relationships, and my thoughts be honorable to You. In Jesus' name, Amen.

AUGUST 12

WHY DOES EVIL PROSPER?
Habakkuk 1:1–6

It seems that no one is safe anywhere these days. Take, for example, the fourth-grade class of James Reeves in Philadelphia. James, a student in the class, had no reason to worry about violence one particular morning recently. After all, the mother of one of his fellow students was sharing with the class about her work as a police officer. As she talked, however, somehow her gun fell to the ground. As it hit, the gun discharged, and James felt a burning along his cheek. The bullet had accidentally grazed him! The ten-year-old is okay, but it must cause his parents to puzzle over exactly when and where they can leave their child safely without wondering if he will be all right.[1]

Like a bullet from nowhere, circumstances can barge into our life and wound us before we even know what is happening. Think of the workers who had their retirements secured by stocks in now-bankrupt companies. Look at the men and women who were let go from their jobs and who are in their forties and fifties. If ever the future seemed insecure, it is now.

Add to all of this the injustice that seems to rule in this world, and we can identify with the prophet Habakkuk when he asked God, "Why do you make me look at injustice? Why do you tolerate

---

1. Nytimes.com, 7 February 2002.

wrong? Destruction and violence are before me; there is strife, and conflict abounds" (v. 3).

God answers the prophet—and us—throughout the rest of the book of Habakkuk. He tells us that injustice and uncertainty will not reign forever. For the moment, it might seem as if the ruthless and unethical are enjoying the fruit and wealth of others they've stepped on in their climb up the ladder of success. But this is not the end of the story. God will bring all injustice to an end. The unrighteous will not ultimately win. In fact, they will suffer for all eternity.

As we come to the end of this devotional, let's keep three things in mind:

1. God desires to help and protect us from the bullets of injustice, so we must pray regularly for His hand to enfold us with safety.
2. God knows what we're going through and will use everything—even the bad things—to accomplish His will.
3. Judgment is coming, so we must keep our life right with God, no matter what everyone around us is doing.

Heavenly Father, please protect me and my family today. You already know what will occur. Please give me the wisdom and strength to react in the right way to today's activities. May I stay strong and faithful in the face of adversity and any injustice I might encounter. In Jesus' name, Amen.

AUGUST 13

EMERGING FROM THE DARKNESS
Habakkuk 1:12–17

How can we take the injustices we see—and experience ourselves—in the world and use them for good? Does God want us to respond to the unfair things that happen to us in a specific way that will please Him?

To better understand how to answer this question, let's go to a wedding in Australia.

The bride and the groom prepare to leave the church. As the couple exits the building, waiting friends lift their hands to fling a parting gift at the couple. What are the wedding guests throwing? We know that some people throw rice; others throw confetti or rose petals. But if you're getting married in Australia, it very well could be that you would be pelted with—butterflies!

The demand for butterflies at Australian weddings has—pardon the pun—taken wing over the last several years. Jill Murray, owner of Butterfly Release, breeds butterflies on a farm south of Perth. She sells a box of orange and black monarch butterflies (wing span: 3.2 inches) for $36.50. Each box holds six monarchs.

When the butterflies come out of the dark, cool box into the warm, sunny atmosphere, they wake up and take flight, surrounding the newlyweds with grace and beauty.[1]

How can this story help us with adversity? This world is spiritually cold and dark. When we believers encounter the inevitable trials of life, we become either bitter or better. If we decide to become better, we move closer to the source of all spiritual warmth and light—Jesus Christ. And as we grow closer to the Lord, we also find ourselves giving testimony of Him in the way we blossom under difficulties. Others—some who are unbelievers, and others who, as believers, are still weak in the faith—watch us take wing and become blessed and are encouraged by our beauty under adversity.

Our growth in Christ and our spreading beauty through a dark world might never have come about had we not experienced the injustices and difficulties of this life.

The next time we encounter troubles, let's keep in mind this thought: it's time to take wing, stand for Christ, and bring beauty into the lives of others.

Dear Lord, I want to bring joy into the lives of others through my difficulties. Help me to give my

1. Yahoo.com/news, 8 February 2002.

tough times to You and lean solely upon Your
strong arms. In Jesus' name, Amen.

THE DANGER OF IMPATIENCE
Habakkuk 2:1–3

Have you ever gotten in a hurry?

One of the areas of my life that I have to monitor constantly is when I'm in the car. I often seem to have patience that lasts only about two seconds. If I'm not careful, I'll get upset with slower drivers or those who hesitate. If you could be in the passenger's seat, you'd probably hear me mutter several times, "Patience, Mark, patience."

I know Christians who are the same way about God's promises. If things don't go exactly right, they immediately lose faith or begin asking, "Why me, God?" A man loses his job and quits going to church because he's angry. A marriage breaks up and the husband grows bitter, refusing to pray or read his Bible. A father sees a family member grow sick and die, and blames God.

In today's passage, we see God telling us that we must take the long view, no matter what occurs in life. God's promises will always come true. Good will come out of bad. The Lord will return to put everything right. Heaven does await all who place their faith in Jesus Christ. What we must remember is that these events might not happen when or as soon as we'd like.

That's where faith comes in.

How's your patience level? Determine today that you will stay patient, no matter what happens, waiting for God to do His work in His own time.

Dear God, help me to remember Your promises to
all believers. No matter what I'm going through
right now, may I keep my focus upon You, not my
temporary situation. In Jesus' name, Amen.

BREAKING THE RULES
Habakkuk 2:11–14

It's confession time. When was the last time you accidentally, or purposely, broke "the rules"? I'm talking about anything from walking on the grass to getting a parking or speeding ticket to breaking line. Were you punished for breaking those rules?

If you've broken the rules, you'd better hope that you never run into someone like a woman we'll simply call "Karen" in Massachusetts. This thirty-eight-year-old woman kicked and beat up a fifty-one-year-old woman when Karen saw her breaking the rules. What terrible thing did the anonymous woman do to receive the beating? She had thirteen items in a twelve-items-or-fewer checkout lane at the supermarket! Karen was arrested for assault and battery with a dangerous weapon—her foot.[1]

Does that "justice" seem a tad unfair? Of course it does. And we see examples like this every day. If the rulings of various legal and legislative institutions sometimes leave you shaking your head, you're not alone. In Proverbs 28:5, we're told why many times the innocent are punished and the rule breakers go free: "Evil men do not understand justice."

One day, however, the "fear of the Lord" will reign everywhere on earth. When that time arrives, the rule breakers will receive proper judgment. True, godly justice will prevail, and believers will receive their rewards.

Which category do you fall into: the godly or the rule breakers? If the Lord were to come back this instant, how would you fare before His throne? If a person were to look solely at your conduct, what would they conclude about your life? Would they see you receiving judgment from God, or would they see you receiving rewards?

True justice. It's coming—soon.

Heavenly Father, may I so conduct my life that
no one will have to wonder if I'm living for You or

---

1. Nytimes.com, 14 February 2002.

if I'm a rule breaker. May I also bring others into
the kingdom of God by sharing the good news of
Jesus Christ with them. In Jesus' name, Amen.

AUGUST 16

A MATURE FAITH
Habakkuk 3:17–19

Today's reading is from the book of Habakkuk. When we first saw this prophet, he was railing about the injustice in the world. He cried out to God, asking why the Lord let so many bad things happen to so many good people. Looking around, he pointed out to the Lord all of the bad people who seemed to be prospering in spite of their evil lifestyle.

At the end of the book, Habakkuk has learned his lesson. He now understands that God might allow the evil to prosper for a time, but judgment will come. His last words reflect a mature faith that does not depend upon present circumstances. The prophet says, in effect, "No matter how bad things might be right now, Lord, I know that you will act to make things right at the proper time. Until that time comes, I will stand faithful."

If that is the definition of mature faith, how do you measure up? Are you willing to trust in God in the bad times as well as in the good times? Perhaps it's time to take a lesson from Habakkuk and place God's Word, not your immediate circumstances, as your ultimate authority.

Dear God, I want to be able to trust in You
always. Beginning today, may the promises in
your Word be my authority, no matter what.
Thank You for loving me and taking care of me.
In Jesus' name, Amen.

FINDING THE GUILTY PARTY!
Zephaniah 1:1–14

"Mister Jones, why didn't you do what I asked you to do?"

Jones begins to sweat. He looks around for some help from his colleagues, but no one is willing to risk the anger of Jones's boss.

"Honest, sir, I did the best I could," Jones stammers. "Someone must have tipped off the man I was supposed to capture. He was waiting and prepared. I barely escaped with my life."

The "Boss" scowls and pulls out a gun. "You know how I deal with treachery, don't you, Jones?"

Jones begins to back away, but there is nowhere to turn. He knows he's about to die. The revolver looks as big as a cannon, and Jones sees the final seconds of his life float before him.

The gun spits fire and Jones closes his eyes in horror. When he finally opens them, he sees the man next to him lying dead on the floor. Jones's boss is smiling grimly. "Taylor was the traitor. He tipped off the man you were trying to capture."

At that point, everyone in the room decides that he will never try to double cross the Boss!

The scene you've just read is a staple in many spy movies. The person everyone thinks will be punished is saved whereas someone else who thinks he is safe is, instead, killed.

The opening verses of Zephaniah created the same consternation in the prophet's audience. The Jews living in Zephaniah's day knew about the "Day of the Lord." They knew that it was a time of judgment and destruction. However, they believed that all of that was going to happen only to their enemies. The prophet stunned them by saying that they were the ones who would be destroyed by God's judgment!

In the New Testament, Jesus tells us that the same thing will happen before God's throne.

> Not everyone who says to me, "Lord, Lord," will enter the kingdom of heaven, but only he who does the will of my Father who is in heaven. Many will say to me on that day, "Lord, Lord, did we not prophesy in

your name, and in your name drive out demons and perform many miracles?" Then I will tell them plainly, "I never knew you. Away from me, you evildoers!" (Matthew 7:21–23)

I love surprises, but I certainly don't want to be surprised on the day of judgment! I don't want to find out that Jesus never knew me, that I had lived my life in vain, that I will be separated from God forever.

What mistake did both Zephaniah's audience and the crowd before God's throne make? They assumed that their own standards of conduct were good enough to get them into heaven. As you and I know, good works are not enough to cancel our debt of sin. We must have a right relationship with Jesus Christ.

If you've not yet done so, I urge you to ensure that you won't be surprised on God's judgment day. Admit that you've sinned, turn away from your sins, and turn to Christ. Ask for His forgiveness, which He bought for you on the Cross. Give Jesus control of your life from this moment forward as you invite Him to be with you forever.

Heavenly Father, I acknowledge my need for Jesus Christ. I want Your Son to be my Lord and Savior. Help me to give You complete control of my life from this moment on. I don't want to be rejected on the day of judgment. I want to be Your child forever. Thank You for Christ's sacrifice that paid for my sins. In Jesus' name, Amen.

AUGUST 18

THE TRUE VALUE OF MONEY
Zephaniah 1:14–18

Perhaps you've heard the story before. It seems that a certain man made a lot of money and was very proud of his accomplishments. The day came when he died and found himself before the door of heaven. The angel in charge of letting people in saw a suitcase in the man's hand and asked, "What do you have there?"

The man swelled with pride and said, "I have all of the wealth that I accumulated while on earth. I've talked with God, and He said I could bring it with me."

The angel frowned but only said, "Could I see what all your wealth looks like?"

"I had it all changed into gold so it would fit in the suitcase," the man replied, opening the precious container. The gold gleamed brightly in the divine light.

The angel opened the door and ushered the man into heaven. "You can bring all that gold with you if you want," he said with amusement. Then, gesturing at the magnificent streets of gold running throughout the celestial city, he added, "But why would you want to work all your life for pavement?"

In verse 18 of today's reading, we see God telling the people that their silver and gold will not save them. In reality, the people's possessions helped lead to their downfall! Used selfishly, money has no real lasting power. Only when we ask God to direct our spending does money become our servant instead of our master.

Do you give ten percent of your income to the Lord as He commands? Doing this will not only help and strengthen your church but also help you get your priorities concerning money and "things" in the right place in your life.

Serve God, not money.

Dear Lord, I don't want money to come between me and You. May I give You the first ten percent of my income every payday, and help me to give it willingly. Use my gift to touch people for the kingdom of heaven. Multiply it to reach around the world for You. In Jesus' name, Amen.

AUGUST 19

It's Time to Seek Shelter
Zephaniah 2:1–3

"It never rains on the golf course."

I had said this many times over the years, continuing around the links in what some people might call gale-force winds. But on this particular autumn day, I finally met my match. My partner and I had already been abandoned by the other two in our four-some. Now, with the wind moaning and the rain moving sideways, I could barely see everyone else on the course moving toward the club house.

"Just one more hole," my partner said—about the same time the first bolt of lightening cracked nearby.

He was driving the golf cart. So I yelled, "We're sitting ducks out here! Head for shelter!"

The cart took off, and I shielded my eyes from the rain. A few moments later, the cart stopped. I knew that the clubhouse was a lot farther away than a few seconds' drive, so I looked up to see where we were. The tallest tree in the area was the "shelter" that my partner had picked for us!

"Get us out of here right now!" I screamed over the wind. We were about ten yards from the tree when the bolt hit, splitting it from top to bottom. Thank goodness we'd already started for the clubhouse, or my last round of golf would have been truly "electrifying."

When is a shelter not a shelter?

If the place you've picked for refuge can't save you from the judgment of God; if it can't help you in times of difficulties, giving you peace; if your "shelter" is, itself, destroyed by the same forces from which you're hiding—then you have a problem.

Where is your shelter in life? In what or in whom do you trust?

God has promised to give us protection from the vagaries of life. He shelters us with His love and grace from condemnation. He gives us moment-by-moment guidance through this world and into eternity.

If you've not yet done so, I encourage you to run to Jesus Christ and allow Him to shelter you, completely and eternally.

Heavenly Father, I don't want to run away from You anymore. Please help me to stay close by Your side, in the shelter of Your arms. I know that You have the grace, strength, and wisdom to protect me from all harm. In Jesus' name, Amen.

ONE—THAT'S ONE—WAY

Zephaniah 2:8–11

We live in a multicultural society. America, above any other nation on earth, can truly be called a melting pot. We are learning respect for others' cultures, cuisine, and clothing. All of this is healthful. Folded subtly into this mix, however, is an ingredient of untruth that can sour both the church and our effectiveness.

Many different cultures, languages, and societies exist. All of them might be equally valid and valuable. But there is only one God, only one heaven, and only one entrance to the path that leads to our heavenly Father. I'm not the one whose word we should or shouldn't take on this subject. If we accept the Bible as God's Word, then we'll discover that the Lord Himself attests that there are many false gods but only one true God.

Zephaniah clearly agreed that Jehovah is the only God. In the New Testament, Jesus unashamedly and unabashedly preached the fact that all but one path to eternity leads to hell and destruction. In the last part of John 14:6, he says, "No one comes to the Father except through me."

Sin is real and powerful. God does not look upon it lightly; neither does He lightly forgive it. That's why Jesus had to pay with His life on the Cross, taking our sins upon Himself and facing rejection by God the Father. When we begin to believe that every religion is equally valid—when we fall for the lie that there are many different paths to God—we not only reject the authority of God's Word but also cheapen the value of Christ's sacrifice for us. After all, if there are many paths to God, there was really no reason Jesus had to come to earth, take our sins upon Himself, be rejected by humankind and God, and be buried in a borrowed tomb.

Thank goodness the story doesn't end in the tomb! Sin is powerful, but Jesus Christ—God, Himself—conquered death and the withering power of our sins forever by rising from the grave and overcoming death.

There is only one way! It leads from the Cross, through the empty tomb, and straight through this world to an eternity with God in heaven.

Believe this truth, follow the path, and proclaim the good news of Jesus Christ.

Dear Lord, I want to be Your follower and Your child. I know that You are the only way to heaven. May my actions and my words conform to my beliefs. May I share Christ without fear today as You give me opportunities. Thank You for allowing Your son, Jesus Christ, to die for my sins. Thank You for your grace. In Jesus' name, Amen.

AUGUST 21

LET'S BE CLEAR
Zephaniah 3:8–13

Excuse me while I absquatulate, but I fear my tendency to divagate renders me a blatherskite, resulting in fleering. Translation: I'd better run before my rambling makes you all laugh and jeer at me.

What does all this mean? It means that I've been looking at an edition of the "World Oxford Dictionary of English" called the *Dictionary of Weird and Wonderful Words*. If you study it well, you might be able to become deipnosophists—someone skilled in after-dinner chat. After all, calling someone a hoddy-noddy sounds much better than telling them they're an idiot. And knowing another word for your big toe—hallux—certainly makes you sound smart![1]

If you've read this book straight through to this point, by now you've been in the major and minor prophets for several months. Perhaps you've noticed that all of these men have proclaimed a terrible warning to their audiences. Maybe you've been a little overwhelmed at the day-after-day messages of destruction, anger, and judgment. So, let me help you put several things in perspective. These men were only obeying their God. And God wanted His people to understand that their wrong lifestyles and attitudes were

1. Excite.com/news, 26 October 2001.

placing them in danger. Therefore, the Lord ensured that His prophets spoke clearly and understandably.

The children of Israel might have disagreed with the prophets' words. They might have grown angry with what Zephaniah and his fellow prophets were saying. But they certainly understood the message from these servants of almighty God.

How clear is the message that you proclaim every day? Do your friends and coworkers see and hear an unambiguous statement that Jesus Christ is your Lord? Do they understand that Christ can change their lives?

Ensure that your life speaks consistently, lovingly, and clearly the good news of Jesus Christ. There's a whole world around you that constantly receives garbled, conflicting messages. In the midst of all of that confusion, the man who simply speaks of God will stand out and be heard.

Dear heavenly Father, I don't want sin in my life to keep me from speaking clearly for Jesus Christ. I don't want to be embarrassed about sharing Christ. I don't want to keep quiet when I should be standing up for You. Please help me to be a consistent ambassador whom everyone understands. In Jesus' name, Amen.

AUGUST 22

YOUR CONSTANT COMPANION
Zephaniah 3:17–20

We don't know the woman's name. In reality, no one seemed to care whether she lived or died. She had long ago lost touch with her relatives. She resided in a large apartment block where her neighbors had not noticed anything wrong.

But something *was* horribly wrong. Because she wasn't paying her rent, the landlord forced open the woman's door to clear out the apartment. That's when accompanying police found the body. The woman, only about forty, had died of natural causes. But the terrible fact of the whole story is that she had been dead for ten months! Nobody had cared enough to see about her. No one had taken the time to try to find her.[1]

I don't know your current situation. But perhaps you're feeling very alone right now. Surrounded by thousands of people (if you're in a city), you still feel as if no one cares. Others have close friends, but you find yourself friendless.

If I've just described you, then the following paragraphs are especially important.

First, are you currently actively involved in a church? I'm not talking about just attending worship on Sunday morning. It's too easy to get lost in the crowd like that. When I say "involved," I mean participating regularly in small group Bible studies where others can get to know you and care about you. It also gives you a chance to help others and, in so doing, develop meaningful relationships with others in your local body of believers. (By the way, when I've talked to Christians who are lonely, it turns out that often they have overlooked ministering to others. They are simply waiting to be ministered to. Rolling up your sleeves, stopping "navel gazing," and focusing on helping those in need can really help you with your loneliness!)

Second, remember what God wants to do for you. Verse 17 from today's reading says, "The LORD your God is with you, he is mighty to save. He will take great delight in you, he will quiet you with his love, he will rejoice over you with singing." Notice that God is with you. No matter who may leave you, be unkind to you, or overlook you, the One who created you will never forsake you. But that's not all. God says that He takes great delight in you. He rejoices over you with singing.

You're not alone! Your heavenly Father, your Creator, your Savior, Jesus Christ, loves you and is with you right now! Thank the Lord for His constant, abiding love.

Dear God, I thank You that I'm not alone. Help me remember that You will always be with me. Also, please help me to show Your love to others who might be lonely. In Jesus' name, Amen.

---

1. Excite.com/news, 1 November 2001.

WORKING SMART
Haggai 1:1–8

At one point in my ministry, a young vagrant came through our town. To his credit, he seemed willing to work for room and board. One of our members had a dairy farm, and he offered to put the young man to work. After several days, I happened to run into the member and asked how his new worker was doing.

"He's not here anymore," the man replied.

I asked if the vagrant had worked or loafed while on the job.

"I'm not sure," the dairy farmer said, rubbing his eyes in frustration. "He sure sweated a lot, but he didn't accomplish anything!"

I'm sure you've heard the term "working smart." The idea behind it is to be sure you're getting the most possible accomplished from your efforts.

In the opening verses of Haggai, God told His people that they weren't "working smart." He pointed out that the hours they spent tilling the ground, tending to their needs, and looking for pleasure were producing little. The reason was that everything they were doing sprang from a selfish heart. They cared more for themselves than for God. The Lord told them to begin focusing upon pleasing Him, and they would see a difference in what their work produced.

Are you "working smart?" Or are your hours of work producing little return because of misplaced priorities? When you place God before everything and everyone else, your accomplishments will be what God intended them to be. You'll be happier, your path through this world will be easier, and you'll feel better about all that you do.

"Work smart." Put God first.

Heavenly Father, I want to produce the very best spiritual fruit possible for You. Help me to put You first in every area of my life. May what I do be pleasing to You, and may it be done with the right motive. I want to "work smart" today by letting You guide my actions, thoughts, and relationships. In Jesus' name, Amen.

SURVIVING LIFE'S DIFFICULTIES
Haggai 1:9–15

If he didn't hurt so much, a sixty-year-old Swedish man would be laughing about his "car wash" experience. The resident of Stockholm was using a high-pressure hose to clean his bus right outside a giant car wash. The hose accidentally hit a sensor and activated the brushes on the car wash. As the brushes began swirling, they caught the hose.

Instead of letting go of the hose, the sixty-year-old man tried to free it. That's when his foot got stuck in one of the brushes! Although he fought the car wash with all of his might, the man lost. The brushes dragged him in and pinned him against one of the machine's rotating bristles. Before it was all over, the man had four broken ribs, a hurt foot—and a great wax job.[1]

Have you ever gotten entangled with life? If so, maybe you've felt like the man in that story. Any time a group of men get together, someone is sure to start talking about a poor decision they've made and its subsequent painful repercussions. But have you noticed that some people seem to have more than what should be their share of difficulties? Sometimes it's just a part of life. At other times, however, the many bad things that occur can be attributed to an unwillingness to learn from previous bad decisions.

In Haggai's day, the people were getting beaten up by life. God told them that the solution to their problems was to focus on Him and His house of worship. To their credit, they heard and began to obey God's instructions, and a new era dawned for the children of Israel.

Focus on God and church—that's not a bad prescription for everyone.

If you want to quit being hurt by life's difficult experiences, stay on God's path and follow His will. Worshiping the Lord while surrounded by other brothers and sisters in Christ will help you go a

---

1. Excite.com, 1 November 2001.

long way toward any spiritual and emotional healing you might need. It will also encourage you to stay on track in your life, giving you a safer and easier way through this world.

> *Dear God, You know how I've been hurt in some key areas of my life. If these hurts have come about because of wrong decisions, please reveal those wrong decisions and attitudes to me. I want to be healed, and I want to have a wholesome life devoted to You. Please help me to focus upon You and upon Your church regularly. In Jesus' name, Amen.*

AUGUST 25

SPIRITUALLY, ARE YOU COLOR-BLIND?
Zechariah 2:8–13

In his autobiography *The Play Goes On,* Neil Simon tells about his brief military experience during World War II. He had enlisted in the Air Force and was pointing toward Officer Candidate School, where he would be trained as either a fighter or a bomber pilot. There was only one problem:

> No one asked if I could drive a car, which I couldn't, but I assumed someone would drive me out to the field and help get me into my plane. I was also found to be color-blind, unable to distinguish some colors from others, particularly blue and brown. This left a very good chance that I could easily bomb London instead of Berlin. I could sense that the Air Force would have to rethink their plans for me.[1]

Are you color-blind? Many men are. But I'm talking about a spiritual color-blindness that does not distinguish between what is God's will and what is a sin. Because of an unfamiliarity with

---

1. Neil Simon, *The Play Goes On* (New York: Simon and Schuster, 1999), 213.

the Bible and an unwillingness to immerse themselves in church, males all across North America not only ruin their own lives but also lead others astray. In 1 Corinthians, Paul tells us that Satan has blinded those who do not believe so that they will be unable to distinguish God's working in this world.

This might be an appropriate time to take a spiritual eye test!

First, as you look at your relationships, can you see God being honored and glorified in what you do and say in them? Second, look at your habits. Can you see them bringing you closer to God and making you a stronger Christian? Third, look at your thoughts. Are you able to keep them focused upon spiritual things and on a better understanding of Jesus Christ? Fourth, look at your Bible study time. Can you see an everyday habit of reading and meditating on God's Word?

If you can't see any of this, it's highly probable that you're colorblind morally and spiritually. The great news is that you can change your spiritual vision through regular study of the Bible and consistent participation in a Bible-believing church.

Start improving your vision today.

Dear God, I realize that I'm not the one who can determine what is always right. May my spiritual wisdom and eyesight become stronger through focusing upon You all day every day. Give me a hunger for studying the Bible and then applying its truths to my life. Help me learn to distinguish Your will for my life in every setting. In Jesus' name, Amen.

AUGUST 26

CLEANSED AND CLOTHED
Zechariah 3:1–7

Good deeds. They don't live up to their reputation.

No, I'm not against doing good, positive things for others and for this world. But some people believe that good works are all you need to please God and get into heaven. Those people will be sadly disappointed when they one day stand before God's throne for the final judgment.

Follow me here.

In the Old Testament, many priests from the line of Aaron offered sacrifices for the people every day of the year. But there was only one high priest, and only he could enter the Holy of Holies to offer a sacrifice for all of the people. If anyone else entered, they would be killed because they'd dared enter the presence of the holy, almighty God.

As we read the third chapter of Zechariah, we see Joshua standing before God. Remember, Joshua isn't just any person; he's a priest. And he's not just any priest; he's the high priest. But when Zechariah sees Joshua in heaven's light, he immediately realizes that the high priest is *filthy!* His good works mean nothing. His high spiritual standing in the community avails him *nothing* when standing before the absolutely pure creator of the universe!

If Joshua, the high priest, needed clean clothes (representing salvation, forgiveness, and grace) from God, then so do you and I. If the high priest couldn't get to heaven on his own merit, where does that leave you and me?

This would be a good time to stop and thank God for His Son's dying on the Cross to pay for your sins. And if you've not yet done so, now is the time to let Christ take away your sins, have control of your life, and cleanse you completely.

Keep on doing good deeds. But first, ensure that you have a relationship with Jesus Christ that has cleansed you and given you an assured place in heaven.

Heavenly Father, I want You in my heart forever.
I thank You for Christ's death on the Cross for
my sins. I accept His sacrifice, turn from my
sinful ways, and give Jesus control of my life.
Thank You for cleansing me now and forever. In
Jesus' name, Amen.

RUSHING TOWARD DOOM
Zechariah 5:1–6

In their book *Joy Breaks,* one of the authors tells about being late for work one morning. Tied up in bumper-to-bumper traffic and frustrated by other drivers, she suddenly saw a young man on a motorcycle blur by, moving from lane to lane.

He's going way too fast, she thought as he weaved past slower cars. Horns honking and fists waving showed that other drivers felt the same way.

Another hundred yards or so, and the traffic slowed to a crawl. *Oh great. Now what?* Those thoughts were suddenly answered as she saw a broken motorcycle and the body of the young boy covered with a sheet. The author concluded, "Somewhere between where I had been and where I was now, this guy had died."[1]

The young man was like so many people today, rushing toward a doom that awaits them just down the road.

The prophet Zechariah saw the judgment of his people getting ready to be poured out upon the whole land. He knew that they were rushing toward an end that would be both painful and destructive. He painted them—and us—as vivid a picture of an impending curse as he could to warn the Israelites and call them back from the brink of catastrophe. We are told that only a small remnant of the people heard and obeyed. The rest hurried forward to their eternal deaths.

Where is your lifestyle taking you? The truly terrible thing about a rush toward destruction is that you seldom go alone. So perhaps we should rephrase the question: Where are you leading your wife and children? Your daily example is being watched carefully. Others, following in your slipstream, will be pulled along by your influence.

On the other hand, if you heed God regularly, if you pay attention to His warnings and loving guidance, you will also influence others. On your way to heaven, you will strongly touch others'

---

1. Patsy Clairmont, Barbara Johnson, Marilyn Meberg, and Luci Swindoll, *Joy Breaks* (Grand Rapids: Zondervan, 1997), 227–28.

lives. One day, walking down the streets of gold, some individuals whom you love very well might come up, give you a hug, and say, "Thank you for leading me in the right direction. Your example kept me from rushing to my destruction. I'm here in heaven largely because of you."

Where are you going? Is it in the right direction? And who is following you?

Dear Lord, help me to listen when You speak. I don't want to ignore Your warnings or Your guidance. Help me to go in the right direction, and may my loved ones follow me on the same path. In Jesus' name, Amen.

AUGUST 28

YOUR BUILDING PROJECT
Zechariah 6:11–15

How good are you at construction projects? I've begun to discover that when it comes to the whole building process, my ignorance knows no bounds. Recently, I've spent quite a few hours at the offices of an architectural firm. We've been meeting with several contractors, discussing a multimillion-dollar project. They've talked about "costs in Division One." They throw around terms such as *tilt-up walls* and *cost-plus* as if everyone knows what they mean!

Thank goodness I have some very gifted men and women in our church whom I can trust both to understand what is being said and to know how to proceed. The building process is moving along well—in spite of me.

What building project has God given you?

In Zechariah's day, it was the temple of God, and the Lord commissioned Joshua, the high priest, to build it. Your project, on the other hand, might be building a positive influence on others. It might be to build a solid, godly family. Perhaps God wants you to construct a life that touches your church family as you teach adults, teenagers, or children.

The one fact to remember in all of this is that *you* have been given a project from God. We all have one. If you don't get busy building, and if you don't stay faithful in the project, God's kingdom here on earth won't resemble what the Great Architect has designed. And we'll all be the poorer if our projects aren't completed.

Get to work—today.

> *Heavenly Father, help me to know what You want*
> *me to do in life. I want to construct a life that*
> *will be pleasing to You. Today, in all that I do,*
> *may I be in the process of building a testimony*
> *that gives honor to You alone. In Jesus' name,*
> *Amen.*

AUGUST 29

WRONG WORSHIP (PART 1)
Malachi 1:6–10

Today, as we begin reading the book of Malachi, we also begin a three-part series of devotionals on "wrong worship." Malachi can be very instructive for us. If we pay close attention and apply what we've read, we can avoid the mistakes that this prophet's countrymen made.

Let's start our study of "wrong worship" by looking at your attitude.

Your attitude will largely determine if you have a true worship experience at church this weekend. Over the years, I've watched people come out of the same worship service with widely different experiences. One Sunday, the power of God fell upon our congregation in an unusual way. At the close of our services, we always give an invitation to respond to Christ. On this particular day, the people flooded the altar, with at least twelve people coming to Christ and well over twenty decisions of various kinds being made.

After the service, people were glowing as they talked about this great spiritual moment—until I encountered someone with a different take on things. That person walked up to me and said, "We ran ten minutes over today. We just can't allow that!"

Again, your attitude determines much of your worship experience at church.

In today's passage, God told His priests that they were just going through the motions, not really accomplishing anything. They had fallen into the trap of believing that *they themselves* could determine how much devotion to give to God. For example, God's commands concerning the requirement that only unflawed animals be sacrificed are explained clearly and forcefully in Leviticus. The priests, however, were leading the people into wrong paths by accepting and sacrificing the poorest animals that were sickly and covered with flaws.

In other words, the people kept the best for themselves and gave the dregs to God!

The Lord spoke from His holy throne, telling both the priests and the people that their attendance at church meant nothing. Their sacrifices were not seen, and atonement for sin was not being made.

Let's apply this incident to your life.

Are you giving God the very best? Do you give Him the best of your income, your gifts, and your time? Is your attitude right when you enter the church for worship?

If some areas in your life need work, begin making those changes today. Change "wrong worship" to a true, heart-felt worship of your Lord and Savior.

Dear God, I don't want just to go through the motions when I come to church. Help me to give You the best of myself in every area of my life. Show me anything that is not under Your control, and give me the strength to relinquish it to Your Lordship. May I truly worship You this day. In Jesus' name, Amen.

WRONG WORSHIP (PART 2)
Malachi 2:11–17

A golfer was irritated by his caddie's nervousness. "Why do you keep looking at your watch?" he asked.

"This isn't my watch," the caddie responded. "It's a compass."

Wrong worship can also occur when we lose our spiritual direction. The Bible tells us that the heart is "desperately wicked." If we depend primarily upon our own emotions and intuition for spiritual direction, we forfeit a spiritual compass upon which we can depend. Our own ideas about right and wrong lead us farther and farther from God's presence.

God told His people in the second chapter of Malachi that they had "divorced" themselves from Him. They had taken other gods and made those false authority figures prominent in their worship. The people believed that they had done nothing wrong because they were still coming to the synagogue, still sacrificing, still singing the psalms, and still lifting up prayers to Jehovah.

What they had to understand—as do we—is that God says He will share His glory with no other gods. Our God demands complete loyalty and complete obedience. To that end, the Lord has given us a means of discovering if we are lost or if we are on the right path. His Word is our compass. The Bible, learned and applied, will lead us toward right worship and toward the center of God's will.

The Israelites had forsaken God's Word. They had begun trusting in the words of false prophets who said pleasing things to them. They allowed their lust for pleasure and wealth to delude them into thinking that they could live primarily for self and still serve God.

It didn't work then, and it doesn't work now.

What is your spiritual compass? If it is anything other than the Bible, your life is in danger of getting off track. Return to regular reading in, meditation upon, and application of God's Word. It will help you get your life straight and make your worship authentic.

Heavenly Father, May I read Your Word and make it my spiritual compass. May its precepts guide me today as Your Holy Spirit applies the Bible's truths to my life. I want to experience authentic worship when I come into Your house. May my actions follow Your commands and bring honor to Your name. In Jesus' name, Amen.

AUGUST 31

WRONG WORSHIP (PART 3)
Malachi 3:6–10

A teacher was trying to help her students learn how to conjugate verbs properly in Spanish. She asked, "How would you say, 'I need money'?"

From the back of the room, a young man yelled, "Love ya, Mom!"

Money. Its influence in this world is tremendous. Its pull on our life can be stronger than we'd like to admit. If we're not careful, Satan will use our lust for money to pull us far from God's will.

God got very blunt with His people in today's reading. He told them that they were robbing Him! The people were shocked. "How are we robbing You?" they asked. The Lord responded by pointing out that they were not bringing to the synagogue ten percent of everything they earned and produced. Again, they were attending church, praying, and so forth. But their lack of generosity toward God revealed a heart of stone ruled by greed, not God.

How much do you give to God? I'm not talking about amount but percentage. God treats all of us equally. He requires the same percentage from the person who earns $400 a month as He does from the person who earns $100,000 a month. Both are required to give a tithe of their income—10 percent.

According to this passage, when you withhold the tithe from God, you are stealing from Him. And, lest you think that the tithe is only an Old Testament concept, Jesus said that we should tithe all of our income to God, and add in right attitudes toward God and our fellowman, as well!

Authentic worship includes returning to God a portion of the blessings that He's poured out upon you. That portion should *begin* with the tithe.

Dear Lord, I want to do the right thing with my income and possessions. Help me to be generous in returning to You that which Your Word says is rightfully Yours. May You multiply the tithes that I give to You through my church to strengthen and add to Your kingdom. In Jesus' name, Amen.

SEPTEMBER 1

BUILD ON YOUR LEGACY
Matthew 1:1–17

On Good Friday in the year that I turned forty, I saw a picture of my father's father for the first time. I had never seen my grandfather because he died long before I was born. No one in our family knew that a picture of him even existed. Then a distant relative discovered a picture and sent it to my mother. She had a negative made of it and then printed copies for me and my siblings.

The picture shows four men standing on the platform of an oil drilling rig. From the looks of the equipment and the clothes the men wore, I would guess that the time was the 1930s. My grandfather worked in the oilfields of Texas and Louisiana. None of the four men was identified in the picture, but I could tell immediately which man was James Terrell Aycock. He was tall and thin and had the facial features that identified him as one of my forebears. He had the face of my father and the body of my children. I belonged to him.

I do not have any financial wealth in my family. We came from humble beginnings, but I still count myself rich in heritage. People on my mother's side were farmers. Family on my father's side were oilfield workers and laborers of various sorts. But these people left me with a rich legacy of family, values, morals, and ideals. I have tried to sort through all of that during my life and separate the positive from the negative. I want to keep the former and trash the latter.

Everybody comes from somewhere—everybody, including Jesus. Matthew's narrative reaches back into the history of Jesus' family and builds on it. As Jesus' life unfolds in the Gospels, we see that He built on the legacy given by both His earthly and His heavenly fathers.

Build on your legacy and pass on the best that your family has to offer. Someday your progeny can look at your picture and say, "I know him. I look a lot like him."

Lord, help me to look at where I came from and to have the wisdom to separate the helpful from the destructive aspects of my heritage. Let me build a legacy that will bless my family for generations. In Christ, Amen.

SEPTEMBER 2

LIVING A REFUGEE LIFE
Matthew 2

The news media tell us regularly about refugees—those hapless groups who are forced from one location to another through the forces of war, disease, social upheaval, or economic strangulation. A friend went to Rwanda as a photojournalist. I will never forget the pictures he brought back. They showed the stories of people who were caught up in a web of events that were not of their own making. Even so, they paid a heavy price for being part of that society.

Jesus was born into a world in social upheaval. The immediate events of His life were amazing, and His early years were dramatic. His parents had to take the baby Jesus to Egypt to escape the persecution of Herod's army. Jesus was a refugee in Egypt. His story includes being the near-victim of state-sponsored terrorism. Herod, the king, tried to have Jesus executed. Can you imagine an army going to "take out" an infant?

In a sense, all followers of Jesus, even today, are refugees. We are in the world but not of it. We live here in all of the world's confusing demands, its exotic pleasures, and its dangers. But we also live in another realm—the kingdom of God. The Scripture calls us "aliens and strangers in the world" (1 Peter 2:11).

I do not like being a refugee. I want my place. I want to belong to my time and to my culture. But God calls all of us to travel lightly because we cannot take much with us. Our suitcase is very small, and only those elements of lasting value can go into it—things like love, joy, peace, kindness, and faithfulness.

A family running for its life gives a clue to the meaning of following Jesus. We are refugees now, but think of the home that awaits us!

Lord, I want so much, and I want it now. You know how I am. Help me to remember that I belong to a Savior who lived lightly but fully. I really do want to be like Him. In His name, Amen.

SEPTEMBER 3

Shortcuts to Success
Matthew 4:1–11

My father hated to see something done in a shabby way. He was not a neurotic perfectionist, but he simply liked things done in an orderly way. If he was going to build or repair something, he took whatever steps were necessary to accomplish his goal. Dad laughed at people who tried to take shortcuts. He would say of that person, "He hit that job with a lick and a promise."

I think about Dad's saying when I read about Jesus' temptations. Read the temptations carefully, and you will see that what the Devil was trying to get Jesus to do was to take shortcuts to success. In the first one, the Devil knew that Jesus was starved because of His fast. The desert was full of oval rocks that looked just like loaves of bread. The Devil urged Jesus to use His divine powers to turn those stones into real bread. Jesus would not do it because His powers were used only as signs pointing people to

God. Besides, the bread of Jesus was not made with flour and yeast.

The second temptation was another shortcut. The Devil had a sure-fire method of stirring up Jesus' popularity with the people. He told Jesus to go up to the highest point of the temple and jump off. Surely He would not get hurt! The seduction of that idea was to turn Jesus into a wonderworker, a circus performer whose tricks would make people flock to Him. But Jesus was not a trickster who tested God.

The final temptation was the most subtle. Jesus had come to save the world, so all He had to do was to worship the Devil and the whole world would be given to Him. But Jesus had only one de-ity—His Father, the Lord of the universe. Jesus said to the Devil (loosely paraphrased), "Go to blazes!"

Let us not take shortcuts to success in our relationship with God. Do not give it "a lick and a promise."

Father, You alone are my Lord. Forgive me when I let anything interfere with my relationship to You. Give me strength. Through Christ, Amen.

SEPTEMBER 4

FINDING THE RIGHT MODEL
Matthew 6:1–15

Prayer is not magic. Magic is defined thus: "The practice of us-ing charms, spells, or rituals to attempt to produce supernatural effects or to control events in nature."[1] Unfortunately, some Chris-tians think this way about prayer.

A friend of mine owns a small mobile home refurbishing busi-ness. He once found a crumpled up piece of paper in one of the mobile homes and gave it to me. The handwritten note contains a "formula" for praying. This is what is scrawled on that note:

> Get 3 glasses of water at 12 o'clock; pray 3 Our Father
> prayers, pray 3 Twenty-Third Psalms. Set all 3 glasses

1. *The American Heritage Dictionary* (Boston: Houghton Mifflin, 2000).

on refrigerator at 5 A.M. in the morning. Go to front door, Say, 'In the name of the Father, in the name of the Son, in the name of the Holy Ghost.' Follow Thursday. Follow Friday. Get all bills, place on a white plate; take your right hand and place over bills. Pray like you never prayed before; offer bills each up to God. Set plate on top of refrigerator; lay your Bible on Psalm 23; take out as you can pay each bill.

Did this formula for prayer work? I guess not. This paper was found in a repossessed mobile home!

Today's reading includes what is commonly called "The Lord's Prayer." Jesus spoke this prayer when His disciples asked Him to teach them to pray. Some people have seen this as an inerrant formula for prayer that should be repeated without change. I do not see it that way. The prayer is certainly a model, a template for how to reach out to God. But what does it really mean? How are we to pray? Are there certain methods and times and postures?

Over the next few days, let us look at this prayer and understand it as a model for our devotional life.

Lord, teach me how to reach out to You in a way that is pleasing to You. Bless even my feeble efforts. In Jesus' name, Amen.

SEPTEMBER 5

DADDY
Matthew 6:9

Jesus gave a model for His followers to use in praying. It is not some magic formula to success, but it is a guide to know what God will listen and respond to. Let us examine the various parts of the prayer.

Verses 9–10 pertain to God's rule over people and their honoring Him as their Lord.

"Our Father . . ."
Jesus spoke in Aramaic, a language similar to Hebrew. He spoke of God as Abba, which is a personal term similar to our term *daddy.* This term expresses our relationship to God and His nature. God is not only the eternal Lord of the universe but also the Father of Jesus and His followers. Someone has noted, "Abba is a term which speaks of God's friendliness and love, as well as of His parental authority; it suggests that the disciples are children who love and trust God and who try to be obedient to Him."
This is a personal term of address. Christians may reach out to God with the realization that He is our heavenly Father who cares for us.

". . . in heaven . . ."
Whereas the term *Father* suggests that God is close and personal, the term *in heaven* reminds us that God is not just a good buddy next door. He is above and beyond us. God is not earthbound or temporary. He is heavenly and everlasting. He is transcendent.

". . . hallowed be your name . . ."
This part of Jesus' model prayer teaches us that God's name is separate from all other names. It is holy, which is the meaning of the word *hallowed.* In the Bible, someone's name referred to his whole character. God's name is hallowed when His nature and purpose are known and reverenced. We should show reverence for God.

Father, teach me to pray as I remember that You love to hear from me. In Jesus' name, Amen.

SEPTEMBER 6

KEEP ON LEARNING
Matthew 6:10–11

Let us continue looking at the Lord's Prayer as a template for our praying.

"Your kingdom come . . ."

God's kingdom is His rule in the hearts and lives of His people. To pray this part of the prayer is to pledge yourself to join God's effort to extend His rule to everyone. This prayer is sincere when we want others to know the lordship of God.

". . . your will be done on earth as it is in heaven."

This is a request that God's purpose be carried out among persons. What is His purpose? A scholar has written, "God's purpose is to create a worldwide family of persons who freely accept God as their God and who receive his love into their lives, and who respond to him by loving him with all their hearts and loving their neighbors as themselves."

This, in a very succinct manner, is what God wills. When we pray "your will be done," we are saying, "Lord, I want what You will for me. I pledge to work for Your purpose in life."

"Give us today our daily bread."

God's care for His children includes their total welfare. The needs of the body are important as are the needs of the soul. Jesus taught that God is interested in our everyday needs. This includes food, certainly, but I think it includes all of our basic needs.

We may properly pray for *all* matters in our daily lives. This could include our home, our job, our health, our relationships with other people, and our deepest physical and emotional needs. Jesus taught that we can pray about everything that makes up daily life. I take that to mean that God invites our prayers regarding our hurts, our hangups, our sexual desires, our loneliness, and anything else we might want to share with Him and have Him assist us with. In short, we may rightly pray about everything that touches our lives.

More than anything else, Lord, I want Your will in my life. Help me to know it when I see it and to make whatever changes might be necessary. In Christ, Amen.

STAY STRONG
Matthew 6:12–13

We continue our look at the prayer that Jesus gave to His disciples as a model. It shows us how to get stronger in our faith by following the spiritual disciplines of forgiveness and resisting temptation.

"Forgive us our debts, as we also have forgiven our debtors."
More will be said about forgiveness later. For now, we can simply note that Jesus made this a matter of importance. Forgiveness opens the door to relationships, with both God and other people.

"And lead us not into temptation, but deliver us from the evil one."
This part of Jesus' prayer has troubled many people. Does God actually tempt us? The word *temptation* in the original language is *peirasmos*. It can mean both "temptation" and "trial." God does not "tempt" people with evil enticement. James 1:13 says, "Let no one say when he is tempted, 'I am tempted by God'; for God cannot be tempted by evil, nor does He Himself tempt anyone" (NKJV).

I think that Jesus meant that we should pray about the trials that come into our lives. His phrase *and lead us not into temptation* means "do not let us fall into a trial so difficult that we will fail." The issue is testing.

We have seen so far that God invites our petitions. In God's grace, our prayers matter to God! Things happen when people pray. "God," said Pascal, a seventeenth-century philosopher, "instituted prayer in order to lend to His creatures the dignity of causality."[1] Our prayers matter.

Since we have been thinking about prayer over the past few days, we noticed that Jesus gave us a model—a template—for our own praying. We can pray about everything—our daily food needs, our relationships, and our desire to join God in what He is doing.

Stay strong. Pray.

---

1. Pascal, *Pensees*, 513.

*Hear the deepest desire of my heart, Lord, as I
seek to strengthen my relationship to You.
Through Jesus, my Lord, Amen.*

FORGIVE THE GUY
Matthew 6:14–15

Jesus concluded His model prayer with these words: "For if you forgive others for their transgressions, your heavenly Father will also forgive you. But if you do not forgive others, then your Father will not forgive your transgressions" (NASB). These are strong and straightforward words. Make no mistake. Genuine forgiveness is not easy! A library says it "forgives" fines, but that is not really forgiveness. Genuine forgiveness is costly to all involved. It cost God the life of His Son to forgive us. It costs our pride and rebellion to accept it. Forgiveness between people is equally costly because we must open the door to people who have betrayed or hurt us. That is not easy.

The alternative—not to forgive—is even worse. "If you do not forgive others, then your Father will not forgive your transgressions." It is that simple and that difficult. Prayer is too important to leave to chance or to misunderstand. After all, prayer is getting in touch with the Lord of all creation, all time, and all space. What could compare with that?

But let's face this fact. Many people have great questions about prayer and think of it as nonsense. Winston Churchill recalled his early life that included rebelling against the idea of faith and prayer. He said, "I passed through a violent and aggressive anti-religious phase. . . . My poise was restored during the next few years by frequent contact with danger. I found that whatever I might think and argue, I did not hesitate to ask for special protection when about to come under the fire of the enemy."[1]

Prayer takes us into the presence of God, who forgives us and calls us to forgive one another. Is there someone you need to forgive?

---

1. Kenneth Cooper, *It's Better to Believe* (Nashville: Thomas Nelson, 1995), 31.

Lord, help me to forgive _____ *. You*
know what happened between us. As You forgave
me, so I forgive _____ *. In Jesus' name,*
Amen.

SEPTEMBER 9

OPEN FOR BUSINESS
Matthew 9:1–8

A guy I know keeps his mind sharp although he is getting up in years. He avoids pickling his brain with alcohol; instead, he keeps it flexible by using it regularly. After he retired as a university professor, he went back to school to study French. When I asked him why, he just smiled and said, "It's fun." When I think about this older friend, I think of him "open for business."

I know another man who seemed to close his mind when he was in his twenties. He went for years without ever reading a book, learning a new skill, trying anything different, intentionally meeting new people, or in general, pushing himself out of a rut. When I think of him, I consider him "closed for business."

Someone once said that a rut is just a grave with the ends kicked out of it. He was on to something.

Look at today's reading. Jesus felt compassion on a crippled man and healed him. You would think that everyone would get excited about such an act of God. But that did not happen. Matthew records, "Some of the teachers of the law said to themselves, 'This fellow is blaspheming!'" (v. 3). They were more concerned with their own preconceived ideas than with the movement of God.

But another group was there. Matthew simply calls them "the crowd." When they saw the miracle, "they were filled with awe; and they praised God" (v. 8). To them, God was not a problem to be contained; He was a reality to be experienced. Two groups saw the same thing but reacted in far different ways. One was "open for business," and the other was "closed for business."

To which group do you belong? Are you genuinely open to God, or do you secretly hope that He does nothing to upset your routine?

Father, sometimes I live in a fog and seem to wander rather than wonder. Help me open my eyes, heart, and mind to You. In Jesus' name, Amen.

FERTILE FOR HIM
Matthew 13:1–9

I worked on a rice farm during the summer between my junior and senior years in high school. One of the most enjoyable events was driving a tractor with a drill that planted the rice in uniform rows. Later, a combine would go through the field and harvest the grain. It was a highly efficient way of working.

The work of God is never quite that efficient. Jesus told a parable about a farmer who also plants his seeds, but his work is not so precise. Some of the seeds fall on the path beside the field. Other seeds end up in the untilled rocky patches. Still others end up among the weeds that choke them out.

But some of the seeds—and this is the saving point—fall on the tilled ground and grow. Their growth makes up for the rest that were lost among the thorns and footpaths. This seed grows and produces up to one hundred times what was sown. That is a 10,000 percent profit! How would you like to get that on your 401(k) plan?

Remember one thing about the hard path, the rocky patches, and the thorny ground, the areas that produce nothing: they are all pretty much *within the same field.* They are all part of us. You and I have this area of experience and thought that is packed down and impervious to the seed. We have outcroppings of the soul that are filled with the stones of rebellion and pride. And we all possess thorns that we protect and even cultivate. The gospel might take hold there for a while, but we are secretly glad when it withers in that place.

Maybe I am speaking for only myself here. But I am all of these areas. Unless I am badly mistaken, you are too. Our task is to let the Lord cultivate *all* of us so that we can be fertile for Him.

Lord, sink the plowshare of Your truth deeply into my soul. Cultivate every area of my life so that it becomes productive for You. Through Jesus, Amen.

SEPTEMBER 11

DYING TO LIVE
Matthew 16:21–28

Today is a terrible anniversary in the life of America. Who can forget where he was on September 11, 2001? Since that day, new words and realities have come into our thinking and speech. We now use words such as *Taliban, Bin Laden, domestic terrorism,* and *homeland security.*

We are tempted to think that the world is "going to hell in a handbasket." But humanity has always known terror, hostilities, and death. Jesus knew what humankind was like. No one needed to teach Him that lesson. Many of His followers, though, were not so sure. They seemed to drift along in a dreamy fog, believing that being on Jesus' team meant that their prospects were about to look up. Jesus regularly clapped His hands and brought them out of their reverie. He told them that some terrible events were about to happen to them.

In today's reading, Jesus predicted His death: "He must be killed" (v. 21). Those words must have been like ice water poured on someone who was sleeping. Peter said, in effect, "That will never happen to you as long as I'm around!" (see v. 22). Big words from a little man. Maybe the others joined in and said the same thing. They were not so much interested in protecting Jesus as in protecting themselves. After all, if He died, what would happen to them?

Jesus wanted no part of this bragging macho talk. He informed them that His death would be followed by something unexpected from the dead—He would rise from the grave! Then He invited His disciples to follow His action: "If anyone would come after me, he must deny himself and take up his cross and follow me" (v. 24).

On this sad anniversary, reflect on what taking up your cross means to you. Always remember: a cross leads to a resurrection.

Lord, I am afraid to take my cross. People will laugh, or misunderstand, or take advantage of me. They did that to Your son. So give me the courage to hoist it onto my shoulders and point it toward a resurrection. In Jesus' name, Amen.

When Discipline Is Hard

Matthew 18:15–20

Dave seeps hostility the way a pine tree seeps tar—bitter, sticky, and potentially deadly. Dave tells everyone that he is a Christian, but people know that if he is what Christianity represents, they want no part of it. Oh, he has a few redeeming qualities, but his actions speak so much louder than his words! Most people avoid him because they do not want to get caught up in the web of his passive-aggressive words and actions.

You might be thinking, "Hey, I know that guy." Most of us know people like him and know that dealing with them is tough, especially in church. Just what do you do with a man who creates havoc everywhere he goes? How does the church exercise some control over him at least to limit the damage he can do?

Jesus gave His followers a step-by-step pattern for confronting people like Dave. Look at the progression of the discipline. First, there should be an attempt to settle differences between just the two individuals. If it can be worked out at that level, great. But if not, go to the next level. The person seeking to correct the problem goes back to the person causing the trouble and takes one or two others with him. Maybe the issue can be resolved there. If not, Jesus said to "tell it to the church" (v. 17).

That is serious business. The point is not to cause a scandal but to prevent one.

If the person causing the problems will not listen even to the church, then you "treat him as you would a pagan or a tax collector" (v. 17). How does the church treat a pagan? It tries to win him to the gospel.

Disciplining a member of a church is difficult work, but it is sometimes necessary for the good of the body. Is there something like this that needs your intervention?

Lord, help me have the courage to get involved if someone is tearing up Your church. Let me act with love and compassion as Jesus taught us. In His name, Amen.

JESUS WAS A MAN
Matthew 21:11

Jesus was not some phantom; neither was He a coward. He looked His enemies in the eyes and said, "Do your worst. I won't back up." He told His followers that He had to go to Jerusalem. That need was theological.

On the surface, Jesus' journey into Jerusalem was disastrous. The week began with adoration. That was followed by rejection, then humiliation, and finally crucifixion. It makes little "sense" in the normal meaning of that word. From God's perspective, however, it was absolutely necessary.

Carl Sandburg wrote a multivolume set of books on the life of Abraham Lincoln. One volume has a chapter titled "Palm Sunday '65." It was about the date of April 9, 1865, when Robert E. Lee surrendered to Ulysses S. Grant at Appomattox Court House in Virginia. On that Palm Sunday, the war ended, and peace began to reign. A few skirmishes flared up here and there until everyone finally got the word, but the war really was over.

That is not a bad analogy to what happened on the day of Jesus' last ride into Jerusalem. God was ready to present His peace plans to men. There would be no compromise. A skirmish broke out on Friday, but men did not yet realize that the battle was over. Jesus faced the forces of evil armed with only the power of self-giving love, but that was enough. God is still seeking to let everyone know that the battle is over and that Christ won.

Where do you stand in relationship to this man Jesus? Do you know Him personally? If not, this would be a great day to say "yes" to Him. Open your life to this Man. You will never be the same.

Lord, I do open my heart to You. Fill me and change my life. In the name of Jesus, Amen.

SEPTEMBER 14

HOLY TEMPER
Matthew 21:12–18

Most of us men have trouble with our tempers. What to do about it is the lesson of the cleansing of the temple. The temple should have been a place of peace, tranquility, and an aura conducive to worship. Instead, it was a place of noise as the traders and pilgrims haggled, swore, and bargained for animals and coins. It was filled with the smell of sheep dung and pigeon droppings. The place that should have been open and inviting was closed and costly.

Jesus was angry—good and angry. He should have been! How could anyone with any moral sensibilities view the temple with its corruption and not be angry? Many modern Christians have great difficulty with anger. We have been taught that to be angry is "wrong." Certainly harboring strong feelings of hostility is wrong. If I am hostile toward my brother, my hostility hurts me much more than it does him. Our responsibility is to deal with the feelings and not let them smolder like coals that will burst into flame at any moment. Paul said, for example, "Therefore each of you must put off falsehood and speak truthfully to his neighbor, for we are all members of one body. 'In your anger do not sin': Do not let the sun go down while you are still angry, and do not give the devil a foothold" (Eph. 4:25–27). The phrase *put off falsehood* means, among other things, that we are to be honest in our feelings, including anger.

Learn to control your anger before it controls you. Jesus got it right. He, not some sports figure or tycoon, is our model.

Father, help me use my anger for righteous purposes, not to explode on those around me simply to make me feel better. In Christ's name, Amen.

EXTRAVAGANT LOVE
Matthew 26:6–13

How would you like a $50,000 shampoo? Does that sound a little extravagant? It is, of course, but it is what the woman in this story gave to Jesus. She was carrying an alabaster jar of perfume extract that was to be used one drop at a time. But instead of rationing out a drop, she impulsively snapped the neck off the bottle and poured the entire contents on Jesus' head.

It was an extravagant, even an insane gesture. That essence was worth a year's wages to common working people. Would you blow a full year's salary on one event? Any event? It is beyond comprehension. How would we pay the bills? Who would feed the kids? What about the taxes? The woman probably never asked such questions of herself. She simply acted impulsively but decidedly. There is a time for rational, methodical thinking. Someone has to look out after the bank account and keep the food on the table. But there is a time to act, to move out with your feelings as well as with your rational thinking. Few people get married by sitting down and saying, "Here are twelve reasons for our getting married, but here are twelve equally strong reasons for our not getting married. Let's flip a coin and see which it will be." In such matters, the heart—feelings—is as important as the mind—thinking.

This woman understood that something about Jesus was different than other men. Pouring a year's salary over His head might not have been "smart," but it surely was intense. Her passion in this matter puts me to shame. Maybe you are included here, too. I am seldom passionate for Christ. I do not mean that we should be "happy clappies" for Jesus all of the time. But have you ever responded to the extravagant love of Jesus? Give as you have been given.

Your extravagant love for me overwhelms me,
Lord. May my response toward You be pleasing as
I respond honestly. In Jesus' name, Amen.

AMAZED ONCE MORE

Mark 1:21–28

The people who heard Jesus teach were "amazed" at His authority. I think of that fact often. One reason is that I have become jaded or negligent or spiritually hard of hearing. I am seldom amazed at what Jesus does. If my confession catches you off guard, good. We should be honest with each other because that is exactly what Jesus was—honest.

Mark notes, "The people were amazed at his teaching, because he taught them as one who had authority, not as the teachers of the law" (v. 22). After Jesus drove the spirit from the man, the people responded, "What is this? A new teaching—and with authority! He even gives orders to evil spirits and they obey him" (v. 27). The term *authority* here is *exousia. Ex* means "out" or "out of," as in our word *exit. Ousia* means "essence," or "inner reality." Jesus' authority was thus His inner reality. He spoke "out of" His "essence." This was integrity and authenticity that had never been seen before or since.

Are you hungry both to hear and to experience truth? Are you tired of living a footnote life, one that takes its meaning and directions from everyone other than Jesus? I am. What I want is authenticity and openness that does not play games. I want my life to count for something in the world beyond the mortgage and the pressures of everyday life. Most of us men are tired of dragging around a religious ball and chain. Let us resolve to live like men. Let us take our cues from the one who spoke out of His essence and who amazed His hearers.

Let's live the truth, tell the truth, and be the truth. Let's be amazed once more.

Lord, amaze us! Fill us with truth so powerful that we say "Wow!" Father, don't let us wither away. Help us to really live. In Jesus' amazing name, Amen.

DESPERATE DISCIPLESHIP
Mark 2:1–12

I have been working on a formula for my spiritual life. See what you think of this: *desperation plus imagination and effort equals success.* Where did I get this? Right from today's reading. You know the story. Some men wanted to take a crippled friend to see Jesus and ask for healing. When they got to the location, their paths were blocked. Everybody else wanted the same thing. They could not get into the front door so they made their own door—in the roof.

I love that! They were not about to be turned back because the way was not paved and they were not escorted by a visible angel. Far too often I hear people say things like, "I just didn't feel that the door was open to me." Well, make another door! Yes, I know that often life really does seem to close off certain paths to us. I know a man who wanted to play in the NFL. He actually made the pros but discovered once he was there that that was really not what he wanted. He backed up and searched for another door.

The paralyzed man had some great friends. They knew his desperation enough that they used their imaginations and put their thinking into action. Jesus noticed their effort and said to the man, "Son, your sins are forgiven" (v. 5). That shook everyone up. At the end of the story, Mark records, "This amazed everyone and they praised God, saying, 'We have never seen anything like this!'" (v. 12).

God, as described in the Bible, is not a boring, safe deity! He is active and surprising. His Son Jesus was, too. I imagine that He laughed aloud when His sermon was interrupted by a bunch of intense guys with enough guts to cut their own path to Him.

Are you desperate? Congratulations. Put on your thinking cap and get busy.

Lord, I'm coming to You, no matter what is in my way. Through Christ, Amen.

BEWARE A BARREN LIFE
Mark 11:12–25

Some religious practices are meant to promote the person doing them rather than to glorify God. That is the insight of today's reading.

This story is tied by Mark with the cleansing of the temple. On the way to the temple, Jesus saw a fig tree that was in full leaf but empty of fruit. He pronounced a curse on it. A fig tree with no fruit was exactly like a temple that produced no spiritual fruit. One commentator noted, "The incident of the fig tree both interprets the cleansing of the temple and is interpreted by the latter incident. Jesus' disappointment with the fig tree is like his disappointment with Israel and the temple, her chief shrine. His judgment pronounced upon the tree is like the threat of God's judgment soon to fall upon the city of Jerusalem."

The cursing of the tree was a prophetic sign. Isaiah had gone naked to show what would happen to the nation (Isa. 20:1–6). Jeremiah smashed a clay pot to symbolize the fate of his nation (Jer. 19:1–13). Ezekiel drew on a clay tablet a city under siege. It was a symbol of the coming siege of Jerusalem (Ezek. 4:1–17). Jesus did not swear at the tree but rather used it as an object lesson for His disciples.

The fig tree's leaves promised fruit, but there was no fruit. The tree's appearance was deceptive. It was a symbol of what Jesus had found in the temple. It, too, looked promising. The temple had a long history and promised seekers that they could find a place of worship, a place that would help them find God. What they found was chaos like the day after Christmas at the mall.

We can get mighty busy doing all sorts of religious stuff. But let us beware of getting so busy that we end up spiritually barren. Slow down enough for the fruit to ripen.

*Prune my branches, Lord, so that I can produce
some fruit for You. In Jesus' name, Amen.*

DO YOU RECOGNIZE HIM?
Mark 14:1–11

One of the ironies of spiritual life is that we tend to get too comfortable with God. This leads to a kind of spiritual amnesia. The early church knew this. After the fourth century, Christian artists began adding new figures to paintings of the nativity. What they added were an ox and a donkey. This came from their interpretation of Isaiah 1:2–3: "Hear, O heavens! Listen, O earth! For the LORD has spoken: 'I reared children and brought them up, but they have rebelled against me. The ox knows his master, the donkey his owner's manger, but Israel does not know, my people do not understand." The Lord is known by even the ox and the donkey, but He is ignored by many people!

Today, many people still scoff at the whole idea of Jesus. They treat His name with contempt and use it as a curse. They make tasteless jokes about Him and use Him as the butt of gross stories. It makes no difference, though, because you cannot laugh God out of existence or joke your way out of moral responsibility.

One man whose life had been changed by a saving experience with Christ was laughed at by his fellow workers. He had been a heavy drinker who spent his paychecks on booze. "Hey, you really don't believe in miracles do you?" they would taunt. "Do you accept the story about Jesus turning water into wine?" He thought for a moment and said, "I can tell you this. He has turned beer into furniture!"

The recognition of who Jesus is for us is the beginning of eternal life. But we need to be clear-eyed about our tendency to turn our backs on Him and forget Him. Mark adds to this section the sad details of Judas Iscariot's betrayal. It is like a light house shining its beam on the shoals that will shipwreck our faith. Don't forget Jesus.

Forgive my tendency to forget You, Lord. I will remember and recognize You. In Christ's name, Amen.

A DANGEROUS MEMORY
Mark 14:12–26

I have an "Old Timer" pocketknife that belonged to my father. I keep it in a drawer, but every time I take it out and look at it I cannot help but think of him. He was not a man of many personal possessions. He never had a record collection or a personal library of favorite books. My dad was a simple man who kept only things such as his clothes and his garden tools. The knife is special. It was uniquely his. I see it and remember that he never went anywhere without it. He used it to cut string and to clean the catch when we went fishing together. It was well used on his job in the oil fields of southern Louisiana. I see that old knife and remember his struggle with lung cancer for a year and a half. It has so many associations for me that I can hardly begin to list them. It brings both smiles and tears.

The Lord's Supper is like that. It might have become a staid and somber event in some modern churches, but it was not that originally. It used bread that reminded the Jews of slavery and tears and backbreaking work. It used wine, dangerous heady stuff that looked like blood. The disciples would never again have a Passover meal without thinking about that last meal with Jesus. They would remember the deep feelings, the strong emotions, the fear, and the hope.

Our remembrance might never be that intense, but it can be a time of reflection that looks both backward and forward. It stirs up a dangerous memory in us because it changes us. We know ourselves to belong to someone beyond us.

Dad's "Old Timer" knife was made to cut things. One thing it cuts is my conscience every time I see it. I remember him and want to make him proud—just like my heavenly Father.

Jog my memory, Lord, so I do not forget You and Your benefits toward me. Stir my memory. In Jesus' name, Amen.

THE GREAT "YET"
Mark 14:32–42

The last Friday of Jesus' life showed Him in an enormous struggle. His inner conflict and the outcome of the struggle was paradoxical. On the one hand, Jesus had come to give His life. On the other hand, He was free not to give it but to escape from Jerusalem and continue to live. Only by being free not to die was He free to give His life willingly. He prayed in all seriousness, "Father, . . . everything is possible for you. Take this cup from me" (v. 36). But then came the great *yet*—"Yet not what I will, but what you will" (v. 36). That willingness to do God's will is what made the difference.

Most people want to cling to life at all costs and will do almost anything to escape death. An ancient Persian story tells of a rich man who was walking in his garden with one of his servants. The servant cried out that he had just encountered Death, who threatened him. The servant begged his master for the use of his fastest horse so he could flee to Teheran, which he could reach that night. The master consented and the servant galloped off at full speed. On returning to the house, the master himself met Death and questioned him, "Why did you terrify and threaten my servant like that?" Death said, "I did not threaten him. I only showed surprise in finding him here when I had planned to meet him in Teheran tonight."

Whatever else the Gethsemane experience might have been, it was at least Jesus' victory in following His Father's will to its completion. The integrity that had given Him authority on Tuesday also carried Him through Friday.

We have worked for many things in life—good careers, family, financial stability, and so on. We want so much, but I hope that we are willing to pray with all seriousness, "Lord, You know my desires, yet not what I want. . . ."

Father, I give You this yet in my life. If You have plans for me other than my own, I will follow them. Show them to me. In Jesus' name, Amen.

THE CROSS AND MY LIFE

Mark 15:33–41

Menelik II was the emperor of Ethiopia from 1889 until 1913. News of a successful new means of dispatching criminals reached him. The news was about a device known as an electric chair. The emperor eagerly ordered one for his country. Unfortunately, no one bothered to warn him that it would never work because Ethiopia at that time had no electricity. Menelik was determined that his new purchase should not go to waste. He converted the electric chair into a throne.

There was another time when an instrument of death became a throne. God decided to give Himself to humanity in a new way in the Incarnation. He fully accepted the risk that people would react to His Son in exactly the same way that people react to everything— some accept, some reject, and some ignore. Jesus died on a cross and was genuinely dead. That He would offer Himself in that way is amazing and incomprehensible.

George Herbert's old poem says it as well as anything else:

> *Love is that liqueur sweet and most divine.*
> *Which my God feels as blood but I as wine.*
> *What is blood to God is life and joy to me!*

Jesus accepted suffering as the way to bring people to God. Henry Nelson Wieman pointed out many years ago that pain and suffering are not the same thing. Suffering is a meaningful, communicable event. According to Wieman, emotional maturity is the willingness to incur suffering that creative good might emerge.

Jesus accepted the suffering on the Cross for the transformation of sinful people to take place. When all is said and done, I really cannot explain that fact. I can only proclaim it. Do you know this Lord who went to the Cross for us?

Lord, what You did for me! I can hardly believe it, much less fully understand it. Thank You for a resurrected life. Through Jesus, Amen.

WHEN GOD SEEMS SILENT

Mark 15:42–47

Our toughest times are those when God seems silent. Do you know what I mean? We pray, go about our lives doing the best we can, and carry on with our religious duties. We reach out to heaven, but no one seems to answer. The Saturday between the Crucifixion and the Resurrection is symbolic of that silence.

Philip Yancey tells of a priest who knew a doctor's family in Paraguay. This doctor spoke out against the human rights abuses of the military regime. To silence him, the local police arrested his teenage son and tortured him to death. The people of the village where he had lived wanted to turn the funeral into a protest march, but the father chose another course of action. Instead of dressing the boy for the funeral, the doctor laid the boy out just as he had come from the prison. His naked body was full of bruises from beatings, scars from the electric shocks, and burns from cigarettes. The body was not laid out in a coffin but was laid on the blood-soaked mattress from the jail. Injustice was on public display.

Yancey wrote, "The Cross of Christ may have overcome evil, but it did not overcome unfairness. For that, Easter is required. Someday, God will restore all physical reality to its proper place under his reign. Until then, it is a good thing to remember that we live out our days on Easter Saturday."[1]

Much of our lives seem to be lived in this "in between" time—not crucifixion but not resurrection either. Perhaps the greatest act of faith is to go on in spite of the seeming silence from God. If life is quiet for you now, carry on. The silence does not last forever.

Lord, I do not always understand Your silence toward me, but I accept Your wisdom. When You are ready, speak that I might hear You. In Christ, Amen.

---

1. Philip Yancey, *Disappointment With God* (Grand Rapids: Zondervan, 1988), 186.

THAT GREAT GETTIN' UP MORNING
Mark 16

On Easter Sunday, Christ broke out of the seeming permanence of death. That breakthrough was a sign of what lies in store for any who will come to Christ as a follower. It was also a sign of the ability of God to break through every form of barrier, hindrance, and grave that stands in His way. This happens in our lives when we accept Him. It happens when God gets "under the skin" of even the most outward pagan.

When George Bush was vice president of the United States, one of his official duties was to represent our country at the funeral of Leonid Brezhnev, the leader of the former Soviet Union. The entire funeral procession was marked by its military precision. A coldness and hollowness enveloped it. Because the Soviet Union was officially atheistic, no comforting prayers or spiritual hymns were sung. Only the marching soldiers, steel helmets, and Marxist rhetoric were offered. No mention of God was made.

Mr. Bush was close to the casket when Mrs. Brezhnev came for her last good-bye. Bush says, "She walked up, took one last look at her husband and there—in the cold, gray center of that totalitarian state, she traced the sign of the cross on her husband's chest. I was stunned. In that simple act, God had broken through the core of the communist system."[1]

That act stuns me, too; but I realize that no system can wall God out just as no tomb can wall God in. Evil had its day on Friday, but Sunday was coming.

Easter Sunday is our day! It is the harbinger of what is to come. Some day all who have lived in Christ will experience resurrection to eternal life. As the old spiritual puts it, "That'll be the great gettin' up morning!"

Include me in that number, Lord, for I want to be with You for eternity. In Jesus' name, Amen.

---

1. George Bush, quoted in *Christianity Today*, 16 October 1987, 37.

No Need for Pretensions
Luke 2:1–7

I have visited the graves of two men who were, in their time, the most powerful men in the world. The first grave was that of Winston Churchill. His grave is a short distance from Blenheim Place near Oxford, England. I had expected that Churchill's grave would be something magnificent. What I found both surprised and disappointed me. It was so small and unpretentious. It looked fairly ordinary and nothing like what I had expected. It was in a small plot with just a few other graves around and looked much like the final resting place of any other man.

Another grave I visited was that of Harry S. Truman. Like that of Churchill, Truman's grave is not very elaborate or large. It is located on the grounds of his Presidential Library in Independence, Missouri, and is well kept but not ornate. Again, I felt a sense of letdown when I saw it.

Think of it—two powerful men and two small, ordinary graves. It was too simple.

If I had gotten to write the story of the coming of the Son of God into the world, I would want grandeur and pretensions. I would make it look like a Hollywood production. Not only that, I would make certain that *everybody* would know about it. But God did not ask me or anyone with my mentality to write the story. Instead, God seems to have gone out of His way to send His Son in a quiet, unpretentious manner.

Read the story again. It is so ordinary. For whatever reasons, God has no need for hype. He has no public relations firm—only a church filled with people like you and me. To my amazement, that is enough.

Lord, help me to hear Your story carefully and to participate in that story on Your terms. Thanks for letting me have a little part. In Jesus' name, Amen.

KEEP ON KNOCKING
Luke 11:9–13

The following ad appeared in a local paper a few years ago, placed by a person calling herself Sister Roberts: "The Southern Born Spiritualist who brings you the solutions to the mysteries of the Deep South, seeks to help many thousands of people who have been Crossed, Have Spells, Can't Hold Money, Want Luck. . . . If you are seeking a sure-fire woman to Aid in Peace, Love and Prosperity in the home, you need to see this woman of God today!" After pointing out how close to God she is, the lady closed with these words in big bold type: "Special This Week: All readings only $5.00 each."

When Jesus said, "Ask, seek, knock," did He mean anything like that? Are we "guaranteed" anything beyond God's care? In Greek, the words *ask, seek,* and *knock* are present imperatives. A present imperative is a command to continuous action. Jesus thus says, "Keep on asking, keep on seeking, keep on knocking." One quick prayer ripped off in a moment of need might or might not be answered. Jesus' point is that we can be assured of God's answer as we continue to seek God's will. Some answers come only after much effort and patience.

We have many needs because life is so unpredictable. The following notice appeared in the window of a coat store in Nottingham, England:

> We have been established for over 100 years and been pleasing and displeasing customers ever since. We have made money and lost money, suffered the effects of coal nationalization, coal rationing, government control, and bad payers. We have been cussed and discussed, messed about, lied to, held up, robbed, and swindled. The only reason we stay in business is to see what happens next.

Life is adventurous. Pray hard. Keep on knocking. The door will open.

Lord, I pray, not to some impersonal force in the universe, but to You, my heavenly Father. You are closer than my own heartbeat. Hear me now. In Jesus' name, Amen.

SEPTEMBER 27

KEEP AN OPEN EAR
Luke 13:1–5

An accident happened at a construction site. Part of the tower that the workers had been erecting fell. Several people were killed and others were injured. The horrible event happened in an instant with no warning.

I am not reading the morning newspaper—I am reading the Bible. Today's reading tells about an accident that all of Jerusalem knew about. A tower fell and killed eighteen men. Was it just a random event, or did it have some significance? Jesus spoke about it while trying to teach people about the unpredictable nature of life. He did not blame the workers, the government, or God. What Jesus did say was something like this: "Keep your ears open to every event in your life."

He called on His hearers to realize that life is fragile. One minute you are working at your job, the next an accident happens and you are facing eternity. Jesus called on people to repent. That did not indicate that the men who were killed in the accident died because they were great sinners. Far from it. They were exactly like everyone else.

When we learn to keep our ears open for the voice of God, we begin to hear messages from unexpected places. An accident can remind us of our need to be ready to stand before God. The birth of a child can teach us about the provision for life's continuance by our heavenly Father. The words *I forgive you* spoken by a spouse can be the Lord's lesson of His similar forgiveness.

In a sense, we learn to listen for these messages with a third ear, one tuned to spiritual frequencies. Much in our lives has no explanation. Jesus did not explain why the tower fell. It just did, but for those who are listening, it taught a needed lesson.

Father, dig the wax out of my spiritual ears so I can really hear You. In Christ's name, Amen.

KNOWING A RISEN SAVIOR
Luke 24:1–12

What do you do with your dashed dreams and smashed hopes? The events of that first Easter gives us clues. Mary's dashed dreams and hopeless outlook had not yet been changed by an encounter with the One for whom Easter is remembered. She still thought that the Son of God was dead! In the 1960s, a movement swept across the country that proclaimed confidently, "God is dead." But that movement is now dead, and people still look to Easter as a lighthouse in a storm.

Some modern people feel as hopeless about life as Mary did. Some singles want a loving and lasting relationship but seem to have trouble establishing it. Some adults feel trapped in their jobs. Some teenagers think that life is a bad joke and end their lives. It is to such people, as well as to the rest of us, that the good news of Easter is directed. Not everyone, though, can see or experience this good news without some help. One of the reasons churches exist is to help people find meaning in life as interpreted through Easter faith. Such faith is a filter that affects every action and claim to truth. If the tomb was emptied because of God, then life takes on a very different meaning than if enemies simply stole Jesus' body.

Mary went to the tomb overwhelmed with grief and hopelessness. At first, she was not in an emotional state to see what had occurred. Eyes of faith are needed to penetrate through the fog of grief and disappointment. Not only that, but a special way of looking at life is needed.

Easter joy is not apparent to many people. They must be taught to "see" what is not openly evident to everyone. When you look at Christ, what do you see?

*Help me see, Lord, really see. I want to know the
risen Savior and live in His resurrected life.
Through His name, Amen.*

SEPTEMBER 29

YOU CAN'T EXTINGUISH THE LIGHT
John 1:1–5

My wife and I have visited Mammoth Cave in Kentucky on several occasions. On the first trip, we were in a group that was guided into the largest underground cavern. The guide had everyone sit as she talked about the history of the cave and the nature of its labyrinth. Then the guide said, "Now everyone get ready because I'm going to show you what the cave looks like in its natural condition." Then she turned out the lights! The darkness was so thick it was disorienting. No one could see anything.

After letting everyone experience complete darkness for a moment, the guide lit one match. The transformation was astounding. That one tiny match illuminated the faces of everyone in that group.

John begins his gospel with the astounding news that the light has come into the world. That light did battle with the darkness in the way the match did in Mammoth Cave. John's conclusion is certain: "The light shines in the darkness, but the darkness has not understood it" (v. 5). Another translation says, "the darkness has never put it out" (PHILLIPS). The meaning is that light penetrates the darkness.

Penetrate the darkness—that is exactly what Christ did. He entered this dark and dangerous world as the source of illumination. He shines in every life that is open to Him. His light shined brightly for about three years of public ministry. Then the forces of darkness banded together and said, "He has to go." One Friday afternoon, they poured water over this flame and laughed as it went out. Little did they know that the light would reignite three days later.

Are you stumbling around in the darkness? If so, why not reach for the light switch?

Father of all light, shine Your beam of love and redemption upon me. Lead me out of the darkness by the power of Your light. In Jesus' name, Amen.

A WORK WELL DONE
John 20:30–31; 21:25

The gospel accounts of the life of Jesus are short. At times, they seem too short. Why did they not offer more details about His teenage years? Why do they not tell about what He looked like? What happened to His earthly father, Joseph? We could ask a thousand questions that have no answers in the Gospels. But they were not written for our questions; they were written to tell us what God has in mind for us.

In today's reading, John says that Jesus did many things that were not recorded in the Gospels. Some of our questions will have to wait for answers. What was recorded, however, is there for a specific purpose: "that you may believe that Jesus is the Christ, the Son of God, and that by believing you may have life in his name" (20:31).

John ends his book with this conclusion: "Jesus did many other things as well. If every one of them were written down, I suppose that even the whole world would not have room for the books that would be written" (21:25). What a statement! I have been in some great libraries. Did John mean that they would not have shelf space for Jesus' words?

I think that John was using an expression to mean that Jesus' work was so important that it could not be contained in ordinary time and space. Everything we need to know is recorded, but there is much more that will have to wait.

Jesus left a work well done. You and I have the opportunity to accept the spiritual life that He offers and to join Him in the ongoing work of His kingdom. That will change us as we help to transform the world.

Maybe heaven will have a library filled with every word that Jesus spoke. Until we find out, we can read the words recorded in Scripture and participate in work well done.

*Lord, I have plenty of questions. Someday You
will tell me all of the answers. Until that time, I
am content to learn, to work, and to serve.
Through Christ, Amen.*

OCTOBER 1

WHEN POWER FALLS

Acts 2:1–14, 37–41

R. C. Sproul is a greatly respected theologian and philosopher. While speaking to a group of people several years ago, he was asked, "What, in your opinion, is the greatest spiritual need in the world today?"

Dr. Sproul replied, "The greatest need in people's lives today is to discover the true identity of God." He went on to say that many unbelievers have rejected God, not because they truly understand who He is, but because they have a false idea of God's personality and character.

Dr. Sproul was then asked, "What, in your opinion, is the greatest spiritual need in the lives of church people?"

The great theologian gave the same answer as before! "To discover the true identity of God. If believers really understood the character and the personality and the nature of God, it would revolutionize their lives."[1]

On the day of Pentecost, both believers and unbelievers got a glimpse of God's power and ability to change lives. Before the day was over, the church had become infused with power, and Jerusalem had seen about three thousand citizens and visitors become followers of Jesus Christ.

When we long to see God and know more of Him, *so that we can better share Him with others,* God reveals Himself to His people. He gives us divine power to handle the problems of life. He gives us an amazing love for others that draws them into a circle of wonderful fellowship. God gives us, in Jesus Christ, both a portrait of Himself and a character map that we are to follow in shaping our lives.

---

1. Bill Hybels, *The God You're Looking For* (Nashville: Nelson, 1997), 4.

Let's ask God, today, to begin revealing Himself to us in a greater and deeper way.

Heavenly Father, I long to know more of You.
May that revelation be used to make me a better
witness and a more consistent Christian. Thank
You for the gift of Your Holy Spirit operating in
my life. May I remember throughout today that
You have given me the power to live for You and
resist temptations. In Jesus' name, Amen.

OCTOBER 2

WE MUST OBEY . . . WHOM?

Acts 4:13–20

Years ago, I got some valuable advice from the manager of a business where I worked. After watching me interact with customers, trying to help them resolve issues with the company, he said, "Mark, sometimes you have to decide whether you want people to like you or respect you." I took that piece of advice and tucked it away in the back of my mind, bringing it forward several times in my life since then.

We want everyone to like us. And we should try to act in a way that will be pleasing to others. But there also comes a time when we might have to choose between being liked and being respected. When that time comes, which way will you go?

Peter and John could have caved in to the demands of the authorities and gotten in their good graces. Simply no longer talking about Christ would have made their lives easier in the city of Jerusalem. But the two apostles had already decided that they answered to a higher authority. They refused the easy way out and stated boldly that they would obey God, not man. In the process, they impressed the religious authorities with their passion.

When others put pressure on you to conform to their ideas of morality, do you give in? During conversations where church or Christian bashing takes place, do you join in, remain silent, or speak up for the Lord? To put it bluntly, have you decided to obey social pressure or God? Is it more important for you to be liked by every-one or respected for the stand you take?

Who—as revealed by your actions and words—is your highest authority?

Father, help me to place You as my highest au-thority. As I go through this day, help me to stand for You, no matter what others might say or do. May I show in a very clear way what a Christian is. In Jesus' name, Amen.

OCTOBER 3

HELPING OTHERS UNDERSTAND

Acts 8:26–39

Bonjour! Je suis tres content de vous ecrire dans ce livre. J'espere bien que vous aimez ce que j'ai ecrit.

No, the proofreader didn't miss some errors in the preceding para-graph; neither did the typesetter. I simply wrote several sentences in French. Translated, it says, "Hello! I am very happy to write to you in this book. I really hope that you like what I've written."

I could have written this entire book in French. (Of course, it would have taken me a lot longer, but that's beside the point!) Why did I write it in English? Because I want you to be able to under-stand the message of the book easily.

In today's passage, we see Philip asking a government official, who is reading a portion of Isaiah, if the official understands what he is reading. It provides an opening for Philip to talk with the official at length and to explain clearly the gospel of Jesus Christ. The result is that the Ethiopian eunuch, one of the most influential people in his government, gives his life to Christ and is baptized. All he needed was for someone to explain the gospel to him clearly.

Sometimes believers make a mistake about the unbelievers around them. They assume that those unbelievers understand the basic message of the Bible. Christians think that their unbelieving friends know how to commit their lives to Christ and experience cleansing and forgiveness.

That simply isn't true.

In most cases, unbelievers have no clue how a person can know they're going to heaven. They know about church, but they might not have any idea about what goes on inside the building. They see some Christians who are inconsistent in their walk, so they put religion out of their mind.

Someone must be a Philip to your friends. Someone has to tell them clearly what Christ has done for them so they can make an intelligent, informed decision about their eternal destination. Will you be that Philip?

Dear Lord, thank You for the gift of salvation through Jesus Christ. Give me the wisdom and desire to speak clearly and compellingly about Christ to my unbelieving friends. Please prepare their hearts for Your message. In Jesus' name, Amen.

OCTOBER 4

GOD IS NO RESPECTER OF PERSONS—ARE YOU?
Acts 10:23–35

While a missionary in France, I started a new church that had very few Christians. Most people in attendance were seekers who eventually gave their lives to Christ. However, one strong family of believers helped make up the core of the church—a wonderful black man named Felix and his wife, Marie Gabrielle. They came from Martinique, and they had children the same age as ours.

Almost from the moment she could talk, our oldest daughter, Amy, played with Felix and Marie Gabrielle's sons. One day, she happened to hear me talking to our mission coordinator about the makeup of our church. I mentioned that we had several black families and several white families. As I named the members, Amy looked stunned. "I never knew they were black!" she said.

Oh, that we could all simply accept others like that without prejudice!

Peter had a tough lesson to learn about God's acceptance of all races. But he learned it! This leader of the Jews was instrumental in helping the council at Jerusalem begin a process that would evangelize the Gentile world. Once he realized that God wanted everyone in the world to hear the gospel, Peter did what he could to help the early church reach that goal.

How are your prejudices? Do you automatically judge people based on their color, gender, speech, or manner of dress? Are you willing to befriend anyone of any race to share Christ with them?

Jesus said that the church is commissioned to go into all the world. If you restrict your witnessing to a certain group of people, you've eliminated much of the world from being able to hear the gospel.

God says that He is "not wanting anyone to perish, but everyone to come to repentance" (2 Peter 3:9). Satan, on the other hand, loves prejudices that keep us from loving and witnessing as we should.

Who will you follow—God or Satan?

Heavenly Father, if I am allowing prejudices to keep me from loving and witnessing for You, help me to give them up. I want to be Your obedient child, helping the church to reach the entire world for Jesus. In Jesus' name, Amen.

OCTOBER 5

SAVED BY GRACE

Romans 3:20–26

Romans can be a difficult book. Paul's great treatise on the power of grace and the weakness of the Law can be somewhat daunting, especially for a new believer. Peter, the apostle, might have been referring to Romans when he said of Paul's writing, "His letters contain some things that are hard to understand" (2 Peter 3:16). But a careful study of this great epistle will be rewarding for the Christian. It also helps us avoid the same mistake that two teenagers made a couple of years ago.

The young men in question were scrap metal thief "wannabes." They were in the process of disassembling an electric tower when they learned an important lesson in construction. Apparently, the teenagers had decided to sell the aluminum supports for scrap. Note the word *supports*. When they took the supports off the tower, guess what happened? One of the young men died as the 160-foot, 10,000-pound tower collapsed and crushed him. The other teen dug himself out from the debris, a sadder but wiser person.[1]

The apostle Paul reminds us forcefully in the book of Romans that grace is the foundational support of a person's salvation. Without the grace of God, we could not have forgiveness of sins and a relationship with Jesus Christ. If we remove the divine support of grace and try to rely solely upon our own good works, life comes crashing down upon us, and we find ourselves destroyed.

Take a moment to thank God for His love and to rest securely in the support of His constant grace.

Dear God, thank You for Your amazing grace, which You show to me every day. Thank You for constantly providing for me, watching over me, and loving me. In Jesus' name, Amen.

OCTOBER 6

HELP WHEN YOU HAVE NO STRENGTH
Romans 5:6–10

The tennis doubles match was going great! The four of us played hard, and we all wanted to win. One of the players on the opposing team tried a drop shot, and I rushed the net. The ball had been sharply angled toward the side of the court, so I made the return and pushed hard off the fence that bordered the area. When I hit the fence, however, the bottom proved to be loose. It gave a little, and my foot slipped through and dropped about an inch off the concrete. SNAP! Just like that, I broke my ankle, and a wave of nausea engulfed me. My friends had to carry me to the car and

---

1. Wendy Northcutt, *The Darwin Awards* (New York: Dutton, 2000), 82.

drive me to the doctor's office, then to the hospital, then to my house. On that day, I could do nothing! I was like a baby again, having to be taken care of by family and friends.

The Bible says that all of us have broken souls. Sin has rendered us completely helpless when it comes to doing anything to repair our ruptured relationship with God. The great news, however, is that Christ comes to us at our weakest moment and offers us the best of health. The Great Physician wants to cure each of us for all eternity.

No matter what you might face today—no matter how weak you might feel in trying to accomplish the tasks before you—God promises to be with you, lift you up, and give you His strength. Trust in the Lord—for everything, for all time.

Heavenly Father, may I remember that You have already promised to heal my broken spirit and soul. As You have touched me with Your grace and forgiveness, now touch me with the strength and wisdom to give You the problems and opportunities of this day. In Jesus' name, Amen.

OCTOBER 7

STAY AWAY FROM SIN!

Romans 6:1—4

In 1792, a man named Ying wrote to his eldest son some advice that we all should heed. The advice concerned the quality of the essays that the son had submitted during his education:

> *Your essays do not lack force*
> *But they require more depth.*
> *Your gold is mixed with sand*
> *And your jade with stones.*[1]

---

1. Frank Ching, *Ancestors: 900 Years in the Life of a Chinese Family* (New York: Fawcett Columbine, 1997), 325.

"Your gold is mixed with sand, and your jade with stones." In other words, some of your reasoning is good, but it is flawed by untruths mixed into the argument.

Paul could have said the same thing in his day. Some Christians were taking the concept of salvation by grace and deciding that they could live any way they wanted! They reasoned that because salvation was through grace, not works, and because they were freed from the Law, how they conducted their lives didn't matter. Such false reasoning threatened the effectiveness and the testimony of the early church.

In today's passage, Paul answers those who have decided to live godless lives while claiming to be Christians. He points out that if a person is truly dead to sin, he should no longer desire to live immorally.

What about you? Are you tolerating something in your life that displeases God? If so, you are taking for granted the precious sacrifice that Jesus made on the Cross. He died to free you from those very sins that you keep casually in your heart.

Remember: *"Almost* means not quite. *Not quite* means not right. *Not right* means wrong. *Wrong* means the opportunity to start again and get it *right!"*[2]

> *Dear Lord, I don't want to be "mostly" right. I want to be fully right with You. Help me not to tolerate anything in my life that does not give You honor and praise. In Jesus' name, Amen.*

OCTOBER 8

THE DEPTH OF GOD'S LOVE

Romans 8:31–39

These verses comprise one of the greatest passages in the Bible. If you've ever doubted God's love for you, I suggest memorizing this Holy Spirit-inspired praise from the pen of the apostle Paul.

---

2. Rob Gilbert, *Bits and Pieces* (Chicago: Economics Press, 1997), 3.

Someone once reportedly asked Joan of Arc why God spoke only to her. Her response is enlightening: "Sir, you are wrong," she said. "God speaks to everyone. I just listen."[1]

Are you listening to God?

In these words from Romans, did you hear your heavenly Father assuring you of His never-ending love? Have you allowed Christ's grace to give you assurance concerning your forgiveness of sins and eternal life? After all, *nothing* can separate you from the love of God in Christ Jesus! Relax—and abide—in God's love today.

> *Dear God, Your grace still amazes me. How You could love a sinner like me is beyond comprehension. Yet, Your Word tells me that I've been cleansed, forgiven, and placed in Your family. Thank You, once again, for Your constant, powerful love. In Jesus' name, Amen.*

OCTOBER 9

BE CAREFUL OF BOASTING
I Corinthians 1:22–31

The patient lay on the psychiatrist's couch. "Doc, I just can't get to sleep at night," he sighed.

"Why is that?"

"I have to solve all of the world's problems."

"Goodness!" the doctor exclaimed. "No wonder you're not sleeping. No one can do that!"

"No, no, Doc. You don't understand. I get most of the problems solved."

"Then what's the problem?"

"It's those ticker tape parades in my honor that keep me awake."[2]

Pride. It can cause a lot of problems, from the boardroom to the bedroom, from the most powerful chairman to the smallest church.

---

1. John C. Maxwell, *The 21 Most Powerful Minutes in a Leader's Day* (Nashville: Nelson, 2000), 70.
2. Sid Behrman, *The Doctor Joke Book* (New York: Barnes and Noble, 1995), 106.

Paul began his letter to the Corinthians by tackling the problem of pride. It was threatening to tear apart that local body of believers. This church had tongues, signs, and miracles. But they sorely lacked love, humility, and spiritual maturity. The apostle reminded the Corinthians that most of them had been saved out of humble circumstances. He gave them an example to follow, saying that he would boast only in the Lord.

Our culture loves to point to self. "We're number one" is a refrain that we hear constantly. "I deserve this" is another popular slogan. But God tells us that humility and an attitude of servanthood are what please Him. The next time you're tempted to point to self but criticize other people, remember Christ's humiliating Himself by taking *your sins* and paying for them.

Today, lift up Christ. Don't put down others.

Father, remind me, as I go through this day, that I am nothing without You. May I accept Your lordship and live as Your faithful servant. May my love of others reflect Your love of me. In Jesus' name, Amen.

OCTOBER 10

HOW MUCH DO YOU KNOW?

1 Corinthians 2:1–5

Today, let's test your knowledge of caffeine. For example, what's the difference between decaffeinated and caffeine-free? Most of us know that caffeine is a drug that is found in coffee, tea, and many soft drinks. Of course, colas do not have naturally high levels of caffeine; bottlers add it to give you, the consumer, a "caffeine high." The fact that it's mildly addictive also helps hook you on their product!

Because caffeine is artificially added to colas, they are labeled "caffeine free" when they contain very little or no caffeine. Coffee and tea, on the other hand, must be labeled "decaffeinated" when little caffeine is present, meaning that the addictive substance has been removed artificially. One other fact: "decaffeinated" does not mean that all of the caffeine is gone; usually about two percent still remains.[1]

Did you already know the preceding facts? In case you didn't glance at the footnote, the reference for this knowledge came from *The Book of Totally Useless Information.*

We live in a world in which more information is available—right at our fingertips (or our computer mouse)—than ever before. Some of that knowledge is extremely important, especially if it helps us become better at our jobs. Other facts, however, might be far less practical. For example, you might know the statistics on every football, basketball, or baseball player who's played in the last ten years. Or maybe (like me) you can name nearly every song you hear, who the composer is, and who sang or played it.

Although knowledge is good, one of the greatest minds in the last two thousand years said, "When I came to you, brothers, I did not come with eloquence or superior wisdom as I proclaimed to you the testimony about God. For I resolved to know nothing while I was with you except Jesus Christ and him crucified" (1 Cor. 2:1–2). If you are not using your knowledge to point others to the Savior, then perhaps you need to reorient your goals and priorities. If you know a lot about nearly everything but know little about God, spiritual qualities, and eternal life, you are certainly wasting your intellect, time, and energy.

Leon, a good friend of mine who is also a fellow church member, went with me one night to visit an unchurched man. The man was cordial but uninterested in our discussions of Jesus Christ—until Leon said, "I've always thought Dale Earnhardt to be one of the greatest drivers to have ever raced." The man's face brightened, and he and Leon talked racing for the next thirty minutes. Leon had seen a picture of the Daytona Speedway, with Earnhardt's number superimposed on the oval circuit. To me, it was just a number. To Leon, who loves auto racing, it meant an opportunity to connect—and connect we did. The man ended up turning his life over to the Lord and joining our church!

Among your friends and acquaintances, strive to be known for how much you love Christ, not for how many "facts" you have in

---

1. Don Voorhees, *The Book of Totally Useless Information* (New York: MJF Books, 1993), 149.

your mental data base. Whatever knowledge you have, ask God to use it for His glory.

> *Lord, I want to be known as someone who loves You and points others to You. Today, help me to use everything I know to help others know about You. In Jesus' name, Amen.*

OCTOBER 11

How High Are Your Standards?
I Corinthians 5:1—7

What are you doing to help keep the church where you're a member a pure, holy body? Before you accuse me of sending you on a witch hunt, understand that I'm talking about *your life*, not others' relationships with Christ.

A woman wrote to *Reader's Digest* telling about an incident with her husband, who has a habit of searching through the refrigerator for a snack—usually while she's preparing a meal.

On this particular occasion, she noticed that he'd looked in the refrigerator for the third time in as many minutes. "Nothing's any different than it was a minute ago," she said.

"I know that," he responded. "It's just that this time I've lowered my standards!"[1]

The problem with the local church in Corinth was that it had lowered its standards. Accepting any type of behavior from its members, the church was no longer holy and pleasing to God. Paul urged the membership to take seriously the sin in its fellowship. He told them that a little sin, left alone, can grow and spread throughout the church.

How are your standards? Are you trying to keep your life completely pure before God? Have you allowed some "little sin" to remain in you, and are you rationalizing that "it's not all that bad"?

Today, put that sin out of your life, confess it to God, and ask for

---

1. "Life in These United States," *Reader's Digest*, May 1992, 133.

His cleansing. Keep yourself pure. In doing so, you'll also help make your church a holier, more effective local body of Christ.

Heavenly Father, I don't want to hinder my church or Your work. I know that every sin, no matter how small, displeases You. Please keep me in the center of Your will, showing me any sin that I need to confess to You. In Jesus' name, Amen.

OCTOBER 12

HOW WELL DO YOU LOVE?

1 Corinthians 13:1–7, 13

How is your love life? No, I'm not talking about the frequency or quality of physical intimacy. Although that aspect is important, the number of books we have detailing how to have a great sex life have not stopped the burgeoning number of divorces in this country. What we really need is to learn how to love as God intended.

Take a closer look at today's passage for clues on how to improve your marriage and every other relationship in your life. Consider the following examples.

- *"Love is patient"* (v. 4). How is your patience with your wife, family, and coworkers? Do you lose your temper easily and frequently? True love doesn't do that.
- *"[Love] is not self-seeking"* (v. 5). How well do you do in giving up your rights at home? Is it always about you? Do you sulk when you don't get your way? The Bible tells you to give up your rights, as Christ did for the church.
- *"[Love] keeps no record of wrongs"* (v. 5). Don't say, "I've forgiven her" if you keep bringing up past problems. True love forgives and, like God, puts away the wrongs forever.
- *"Love never fails"* (v. 8). Aren't you glad that you don't have to worry about God deciding that He's no longer

in love with you? You should give that same type of love to your wife and children. Don't ever threaten to withdraw love if their actions don't match what you want. *Withdrawn love was never proper love to begin with.* Your children will learn about God's love for them by looking at your love for your wife.

For those of you who find yourselves as single parents, ask God to help you live before your children a life that reflects Christ's love at all times. In any future relationship that you might have, ask God to make your marriage one that will be a model of godly love to the end of your days.

Read today's passage one more time. It will improve your love life!

Dear God, may my family learn about Your love by seeing my example of love toward them. I want to love my wife the way You love me. Help me to give up rights, forgive generously, and never quit loving my family. In Jesus' name, Amen.

OCTOBER 13

ENCOURAGEMENT TO STAND FIRM
1 Corinthians 15:50–58

As Paul prepared to close his letter to the Corinthians, he addressed head-on the most feared, mysterious subject of humankind: death. This great servant of God brilliantly explained what happens to the Christian at death, pulling aside that black curtain and revealing the splendor of heaven. Then, ever practical, the apostle applied this knowledge about heaven and eternity to the earthly life of the believer. He said that we are to stand firm, no matter what life might bring our way. We can do so because of the assurance that a better life awaits us around the throne of God in heaven.

The believer should shun a timid life that makes no difference. As Teddy Roosevelt once said, "Far better it is to dare mighty things, to win glorious triumphs, even though checkered by failure, than to take rank with those poor spirits who neither enjoy much nor suffer much because they live in the gray twilight that knows neither victory nor defeat."[1]

I don't know what is happening in your life right now. However, God tells me that you will one day know ultimate victory! Therefore, stand up for God, be faithful in adversity, and act boldly for the Lord's kingdom. After all, the triumphs that you gain for God on earth's stage will resonate throughout all eternity!

Father, thank You for the assurance of heaven.
Because it is my ultimate destination, may I live
faithfully and boldly for You today and every day.
In Jesus' name, Amen.

OCTOBER 14

A TRAIL OF COMFORT
2 Corinthians 1:1–5

Did you ever wonder why some jets leave a cloud-like trail behind them whereas others do not? Let's begin by getting our terms right. The proper name for the trails is *contrails*. They are formed from condensed water vapor. Knowing this fact also gives us a clue to answering our question.

Jet engines release water vapor into the air from their exhaust. For that water vapor to turn into a contrail, it must hit and then mix with the cold air of the atmosphere. Only jets that fly at high altitudes will encounter air cold enough to leave a visible symbol that they've been in the area.[2]

Do you want to know how we can make a difference in this world that will last far beyond the moment? God's Word tells us that we'll fly high by stooping low to help those who have fallen on hard times. "Praise be to the God and Father of our Lord Jesus

---

1. Tim Kimmel, *Basic Training for a Few Good Men* (Nashville: Nelson, 1997), 136.
2. Don Voorhees, *The Book of Totally Useless Information* (New York: MJF Books, 1993), 8.

Christ, the Father of compassion and the God of all comfort, who comforts us in all our troubles, so that we can comfort those in any trouble with the comfort we ourselves have received from God" (vv. 3–4).

In other words, the Lord wants us to pass along the divine comfort that we receive from Him.

Let's each take a mental inventory of our church. Who is having a hard time? Who needs financial help? What grieving man or woman recently lost a spouse and is suffering from shock and loneliness? How many of our fellow believers need a kind word from someone who cares?

Taking a few minutes of our time, and maybe some of our money, to lift and comfort those who are hurting will help in ways far greater than you or I can imagine. God can multiply our "five loaves and two fish" of comfort and feed a multitude with the spirit that it engenders.

If we'll all look around, we will see someone who needs the comfort of our Christian love today.

Lord, help me to make a difference in the lives of others. Show me those who could benefit from what I have to offer as a believer. May I be willing to share my blessings with others that their lives, our church, and Your kingdom might be enriched. In Jesus' name, Amen.

OCTOBER 15

STANDING FIRM ON THE ROCK OF AGES
2 Corinthians 1:20–22

At every home game of the Clemson Tigers since 1942, the same scenario takes place. Eight minutes before kickoff, the football team gathers at the top of the hill at the east end of the field. A cannon fires, the band plays "The Tiger Rag," and the crowd begins to roar. In this atmosphere of excitement, the players take turns rubbing a rock that supposedly grants mystical powers. Then the Tigers run down the hill and onto the field.

"The rock has strange powers," says former Clemson star and Cleveland Browns player Michael Dean Perry. "When you rub it, and run the hill, the adrenaline flows. It's the most emotional experience I've ever had."[1]

There is another Rock far more solid than any earthly foundation. Jesus Christ, the Rock of Ages, is neither a tradition nor simply a beloved myth. The Son of God is fully alive today. His power—the power that created the universe—is available to you today. Place your life in His hands, and He will guide you, protect you, and strengthen you.

Rock is a great foundation on which to build. And Jesus Christ, fully God, the Rock of Ages, is a sure foundation that will never fail. Rest in His promises today.

Dear Lord, help me to place my trust fully in You today. Through the power of Your son, Jesus Christ, may I realize that nothing I face today is too difficult to overcome. Thank You that you keep all of Your promises. May I be as faithful to You as You are to me. In Jesus' name, Amen.

OCTOBER 16

THE GIFT THAT KEEPS US FAITHFUL
2 Corinthians 4:5–18

As a child, Eleanor Sass had to be hospitalized for appendicitis. In the same hospital room, a girl named Mollie was fighting a losing battle against depression and the prospect of never walking again.

A car had hit young Mollie while she was riding a bicycle. Her legs badly broken, she had suffered through many operations. Now Mollie faced what looked to be a bleak future. She responded to her situation by falling into depression. Uncooperative with her nurses, she refused to participate in therapy and spent most of her days crying.

---

1. Don Martin, *Team Think* (New York: Penguin Books, 1993), 98.

Mollie's only bright spot of the day occurred when the mail arrived. It would usually contain some sort of gift for her: books, games, stuffed toys—appropriate gifts for a bedridden child. But one day, the mail held a different sort of gift. Sent from an aunt far away, the package contained a pair of beautiful black patent leather shoes. The nurses could be heard grumbling about "people who don't use their heads," but Mollie paid no attention to them. She was too busy putting the shoes on her hands and walking them up and down her blanket.

From that moment, Mollie's attitude seemed to change. She became cooperative, her depression lifted, and she began therapy. One day, Eleanor heard that her friend had finally left the hospital. And, best of all, Mollie had walked out, wearing her beautiful new shoes.[1]

Times get rough for all of us. But when the difficult times come, we should remember God's gift to us. That gift should motivate us to "keep on keeping on." It certainly made the vital difference in Paul's life: "We are hard pressed on every side, but not crushed; perplexed, but not in despair; persecuted, but not abandoned; struck down, but not destroyed" (vv. 8–9).

What was Paul's secret? What is God's gift to you that can keep you strong?

The apostle gives us a glimpse into his source of strength in the last part of today's passage. Paul knew that heaven awaited him. He realized that his current situation, though difficult, was only temporary. Therefore, that great man of God kept his eyes—his attention—fixed constantly on his future eternal home.

Where is your attention? Are you fixated on your current problems or on your promised paradise? Does Satan use the trials you're undergoing to rob you of joy, or do you entrust them to your heavenly Father, knowing that one day they will vanish in the eternal light of heaven?

God has given you the gift of eternal life in His presence. One day, you'll walk on streets of gold, surrounded by angels and other believers, unhindered by physical, emotional, or spiritual problems. Keep your life focused on that promise. It can help you walk out of a debilitating attitude of depression and hopelessness.

1. Medard Laz, *Love Adds a Little Chocolate* (New York: Warner Books, 1997), 161.

Dear Lord, thank You for the gift of eternal life and heaven. Help me to remember that heaven is my future, ultimate destination. Today, may I keep my eyes fixed on You and not on all of my problems or difficult situations. Thank You that I will win the victory in Jesus Christ! In Jesus' name, Amen.

OCTOBER 17

HE TOOK OUR PLACE
2 Corinthians 5:17–21

In her book, *Mama, Get the Hammer, There's a Fly on Papa's Head!* (what a great title!), Barbara Johnson confesses that she once got a speeding ticket. As a result, she had to go to an all-day traffic school at eight o'clock one Saturday morning. When Barbara arrived, she showed the attendant her traffic ticket and the summons to appear in traffic school. This was not enough for the attendant, however. "I'm sorry," the woman said, "but I also need to see your driver's license."

When Barbara asked why they needed to see her driver's license in addition to all of the other documentation, the woman smiled and gave this explanation. "Some violators—particularly professional people—try to hire people to sit in for them at traffic school. We have to check every license to be sure the person coming to traffic school is the same person who got the ticket!"[1]

In today's Scripture, Paul reminds us that Jesus Christ stood in for us. Because of our sins, we faced a court far more severe than any earthly seat of justice. A punishment that would last for all of eternity threatened even the best of us. But Jesus took our sins upon Himself, stood in our place on the Cross, faced rejection by God, and endured death. In other words, He paid our fine so that we could go free.

Take a moment to thank God for the tremendous gift of Christ's

---

1. Barbara Johnson, *Mama, Get the Hammer, There's a Fly on Papa's Head!* (Dallas: Word, 1994), 115.

sacrifice. Promise the heavenly Father that you will live in the light of His grace and tell others the good news that Jesus has for them.

> *Dear Lord, how I thank You for allowing Your Son to stand in for me! I don't deserve Your grace and mercy, but I want to live every moment today aware of Your love. May my actions and thoughts reflect a life lived totally for You. In Jesus' name, Amen.*

OCTOBER 18

WHICH GOSPEL?

Galatians 1:6–9

It might be good to stop for a moment and ask yourself the same question that Paul posed to the Galatians at the very beginning of his letter to their church. "What gospel are you following? Have you left the gospel preached by Paul?"

Heretics had infiltrated the church of Galatia. These false teachers wanted the new believers to reject salvation by grace. They urged the church members to go back to believing that good works and adherance to the Law would save them. Paul was blunt in his condemnation of those who tried to preach another gospel. "But even if we or an angel from heaven should preach a gospel other than the one we preached to you, let him be eternally condemned" (v. 8). The rest of his letter to the Galatians is a restatement of the gospel that he received directly from God—salvation by grace alone.

What gospel are you following? After all, many different voices are clamoring for your attention, each proclaiming loudly that it is the answer to your problems. Perhaps you think it's possible to mix different gospels, taking a little of this and a smidgen of that, combining them to fit your lifestyle.

Mixing different gospels together to come up with your own personal favorite has two problems. First, when you are the one making the decisions about what you will and won't believe, you've made yourself god. Second, when the gospel of Jesus Christ and salvation by grace are mixed with any other philosophy, it is no longer the real gospel.

Paul was uncompromising on this point. If you read further in Galatians, you'll see that he stood against Peter and the council at Jerusalem to defend salvation by grace!

Have you drifted? Have you begun mixing a bit of this and that to what God says in His Word, the Bible? Are you compromising, in small ways, the commandments that the Lord has given you?

Ask God to keep your beliefs, your relationships, your thoughts, and your entire lifestyle pure before Him. Don't drift. Don't compromise. Stay committed to the gospel revealed by your Savior, Jesus Christ.

Dear God, I do not want to be found guilty of watering down the authority of Your Word. I desire to hold firmly to salvation by grace alone. May I never compromise my beliefs to accommodate a wrong lifestyle. Keep me pure before You. In Jesus' name, Amen.

OCTOBER 19

THE TREE THAT SAVES
Galatians 2:20–3:1

The tree stands in the middle of nowhere.

It's not particularly impressive, reaching a height of only fifteen feet. There are far more beautiful sights in Australia and more lush surroundings. To find the tree, you have to go to Daly Waters, then drive a couple of miles down a dirt track. At the edge of a large clearing, you'll see a sign saying that you've found the Stuart Tree.

John McDouall Stuart has been proclaimed by many as Australia's greatest explorer. He led through the country's interior three expeditions that nearly killed him but saved Australia. The intense heat and strong sunlight rendered him nearly blind on two of his trips. On the second expedition, he became ill with scurvy. His body became, in the words of one of his lieutenants, "a mass of sores that will not heal." The skin "hung from the roof of his mouth, his tongue became swollen and he was incapable of talking." He was carried the last 400 miles on a stretcher, and each day his colleagues expected to find him dead.

Not only did he survive this second expedition but also within a month of returning home he was up and ready for another trip! This time, Stuart was determined to find a way through the interior of Australia—or die trying. For a while, it looked as if he and his party would die. His horses (and men) were about to fall out because of lack of water, until they stumbled upon a stream of drinkable water at what later became Daly Waters. Refreshed, Stuart and his party pressed on, and in 1862, nine months after setting out from Adelaide, they reached the Timor Sea. For the first time, someone had found a practical route through the heart of the continent. Within a decade, a telegraph line ran from Adelaide to Darwin, putting Australia in direct touch with the rest of the world.

When Stuart, dying of thirst, finally found Daly Waters, he showed his delight and appreciation by carving an *S* into a big gum tree. Today, the tree consists of only a fifteen-foot-high chunk of long-dead wood. But what it represents makes it valuable to the grateful citizens who make the trek to see the modern beginnings of their country.[1]

The Roman cross was only a blood-stained piece of wood. In its day, the cross was a symbol of shame, a place where only the worst criminals shed their blood and died a horrible death. Because Jesus Christ died on the Cross, however, it has been transformed forever in our eyes. Our Savior found a way for us from the outback of sin straight into the heart of God and His offer of abundant life. His thirst, His anguish, and His loneliness provided us with the water of eternal life, eternal peace, and never-ending fellowship with God.

Heavenly Father, thank You for loving me enough
to give Your most precious, only Son to die for me.
May Christ's sacrifice for me not be in vain.
Help me to honor You and tell of Your love today.
In Jesus' name, Amen.

---

1. Bill Bryson, *In a Sunburned Country* (New York: Broadway Books, 2000), 237–38.

THE CONTRACT IS SIGNED, SEALED, AND DELIVERED
Galatians 3:13–17

Our church has just finished signing a multitude of contracts in preparation for building new facilities at a new location. If all goes well, fourteen months from now, our church family will be worshiping at a site designed to reach many more seekers.

We began the process by signing a contract to buy the land. The next contract aligned us with an architectural firm, which led to a contract with the construction firm that is building our new church. Meanwhile, another church contacted us about buying our old facilities because a third church wanted to buy theirs! More contracts, and two other churches had new homes.

All of these things will take place because of the value we place in contracts.

Paul tells us that it is the same with God. He signed a contract with Abraham that is still in effect today: *"[God] redeemed us in order that the blessing given to Abraham might come to the Gentiles through Christ Jesus, so that by faith we might receive the promise of the Spirit"* (v. 14).

Men will occasionally break contracts; God never does. We can trust in His Word and claim His promises. For the New Testament believer, God signed His contract of salvation with the blood of Jesus Christ. Our covenant of grace has been signed, sealed, and delivered!

> *Dear Lord, I thank You that Your Word is trustworthy. May I claim Your promises in faith and live out Your grace daily. In Jesus' name, Amen.*

OCTOBER 21

SLAVE OR FREE?

Galatians 5:1, 13–16

It's hard to understand. Some people prefer slavery to freedom!

When Moses liberated the Israelites from slavery in Egypt, some of the people groaned about their freedom and wished to be under the yoke of bondage once again. All they could focus upon was the good food that they had had in that foreign land. They conveniently forgot the beatings and murders that their people had endured.

When communism was finally overthrown in Russia, some citizens openly longed for "the good old days" under a military dictatorship that robbed them of individual freedoms and the right to advance in their careers. All they could remember were the free housing, cheap food, and guaranteed jobs for life. They conveniently forgot the long lines, empty stores, and bleak lifestyle that a communist state produced.

Paul said that the Galatians would fit right into either of the preceding groups. He told them that they were now free in Christ, but if they kept following false teachers, they would enslave themselves to the Law and sin once again. They might find some comfort in the old rituals, but they forgot that slavery to the Law brings only destruction and separation from God forever. Paul encouraged them—and us—to remain free by living and walking in the light of Christ and His saving grace.

Slavery to sin or freedom in Christ—which do you choose?

Lord, I want You truly to be my Lord and Master. May I live in Your freedom every day of my life. I don't want to go back to the way I was before I knew You. Please keep me from temptation today. In Jesus' name, Amen.

THE SEAL OF OWNERSHIP
Ephesians 1:11–14

"Pastor, I'm embarrassed about something." The woman stood in the hall outside my office, holding something behind her back. A steady stream of worship attenders turned curious heads, but the woman was determined to finish her confession.

She thrust a book into my hands—a book I hadn't seen for almost ten years!

"Where did you find this?" I asked.

The woman hung her head. "It's been on my bookshelf for as long as I can remember. I thought it was mine. Then, a couple of days ago, my husband took the book down and began reading it. He called me over, pointed to something on the flyleaf, and asked, 'What is this?' Pastor, it was a seal that had your name on it. Then I remembered, I'd borrowed this book from you years ago!"

We straightened out the misunderstanding, and I thanked the woman for returning my book—finally. Whenever I buy a book, I take out my "seal" that looks like one that a notary public might employ. I crimp the pages in several different places in the book to remind borrowers that the book belongs to me. I know my books because of my personal seal upon them.

God has also placed his personal seal upon you. If you have given Jesus Christ your sins and asked Him to take control of your life, you've been sealed with the Holy Spirit. God's mark is upon you, and it means that you'll never be the same. But it also means that God knows those who belong to Him.

Take a moment to thank God for having sealed you until the day of redemption.

Heavenly Father, thank You for sealing me to Yourself. With Your mark of ownership upon me, may I represent You consistently to a watching world. In Jesus' name, Amen.

A RICH FUTURE

Ephesians 2:4–9

Not long ago, I was eating lunch with a couple of friends at a Chinese restaurant. One of the guys had been going through some tough times, and we were talking with him about it. At the end of the meal, we all received fortune cookies and shared what each one said. The friend who was going through hard times cracked open his fortune cookie and began to laugh.

"What's so funny?" I asked.

He held up the cookie for us all to see. "It's empty. There's nothing. I guess it represents an empty future!"

Fortunately, my friend knew that just the opposite was true. As a mature believer, he realized that the setbacks occurring in his life were only temporary. The grace Christ's sacrifice bought for us on the Cross ensures that Christians will share a rich future in heaven.

Satan wants us to forget the great inheritance that awaits us. If he can get our mind off of eternal riches and onto temporary problems and meaningless acquisitions, then he's gone a long way in negating our influence for good in this world. Reading devotionals like this and a regular dose of the Bible every day will keep us focused on all that the Lord has promised to those who love Him.

Grace, forgiveness of sins, salvation, adoption into God's family, guidance through this life, and assurance of living forever in the Father's presence—what a rich future we have!

Lord, I thank You for the future that awaits me. Help me to remember my calling and my future home throughout this day. May everything I do reflect my love for You. In Jesus' name, Amen.

GETTING TO THE ROOT OF THE ISSUE
Ephesians 3:14–21

When our church put out our new plans for bids, we had a certain budget in mind. But when the bids came in, we were shocked to say the least. The *low* bid was more than a million dollars over what we'd anticipated! Thankfully, the Lord actually worked through that overage to help us have a strong building plan of which we could all be proud.

The main culprit in the overage, we discovered, was the amount we'd budgeted for site work. Because a strong, sturdy foundation is vital to any building, the contractors had realized a large percentage of the costs for the new facilities would go into dirt work and putting down a good base.

What's true for buildings is also true for believers.

During my years in the pastorate, I've seen some church members who initially blazed a brilliant path. In time, however, flaws began to make themselves seen in their attitudes or behavior. Eventually, if not corrected, those flaws would sideline the worker and render him or her practically useless for Christ.

The reason for these flaws could almost always be traced back to a poor foundation in the person's spiritual life. Time was not taken to learn the basics of the Christian life, no Scripture memory took place, and the discipline of daily time with God never became a habit.

If you construct a large building without a solid foundation, eventually it will develop cracks. It can be the same with Christians.

How is your foundation? You know Christ, but are you also reading His Word, memorizing His promises, and developing your character to resemble His? Take the time to learn from the One who gave Himself for you. That foundation will give you a strong life and make you a consistent witness for the Lord.

Dear God, I want to have a strong foundation. Help me discipline myself to give You the necessary time in my life each day. May I not be so bent on doing other things that I miss out on

committing Your Word to memory and letting You
speak to me. In Jesus' name, Amen.

OCTOBER 25

LOVE, MARRIAGE, AND GOD
Ephesians 5:25–28

Laura Jensen Walker is the author of *Dated Jekyll, Married Hyde*. Tongue in cheek (sort of), she says of her husband,

> I married a whiner.
> Whenever my husband isn't feeling well, I know it.
> I've never known anyone to make such a fuss about a headache.
> Or allergies.
> My girlfriends tell me their husbands are the same way. They just can't cope with pain and discomfort the same way that women can.
> That's why women have the babies.
> And my reaction when my husband starts to whine about his splitting head or stopped-up sinuses?
> Take some Tylenol.
> Blow your nose.
> *Deal* with it.[1]

If you're married, what would your wife say about you?

We men are pretty good at remembering Paul's commandment that says the husband is the head of the house. But we often forget that Paul also said we are to love our wives as Christ loved the church and gave Himself for it.

If you're the head of the house, that means several things:

1. *You* will lead in having a family altar every day.
2. *You* will set the example of good use of time for God

---

1. Laura Jensen Walker, *Dated Jekyll, Married Hyde* (Minneapolis: Bethany House, 1997), 35.

by not "vegging out" in front of the television every evening.
3. *You* will model God's love for your family by showing consistent, forgiving love.

If you are going to follow Paul's commandment to love your wife as Christ loved the church, you will:

1. Regularly give up your rights.
2. Seek her happiness and fulfillment, putting it above your own.
3. Be a holy, spiritual example of Christlike love.
4. Lead the way in church attendance, daily Bible reading, and spending time with your wife.

I don't know what your wife thinks about you as a husband, but I can guarantee that if you'll begin to put into practice the life qualities listed here, it should change her opinion for the better! Love your wife as God intended you to love her, and you'll go a long way toward having a "marriage made in heaven."

Lord, I thank You for my wife. May I lift her up by showing Your love for her through my words and actions. Help me to be a godly husband and a true spiritual leader of my family. In Jesus' name, Amen.

OCTOBER 26

How Do You Respond to Trials?
Philippians 1:12–18

In today's Scripture passage, we get a glimpse into one of the major reasons Paul became such a mighty servant of God. Teamed with Barnabas, he became the first missionary of the New Testament, the first church planter, the Lord's primary evangelist, and new believers' preeminent Bible teacher! As we open the letter to the Philippians, however, we find Paul confined to a prison and bound in chains.

Wasn't Paul doing a great work for God? Why would the Lord allow this great apostle's church planting to cease? Didn't Jesus know that Paul was suffering from this unjust imprisonment?

It's interesting to note that Paul never complained or asked, "Why me, Lord?" in any of his writings. Instead, he wisely realized that God could—and *would*—use everything in his life to further the work of the kingdom. Even the imprisonment and chains, given to the Lord, became instruments of evangelism and teaching. For example, we now know that some of Paul's richest writings took place while he was in prison. Those "prison epistles" have far outlasted any of the coliseums and palaces built by emperors of that day.

What about your own life? How are you responding to any difficulties that you might be experiencing? Have you fallen into the trap of saying, "Why me, Lord?" Have you grumbled that you don't deserve this?

I don't know what God's will is concerning the situation that you face right now. But let me tell you several things that I *do* know. First, God wants to give you the strength and the peace to come through your trial victoriously. Second, He wants to use your situation for His glory, touching the lives of others in a positive way. Third, God wants you to become a stronger, deeper Christian because of it.

Give your chains to God. He'll lighten their load and use them to bring spiritual freedom to those who are watching your faithful, godly struggle.

Heavenly Father, I don't want to suffer in vain. If it is Your will, please relieve me of my current difficulties. In any case, help me to be faithful to You no matter what happens. Use me and my situation for Your glory, and may I emerge victorious for You. In Jesus' name, Amen.

PERMITTED TO SUFFER
Philippians 1:27–2:2

Did you see that word? Look again at verse 29. In the *New American Standard Bible*, the *New International Version*, the *New King James Version*, and the *New Revised Standard Version*, Paul uses the word *granted*.

Granted? God "grants" us the privilege of suffering?

Obviously, we've been looking at suffering in the wrong way! We've imagined that suffering is something to be avoided. We don't want to experience physical, emotional, or spiritual pain. But Paul's explosive statement means that we might need to reexamine how we react to suffering.

Think about this with me for a moment. If God is granting us the "privilege" of suffering for Him, it means there's something good in it for us. For example, one of the prime ways we grow in the Lord and grow to be like the character of the Lord is to experience trials. When God allows us to suffer, it means that He loves us enough to help us grow closer to Him.

Another key element we often overlook is that by granting us the privilege of suffering for God, the Lord is saying, "I have confidence in you. I know that you are strong enough to handle this and be a witness for Me."

No wonder Paul said that our suffering for the Lord is a tremendous privilege. Through suffering we grow in Him, and by suffering God expresses His confidence that we will stand firm in Christ.

Heavenly Father, help me to praise You in every circumstance. May You use my current and future trials to show others how You give strength during difficult times. May I grow closer to You and develop a more godly character. Help me to stand firm today. In Jesus' name, Amen.

DEVELOPING A SERVANT'S HEART
Philippians 2:4–11

In 1978, a savage flood swept through the hill country of Texas. Sherry Cooper, a survivor, tells how her mother perished needlessly in the swirling waters. "My mother . . . did not climb the tree with us. She lost her way before we got to the tree." It seems that this woman kept records of everything and was afraid of losing it all.

The family had formed a human chain to help one another move to safety. Holding hands, they struggled through the rising flood to a tree that offered shelter. Sherry's mother, however, had insurance papers gathered up in her hands. She wouldn't let go of them to accept the help of others, and so she was washed away.[1]

What are you holding onto that keeps you from living the abundant life that God promises?

Jesus, the example we are to follow, gave up everything to submit to His heavenly Father's will. His complete obedience not only bought us forgiveness of sins but also assures that one day everyone, everywhere will honor Jesus Christ as Lord of all.

If it's pride you need to let go of, then give it to God. If there's a favorite sin you've clung to for years, confess it, and let God cleanse you and free you from bondage. If wealth and the acquisition of power have a grip on your life, ask God to make Him, not temporary baubles, the first priority in your life.

Giving everything and everyone in your life to the Lord gives you a wonderful freedom! It allows you to empty your hands and grasp the hand of God. No flood can sweep you away when you're in the shelter of God's arms.

Dear Lord, please identify for me the things I'm holding onto that are displeasing to You. Help me to give them to You, and discover the freedom and abundant life that You've promised to your children. I want to be firmly in Your hands today. In Jesus' name, Amen.

---

1. *Proclaim: The Journal of Biblical Preaching*, 20 November 2000, 34–35.

REMOVING THE STING OF DEATH
Philippians 3:8–15

Stanley Collins tells of an experience from his days with the British Army in World War II. While out on patrol, he and another soldier came upon an unexploded land mine. They carefully marked its location and moved on. Later that night, Collins says he walked into his tent and nearly passed out. There was his buddy, resting his head on the same mine! Then Collins discovered that the soldier had removed the firing pin, rendering the mine harmless. What had once been an instrument of destruction had become, in his words, "a pillow for a weary soldier."[1]

As Paul contemplated his approaching death, only excitement to see God had a place in his thoughts. He had no fear, no uncertainty, and no panic. The apostle knew what we need to remember: Christ's resurrection from the tomb has removed the sting of death.

Others might face the cessation of life on earth with unrelieved sorrow. For the believer, however, death means merely temporary separation from loved ones. We *know* that heaven awaits those who have trusted in Christ as Savior. With God as our guide when we take that last breath, death simply becomes a portal through which we pass that opens to wonderful, eternal glory.

*Father, thank You for transforming death from
something to be feared into the way we come to
live with You forever. Thank You for Christ's
resurrection from the tomb, which signals the
removal of the sting of death forever.
In Jesus' name, Amen.*

---

1. Ray Pritchard, *In the Shadow of the Cross: The Deeper Meaning of Calvary* (Nashville: Broadman and Holman, 2001), 102.

A REASON TO LIVE

Colossians 1:11–20

In one of his novels, George Moore writes about Irish peasants who were given government jobs of building roads during the Depression. The men were glad to have a meaningful way of making money and sang songs while they worked. But then something happened. They discovered that the roads they were building led nowhere, expired in peat bogs, or simply petered out.

When the workers discovered this, their joy disappeared. They knew that their work meant nothing. The government was simply looking for a way to give them money to help them survive. In the words of the novelist, "The roads to nowhere are difficult to build. For a man to work well and to sing as he works, there must be an end in view."[1]

As believers, we have many reasons to live—joyously. Let's examine today's passage to discover some of those reasons.

1. We are "strengthened with all power" (v. 11).
2. We have been made partakers of "the inheritance of the saints in the kingdom of light" (v. 12).
3. We have been "rescued . . . from the dominion of [spiritual] darkness" (v. 13).
4. We have "forgiveness of sins" through Christ Jesus (v. 14).

Our lives are not meaningless—and they lead somewhere.

With heaven as our final destination and God as our provider of power in this world, we have everything to live for. Let's rejoice in that knowledge!

> *Dear God, thank You for giving me a divine*
> *purpose. May my life return rich dividends from*
> *the investment that You've made in me.*
> *In Jesus' name, Amen.*

---

1. Quoted in John Haughey, S. J., *The Conspiracy of God* (Garden City: Doubleday, 1973), 35.

WHAT ARE YOU THINKING ABOUT?

Colossians 3:1–10

I'm *still* on a diet.

Right now it's 12:30 in the afternoon. Guess what I'm thinking about. If you guessed "food," then you're absolutely right. However, my thoughts on food have begun to change. For example, I used to want a hamburger with fries, or some chips, hot sauce, and a burrito with chili and cheese. Now, I'm staying away from fried foods, and my Mexican restaurant visits consist of helpings of grilled chicken salads with salsa sauce as dressing. Sitting beside my left elbow is a glass of water, not Coke. Accompanying it is a bag of dried fruit, not Doritos.

In other words, my thoughts about eating are changing—for the better. If I'm going to keep off the weight I've lost, I have to develop new ways of thinking about food that also lead to new, healthier habits.

The Bible tells us that we need to do the same thing when it comes to our spiritual life. We cannot focus on the same things that used to occupy our minds when we were not followers of Christ. Those who have not yet learned this lesson and put it into practice are doomed to a lifetime of spiritual wavering that produces little of lasting value.

Let's decide to let the Holy Spirit examine our lives closely. Let's ask Him to investigate our viewing habits and reading material. Let's let Him peer over our shoulders at the computer screen as we log onto the Internet. Let's permit Him to follow us and rate our use of leisure time.

In short, we all need to focus on only what is good, holy, and of benefit. We all have twenty-four hours every day. Let's ask God to show us how best to use that time for Him.

Father, I ask You, right now, to examine every
aspect of my life. Please show me where I'm
focused on the wrong things or wrong individuals.
Help me to give You access to even the deepest

areas of my life. I want to focus upon You and Your Word above anything else. In Jesus' name, Amen.

AUTHENTICITY TAKES TIME

1 Thessalonians 1

Becoming real takes time. We go along through life being squeezed by a thousand influences that we might not even recognize. Then we have an encounter with Christ, and things begin to change. We start to become real.

Paul writes that the church in Thessalonica began to imitate him and become real. That takes time and effort. It reminds me of a passage from my favorite children's book, *The Velveteen Rabbit*. In it is a conversation between the Skin Horse and the Rabbit. It goes like this:

"What is REAL?" asked the Rabbit one day. . . . "Does it mean having things that buzz inside you and a stick-out handle?"

"Real isn't how you are made," said the Skin Horse. "It's a thing that happens to you. When a child loves you for a long, long time, not just to play with, but REALLY loves you, then you become Real."

"Does it hurt?" asked the Rabbit.

"Sometimes," said the Skin Horse, for he was always truthful. "When you are Real you don't mind being hurt."

"Does it happen all at once, like being wound up," he asked, "or bit by bit?"

"It doesn't happen all at once," said the Skin Horse. "You become. It takes a long time. That's why it doesn't often happen to people who break easily, or have sharp edges, or who have to be carefully kept. Generally, by the time you are Real, most of your hair has been loved off, and your eyes drop out and you get loose in the joints and very shabby. But these things don't matter at all, because once you are Real you can't be ugly, except to people who don't understand."[1]

Authenticity takes time, so if you are feeling loose in the joints and a bit frayed at the edges, rejoice. You might just be making some progress!

Father, keep me from being a fake and a fraud.
Help me be a child of God and live like it. In the
name of Jesus, who lived an authentic life, Amen.

BOTH SIDES OF PARENTHOOD
1 Thessalonians 2:6–12

I have always loved Joni Mitchell's song "Both Sides Now." It proclaims, "I've looked at clouds from both sides now." That change of perspective changed the singer. Perhaps that is how Paul felt when he considered his ministry.

Speaking to the church, he said, "We were gentle among you, like a mother caring for her little children" (v. 7). A little later he said, "For you know that we dealt with each of you as a father deals with his own children" (v. 11). Isn't that amazing? Paul could refer to himself as being like both a mother and a father.

When my children were born, that was a lesson I had to learn. I had already decided to be more involved in their lives than my father was in mine. Because of both his work schedule and his temperament, my Dad was pretty much hands-off in my rearing. But I wanted to be different. I had some flexibility in my schedule, so I was very involved in rearing my boys. I washed their dirty diapers, helped feed them, played with them, and generally was involved in every step of their growth and development. At the time, I never thought about any part of that being masculine or feminine. Changing diapers did not offend my sense of being a man.

---

1. Margery Williams, *The Velveteen Rabbit* (Philadelphia: Running Press, 1981), 14–16.

I can tell you this. Whatever benefit my sons might have received from my involvement, I am the one who profited. I grew as a human being and learned to love those boys with a passion. When you care about somebody, you do whatever you can to help them. It is not a matter of being a "mother" or a "father"; it is a matter of being a whole, healthy human being.

Both sides of parenthood are necessary and both are rewarding. If you have kids at home, be involved in everything in their lives. They will thank you later, but you will thank yourself.

Lord, You have been both gentle and tough with me. You always know when I need each. Help me be my best for my family. In Jesus' name, Amen.

NOVEMBER 3

AN ENCOURAGING WORD
1 Thessalonians

The old cowboy song "Home on the Range" includes the phrase "where seldom is heard a discouraging word." How I wish that were true today! We are bombarded on every side by messages that do little to build us up. Wars and rumors of wars, stock market jitters, scandals, disease—all of it merges into a gray, gelatinous blob in our minds. We are like men suffocating for lack of a good word.

A story is told about the ancient Greek philosopher Socrates. A young man went to him and said, "Be my teacher. I want to learn everything you know." Socrates took the young man down to the Mediterranean Sea and pushed him under the water and held him a while. When he pulled him up, Socrates asked the young man, "What do you want?" The man said, "I want to learn." The teacher pushed him under again, held him longer, and again asked what he wanted. His answer still was, "I want to learn." Finally, Socrates held him under for a long time. When he pulled him up and asked, "What do you want?" The young man shouted, "I want air!" The philosopher said, "When you want learning as much as you want air, then you will be ready to study with me."

Paul said that young Timothy had brought him news that encouraged him. Paul had established the church in Thessalonica. When he left it to plant other churches, he was desperate for news from the church. Had they forgotten everything that he had taught them, or did they remember and put it into practice? Paul wondered until Timothy came with good news.

Do you need an encouraging word? If so, then put yourself around people who will deliver it. I avoid some people because they have a perpetual black cloud over their heart. Do your family and your associates need good news from you?

Don't rain on other people's parade.

Lord, I have a good word to share with people because You have given me that word. My relationship with You generates that message. Help me give freely as I have received. In Jesus' name, Amen.

PLEASING GOD

I Thessalonians 4:1–12

As a pastor, I am sometimes asked, "How can I live a life that is pleasing to God?" Today's section of Scripture is a good place to start. Paul told the church, "We instructed you how to live in order to please God" (v. 1). What were his instructions?

First, we should be sanctified. That word means changed to be like Christ. In particular, we should learn to control our bodies and desires. Paul said to "avoid sexual immorality" (v. 3). For one thing, that means to think with our brains, not our bodies.

William Backus is the author of a book titled *Finding the Freedom of Self-Control*. He suggests several steps in learning self-control. First, take issues one at a time. If you have several problems to work on, choose the one that is most important and deal with it first. Then move on to the others. Second, begin to work on self-control issues with a prayer of repentance. Backus says, "Believe that God will, through Christ, not merely forgive your sins, but

347

take them away and replace them with the self-control you need for change." Next, use a self-control journal. In a small pocket notebook, record behavior that involves self-control issues. The reason? "Recording episodes of failure and success in the particular self-control area you are working on will allow you to see concrete evidence of change and improvement." Finally, do it now! Work on your issues when they arise instead of putting it off until later.[1]

Paul also mentions several other elements of a life that pleases God: "brotherly love" (v. 9), "mind your own business and . . . work with your hands" (v. 11). All of this shows that a man who has the self-control can behave himself in every area of life. That is not always easy, but it is always worthwhile.

Heavenly Father, I do want my life to be pleasing to You. Help me develop the skills to live that way. In Christ's name, Amen.

NOVEMBER 5

WAITING FOR THE SON TO SHINE
I Thessalonians 5:1–11

"When is Jesus coming back, preacher? I heard it was going to be soon." This was the beginning of a conversation I had with a man on a sidewalk near our church. Someone had broken into his truck the night before and stolen his battery. The truck's owner was tired of the struggle to live with dignity in that neighborhood. He wanted Jesus to come back and pull him out of his hum-drum life.

He certainly asked a good question about when Jesus would return. A wide variety of opinions exist about that issue. I have studied them and think that Paul's suggestion in today's reading is worth taking seriously. He says in effect that we need not worry about that because we will be so busy serving God. The event will take place "like a thief in the night" (v. 2), that is, without warning

1. William Backus, *Finding the Freedom of Self-Control* (Minneapolis: Bethany House Publishers, 1987), 49.

or fanfare. We await that day but must not speculate idly about when it will happen. So what should we do in the meantime?

Paul gives us our marching orders. First, because we are "sons of the light" (v. 5), we should act like that all of the time. We are to be "alert" (v. 6). We are to keep our mind and ears open. Because no one knows when Christ will return, we are always to be awake mentally.

Second, we are to be "self-controlled" (v. 6). A "Frank and Ernest" cartoon has the two men looking at a book that one of them is holding. Its title is *"No" Thyself.* Frank explains, "It's about self-control." That is a great image. We learn to say "no" to some things so we can say "yes" to others.

When will Christ return? I don't know. What I do know is that I will be at my duty post until we meet.

Lord, Your Son's return will change everything for us. Please understand our impatience. Through the name of Jesus, Amen.

BRAGGING ON YOU
2 Thessalonians 1:3–4, 11–12

When I was about seven or eight, I walked into the living room with my BB gun slung over my shoulder. As I passed in front of the old Zenith black-and-white TV, the BB gun went off and shot out the picture tube. Panic and fear seized me, and I was sure that my parents would too. Instead, they sized up the situation and peered into the face of a terrified little soldier whose world seemed to have shattered along with the picture tube. A loving mother and father decided then and there that their little boy was worth far more than an old Zenith. They assured me that it was not my fault, and that the BB had not even come close to the TV. It just "happened" to explode about the same time as I passed in front of it. To a terrified seven- or eight-year-old kid such an explanation seemed perfectly logical, and I happily accepted that as the true account of the death of the TV.

Only later did I figure out what really happened, and why my parents had "stretched" the facts a bit. That incident has played in my memory for years. Its message is loud and clear.

To be loved, bragged on, protected, upheld—choose whatever word you want. The fact is that every child needs to feel special to his parents. We learn all too soon that the rest of the world does not view us that way. But if we have family support, we can deal with the rest of the world.

In today's reading, Paul wrote to the church as if they were his child. He bragged on them and encouraged their growth. Who wouldn't when someone says, "We constantly pray for you, that our God may count you worthy of his calling" (v. 11).

Brag on, Paul. We need it.

Thank You, Father, for sending us people to brag on us and encourage us. Even if those people seem scarce now, remind us that Your Son is doing that for us right now in Your presence. In His name, Amen.

NOVEMBER 7

SPECIAL IN HIS SIGHT
2 Thessalonians 2:13–15

When I was a child and felt sick, my mother often made me soft-boiled eggs because they soothed my stomach. She tucked me into bed, ensured that I had everything I needed, and cooked her wonderful delicacy. When I ate those eggs, I knew that they were somehow a part of the healing process that was mysterious to me. The eggs themselves had no special healing powers, but getting them from my mother's loving hands had some wonderful effects on me.

I have not eaten a soft-boiled egg in years, but I certainly remember them and what they meant to me.

On several occasions when I was young, my father chewed me out and pointed out how I was acting like an idiot. Why? Because I was doing something dangerous—even lethal. Although I did not like being scolded, I knew that he was doing that for my own good. I felt special being protected by Dad like that.

Our heavenly Father stands by us that way. Paul says, "God chose you to be saved" (v. 13). He wants us in a relationship with Himself. In His sight, we are special. Do you know the Lord in that way? If not, please accept the fact that He loves you and wants you in His family.

Lord, am I really special to You? If so, I resolve to act like I belong in Your family. In Jesus' name, Amen.

NOVEMBER 8

STRONG ENOUGH TO ASK FOR HELP
2 Thessalonians 3:1–5

Why is asking for help considered an "unmanly" thing? You have heard all the old jokes about men asking for directions. We go along on the journey, guessing and hoping that we know the way rather than being certain. The situation reminds me of the story of an airline pilot who announced to his passengers, "Folks, we have a malfunction in our navigational equipment, so we don't exactly know where we are going. But you might be interested to know that we are making good time getting there!"

Consider what Paul did in today's reading. As he had done many times, he asked the church for help. He said, "Pray for us" (v. 1). Did you realize that requesting prayer is asking for help? It is admitting that we do not have all of the resources at our disposal to accomplish everything we desire. Well, "Duh!" Of course we don't.

Paul said that he knew who *does* have all of those resources, though. Jesus would be able to "encourage your hearts" (2 Thess. 2:17). When spirits are flagging and hope seems just a distant daydream, Jesus gives us what we need. Also, according to Paul, He will "strengthen you in every good deed and word" (v. 17). Think of what that means. Jesus, the unique Son of God, is able to give us strength for our actions and for our speaking. No wonder Paul, and all of the other biblical writers, turned to Him for help. The good news is that we can, too.

Are you heading down a path with which you are not familiar? Do you think you are going the wrong way? Do you feel lost? One of life's ironies is that we drive faster when we are lost. Stop if necessary. Get your bearings. Lay out the plans for the rest of the journey. Be strong enough to ask for help.

Lord, I call out to You from the depths of my heart. You know my needs. Strengthen me and encourage me. I need both. In Jesus' name, Amen.

NOVEMBER 9

LAZY
2 Thessalonians 3:6–14

Jerry and Rita were my distant cousins. They came to visit us when I was about twelve. They arrived on a bus with their three children. My parents were a little surprised when they called and asked them to come to the bus station to get them. This little family looked like a group of refugees, with their few possessions and disheveled appearance.

Their story came out over the several days they were with us. Jerry had been "out of work" for a while. They did not have a home because they had been evicted from their apartment. We found out that they went from family member to family member staying as long as they were allowed to. What was clear to everyone, including me at an early age, was that Jerry had no intention of getting a job. He was content to mooch off relatives.

After they were with us for three or four days, my mother asked them, "What bus are you taking home tomorrow?" They got the hint. She took them to the bus station the next day, and they went to his mother's house. We found out later that they "got religion" and started freeloading off churches. When one church would tire of helping them, they simply went to another and "got saved."

Strange how I can remember that incident forty years later. My father worked hard and had no use for anyone who would not work. I do not know if he got his attitude from today's Scripture, but he might have. Paul worked hard too. He was a tentmaker and earned his own living wherever he went. In some places, he ran into people like my cousins. When he did, his teaching was plain: "If a man will not work, he shall not eat" (v. 10).

Let us be about our Father's business with energy and honesty. We learn while we earn. Let us not be lazy.

Lord, as I work to earn a living for myself and the ones I love, help me be about Your work at the same time. In Christ's name, Amen.

NOVEMBER 10

RELIGIOUS CONTROVERSY
1 Timothy 1:3–11

I know a man who loves to argue his religious opinions. I mean he *loves* to argue! This fellow thinks that God must have given all of His truth to only one person in every generation, and this guy is that person for *this* generation. He is blunt to the point of being aggressively offensive. If he collars you, watch out. You're in for quite a debate.

Most of us are not like that. We have faith, and faith has specific content. We learn certain things about God, Jesus, the Holy Spirit, the nature of the Bible, the makeup of the church, and so on. Study and work are required if we are to grow and gain knowledge. But when our knowledge—or our opinions—becomes a weapon, then we have moved in the wrong direction.

Paul wrote to his young protégé, Timothy, to instruct him about how to live his faith. One way is by avoiding, if possible, all religious controversies. We know from reading Paul's letters, however, that at times he defended himself and his work vigorously. But he never went out of his way to attack and offend people. Quite the opposite, he was "all things to all men" (1 Cor. 9:22) to win them. He told Timothy to stay away from false teachers who enjoy controversy. Why? Because they would waste his time and get him off track.

The goal of this teaching is love. This love "comes from a pure heart and a good conscience and a sincere faith" (1 Tim. 1:5). The goal is to build people up rather than tear them down. Whatever builds people in their faith "conforms to the glorious gospel" (v. 11). The man I mentioned earlier seems to have a different goal. He seems to want to prove to everyone how smart he is. That is a long way from showing how loving God is.

I share my faith with people, but I try not to beat them over the head with it. I would rather plant seeds than cut forests.

Lord, help me get the mix right. But whatever I do, help me do it with the motivating love that comes from You. In the name of Him who is both grace and truth—Jesus—Amen.

WHAT GOD REALLY WANTS
I Timothy 2:1–7

Do you ever wonder about what God might actually want? We hear many things, and everyone seems to have an opinion. But what does the Scripture say about this? In today's reading, Paul hits this matter head-on. He writes that God "wants all men to be saved and to come to a knowledge of the truth" (v. 4).

What does "be saved" mean? It means to surrender our lives to Christ, who gives us a spiritual retrofit. He changes us to be ready to serve in His kingdom. We cannot do that by ourselves. Salvation is a personal relationship with Christ that transforms our outlook and our destiny. God wants that for all people. Did you get that? He wants it for everyone, including you. That is why we tell people about our faith. That is why churches do outreach and evangelism. After all, this is not a secret that we are protecting; it is good news that we are sharing.

God wants all people to be saved and to come to a knowledge of the truth. What is that truth? Paul tells us: "For there is one God and one mediator between God and men, the man Christ Jesus, who gave himself as a ransom for all men" (vv. 5–6). Although we live in a world of many religious claims, they are not all the same. Well-meaning people sometimes say, "All religions point us in the same direction." Actually, they do not. Biblical faith tells us that there is only one God, not many. There is only one mediator between us and God, not many.

What does God want? He wants us to understand how much He loves us. He gave His only Son to be our Savior. Then He wants us to tell somebody else about what happened to us.

It is not such a mystery after all, is it?

Lord, thank You for wanting to include me in Your family. Let me tell someone else about what You have done for me. In the name of our Mediator, Jesus Christ, Amen.

NOVEMBER 12

SERVING THE CHURCH
1 Timothy 3:1–13

Some churches call them deacons, others call them elders, still others call them overseers, and some refer to them as bishops. Although the terms are used in various ways, they refer to men who are willing to serve the church. The key word here is *serve.*

Great confusion abounds about the meaning of service in the church. Get a group of pastors together and ask them about their board or their deacons or their elders. They will look at each other with a knowing smile and a rueful expression. Why? Because they have had too many battles with those men.

Disagreements can be very helpful in moving ministry in the direction it needs to go. Minds sharpen minds. Looking at problems and opportunities can be extremely beneficial. But when someone begins to think of the power given him as a weapon, watch out! We should understand that there is a difference between "power with" and "power over." Together, we have "power with" each other to serve Christ and His cause. We make a mistake, however, when we think that we have "power over" someone else and try to accomplish *our* goals rather than those of God.

I want you to do something very difficult today. I want you to examine your attitudes about serving your church. Notice that I did not ask you if you *do* serve. I assume that every man *should* serve in some way. What I am asking is this: Do you think of your service as sharing power with your minister to move the work of the church forward, or do you see yourself as his or her boss?

Many churches are virtually run by women. God bless them! But where are our male leaders? Christ has called *men* to serve Him. Don't go AWOL.

Lord, You have given me gifts and insight to be Your servant. Help me use the power from You to join with others to serve Your church. In Jesus' name, Amen.

NOVEMBER 13

I ACCEPT ALL GOOD GIFTS
1 Timothy 4:1–5

Around this time of year, Americans begin to gear up for Thanksgiving. At my house, I begin to look for turkeys on sale. I usually buy one or two and cook them in my charcoal smoker. The process takes all night, but the dinner is worth the effort. I once lived in a place that had two hickory trees in the yard. Our sons and I would gather all of the nuts from those trees and save them to mix with the charcoal. They gave a great hickory flavor to our favorite bird.

I mention this little slice from my family's life to point out that we often enjoy the simple things of life. In fact, life is pretty much made up of the routines of simplicity and naturalness. The apostle Paul ridiculed teachers of his day who tried to deny their followers the everyday pleasures of life—marriage and good food in particular. They tried to make themselves superspiritual by forbidding certain things that, according to them, would bring them closer to God. But would it?

When I was in my teens during the 1960s, every pothead could cite verses 4–5 of today's reading. I remember having an argument with a student who said that the Bible says that everything, including marijuana, is God-given and good, so why should people make laws against it? I replied that hemlock was natural too, but I did not see him lacing his tea with it!

Paul was not into harsh practices. On the contrary, he was trying to get people to realize that our relationship to God is not based on what we eat or avoid, or whether we marry or remain single. Food and relationships are gifts from God that are available if we choose them. I don't know about you, but I will accept any gift that God wants to give me.

Thank You for the good gifts that You place in my path. I accept all that You have for me. In Jesus' name, Amen.

NOVEMBER 14

TAKING CARE OF BUSINESS AT HOME
I Timothy 5:8

I love the story of the football coach who watched his team fail at even the basic moves on the field. He gathered the team in the locker room and began by holding up a football saying, "Gentlemen, this is a football." The basics are essential for not only the gridiron and the business place but also the home.

I have been in far too many homes that seem more like a gathering of strangers than a close-knit fellowship. Paul directed the white-hot light of God's truth on the home when he wrote, "If anyone does not provide for his relatives, and especially for his immediate family, he has denied the faith and is worse than an unbeliever" (v. 8). That is one of the biblical statements that I sometimes want to show people and ask, "What part of that don't you understand?"

Friends might come and go, and work associates seem as though they enter and exit our lives through a revolving door. But family is forever. That is why families have so much potential for blessing us or cursing us. Part of the very Word of God to men is that we are to take care of our families. We often think of that in financial terms and feel guilty if we are out of work. But that taking care of family is deeper. It involves the financial, certainly, but also the emotional and spiritual.

I heard of a man who arrived at the airport and was met by his wife and their two children. He swept them up in his arms and kissed them and told them how much he loved them. Another passenger who saw this asked him, "Wow, how long were you away?" "Two days," he answered. The other man said, "If I ever get married, I hope I have a family like yours." As he walked away with his family, the first man turned back and said, "Don't hope. Decide."

Lord, I have decided. I will give my best to my family. If something else has to be left undone, so be it. My family members come first. Give me the strength to carry this out. Through Christ, my Lord, Amen.

NOVEMBER 15

BUILDING YOUR LEGACY
1 Timothy 5:22–25

We build our lives day by day, decision by decision. Both the small and the large choices we make add to the mix as we build our legacy. You might be tempted to say, "Wait a minute. I'm not wealthy, so how can I leave a legacy?" Our legacy is not just what is specified in our will. It is the moral influence that we have had on other people. It is the trail through life that we have left behind us.

A legacy is what my father left behind that comes to mind when I think about him. He was as rock-solid a man as I have ever known. Although he was not well educated, he was intelligent. He was of the old school, and when he gave his word on something, you could take his word to the bank. His "yes" was "yes," and his "no" was "no." He did things for other people but stayed out of their business. Although he was not a highly emotional or physically demonstrative man, I had no doubt that he loved his family.

We all leave a legacy. That is what Paul writes about in today's

Scripture. Both our sins and our good deeds leave a wake behind us. Both are part of our legacy, but the sins should be minor, and our virtues should be major. That does not mean that we sit around like Little Jack Horner in the children's poem, thinking, *What a good boy am I!* It means that we own up to our attitudes and actions and realize that each day is a brick in the foundation of our legacy. Do we build with care and forethought, or do we blunder through life little knowing or caring what we leave behind?

What are you leaving in *your* wake?

> *Lord, I am Your man as best I can be. Help me develop a plan for building a positive legacy for everyone associated with me. In Jesus' name, Amen.*

NOVEMBER 16

FINANCIAL PEACE

1 Timothy 6:3–10

Author and counselor Dave Ramsay has a book with an intriguing title—*Financial Peace*. That book is different from many financial guides in that it does not discuss dollars and cents as much as it does common sense. Ramsay says that we have to come to grips with our attitudes about money. Only when we examine our attitudes and actions can we gain financial peace. Otherwise, we will be at the mercy of every whim or gimmick that comes along. When asked where he gets this idea, Ramsay says he got it out of the Bible and just packaged it differently.

Today's reading is one of those places in the Bible that often pulls us up short. So much in our culture tells us to do whatever it takes to make as much money as possible. But look at the other side of that concept: "For the love of money is a root of all kinds of evil. Some people, eager for money, have wandered from the faith and pierced themselves with many griefs" (v. 10). The whatever-it-takes attitude of gaining money is shown to be what it is—spiritual fraud. Does this mean that money is bad and we should never think about it? Hardly. Money is a tool that we use and control or it controls us. One of the best things we can do is to develop a wise attitude about money so that whatever we have is a blessing from God.

The biblical warning that people who chase money pierce themselves with many griefs is a startling STOP sign. Life is short, way too short to be chasing small strips of green paper. God is the goal of our lives, not cash. If you have money, thank God for it and use it wisely. If you don't have much, thank God for the freedom that you have not to worry about it. Whichever your circumstances, learn to gain financial peace.

Your Son gave up the riches of heaven for our sake, Father. Help us to use our resources for His sake. In His name, Amen.

NOVEMBER 17

BUT YOU. . . .
1 Timothy 6:11–21

One of the problems that I have always had in my spiritual life is how to live in the world and really make a difference and, at the same time, be different from people who do not know Christ. Is that a difficulty for you too? The New Testament reflects this dilemma. On one hand, we live in a world of dark forces and evil. On the other hand, we inhabit an environment of grace and peace ruled by Jesus Christ. How do we deal with these opposite poles?

Paul addressed this issue when he wrote to his young protégé, Timothy. He began verse 11 with the words, *But you. . . .* Here is the separation from the rest of the world, a differentiation that characterizes a man of God. Paul had been discussing people who had made their faith useless by their actions. Instead of pursuing the fruit of the Spirit, they were into controversies, power trips, and money.

Then, thinking of Timothy and those like him, Paul drew a line in the sand and said in effect, "But you. . . ." Yes, they might be filled with rage and envy, but you must be like Christ. They might spend their lives chasing a large bank account, but you remember the source of your real riches. They might be tickled at every teaching that comes down the road, but you remember that the Word of God is the truth.

I think about those separating words, *But you.* They remind me that I have made some decisions that help define my actions and my attitudes. Others might go in this direction, but I need to go in another. Others might zero in on what they define as their goals, but I try to keep my eyes on Jesus.

> *Lord, You know that I want to be "one of the guys" and do guy stuff. Remind me that I can be a real man and celebrate my masculinity without going out of my mind and off my course. Keep me straight. In Christ's name, Amen.*

NOVEMBER 18

BETTER THAN FORT KNOX
2 Timothy 1:12

My first pastorate nearly thirty years ago was near Fort Knox, Kentucky. I knew the significance of that place, not just as a military base, but as a repository for the nation's gold supply. The old James Bond movie *Goldfinger* supposedly showed the inside of the vault where the gold was kept. At least it stoked the imaginations of many people who wondered about what kind of security measures were involved in such a venture.

When I think of security, I think not of Fort Knox but of my relationship with God. Even the best human security can fail. Just recently in the state where I live, several valuable paintings were stolen from a private residence. The security system was supposed to be elaborate and virtually foolproof. But you know the old saying: "They'll find a better fool."

Paul writes to his young protégé, Timothy, about the trustworthiness of God's hand upon us. Thinking about the Lord's character, Paul wrote "that He is able to guard what I have entrusted to Him until that day" (v. 12 NASB). Imagine that—God's standing guard over our relationship! What enemy could storm the gate with such a sentry? What power could come with stealth and steal our treasures? Who could defeat such a formidable foe? The answer, of course, is no one.

We can take great comfort in this image of God guarding our faith. We believe, and something happens within us to transform us to be like Jesus. That does not happen by only our will power; it is the grace of God that changes us. When we say "yes" to God, He assumes a sentry stance over us. That is not just a metaphor; it is a fact.

Remember that your standing with God in faith is better than gold in a vault. He is able to take care of you.

Father, guard my heart, my mind, and my soul by Your power. Keep me for Yourself and help me live like Your child. Through Christ, my Lord, Amen.

NOVEMBER 19

KEEP YOUR EYE ON THE TARGET
2 Timothy 2:1–7

When my sons were in high school, I bought them both a shotgun. They are beauties—Remington 12-gauge pumps. Before I let them go out hunting, I took them to gun-safety classes that had required attendance and a test at the end. If they passed the course, they could get their certification. The first night of class, the instructor told the group that the most important things in hunting are to keep your eye on the target and never to point your gun at anything that is not the target. He said that we would be amazed at some of the places gun barrels end up pointing.

That is not such a radical message. The Bible tells us, in many different ways, the same thing. When we know that our target in faith is a sustaining relationship to God, we keep pointing in that direction. Otherwise, we are like a tumbleweed blowing through the desert. Paul tells us to remember three kinds of men as we think about this truth.

The first is a soldier. A good soldier knows that his goal is to serve his nation by following orders. He does not invent his own goals but accepts those of his superiors. The second kind of man that Paul mentions is an athlete. He trains hard to compete for a prize. He has to follow the rules of the game, or he will get disqualified and never reach his target. The third kind of man is a farmer. He knows that soil preparation and planting are necessary if he wants to achieve his objective—a harvest.

If I were to ask you what your target in life is, how would you answer? To make a million dollars? To run your own company? To have a happy family life? Those are not bad goals, but by themselves they are not big enough. Let us make our target in life loyalty to God.

Lord, more than anything else in life, I want my goal to be becoming Your man. Help me keep my eyes on that target. In Jesus' name, Amen.

NOVEMBER 20

Approved by God
2 Timothy 2:14–19

Several organizations exist to give approval or denial to certain products. Underwriters Laboratory was set up to check on compliance with electrical safety codes. Consumer Reports rates a wide variety of products and tries to give an objective evaluation of them. Good Housekeeping does the same thing for household items. An item that is given the Good Housekeeping Seal of Approval is seen as being above the competition.

What would you think of a seal of approval given to a life? Who would be qualified to do such a thing? In today's reading, Paul tells us that we can work toward getting the approval of the Lord. I suppose that we could call it the "God Housekeeping Seal of Approval."

This is not a trivial pursuit. One of the ways we do this is by keeping ourselves squarely in relationship with God. This goal involves being serious in how we handle "the word of truth" (v. 15). I always cringe when I see a Bible in a car on the back dashboard where it curls up like a banana peel in the sun. We avoid "godless chatter," which is trash talk that pulls us away from God.

I am not ashamed to say that I want to be approved by God. That does not necessarily mean that we will not have a successful life in the normal sense of the word. In fact, I believe that faith takes us closer to a life of success than does any other stance. But being approved by God is more than conventional success. It is His saying to us, "Well done, son. I'm proud of you. You have faced all of the trials set before you; you kept going and did not fail." Now *that* is what I want to hear!

How about you?

Give me that word of approval, Father. I'll do my best to make You proud. Through Christ, Amen.

NOVEMBER 21

AN OPEN-FACED LIFE
2 Timothy 3:10–17

I know two men who exemplify two very different approaches to life. One, Jim, is closed. He does not get close to people and keeps everyone at arm's distance. He does not talk about himself much, although he will argue football for hours. Jim pretty much lives within himself. People are uncomfortable around him because they never know what he is thinking or feeling.

Dan is very different. He is open and transparent. People love being around him because he says what he thinks and lets other people know how much he likes them. His behavior is not a put-on; he really does like people, and that is why he has many friends.

You and I probably fit somewhere in between these two poles. We face the constant challenge of being open and honest about who we are and of what we are capable. When Paul wrote to Timothy, he reminded his young protégé that he had seen Paul up close and knew all about him. Paul even listed the things about which he was open: his teaching, way of life, purpose, faith, patience, love, endurance, and even the persecutions that he suffered. His life was an open book with nothing to hide.

I have found through the years that there is a time to be strong and invulnerable. There is also a time to be up front and let people know that I do not have a big S on my chest for "Superpastor." Some people will exploit that openness, but most people seem to appreciate it because it allows them to be themselves. They do not have to put on airs or act superspiritual around me because I am not perfect either. I am a disciple in the making with a long way to go, but I have already come a long way.

How about you?

Lord, help me to be open before You and everyone else. Let my life be a beacon and not a stumbling block. Through Jesus, Amen.

NOVEMBER 22

READY TO LIVE, READY TO DIE
2 Timothy 4:6–8

Paul was weary—very weary. His travels had worn him out physically. His travails had worn him out emotionally. But in the midst of all of his difficulties, he knew that he had lived—really lived. Because he had done his best, Paul knew that he could face anything that life or death brought his way.

We do not have to be as courageous as Paul to face life. I have never known anyone quite like him, but I have known many people who have done their best in their own quiet way and who were also ready to face whatever life gave them.

My father had lung cancer. A surgeon removed part of one lung and thought that he had gotten it all, but it came back after a while. Dad went through some chemotherapy, but it seemed to hurt him more than it helped, so he stopped treatments. He faced his death with the kind of courage that I had always known him to have. I remember when he and my mother went to their lawyer to get their legal affairs in order. I went to see him one day shortly before he went into the hospital for the last time. We sat at their table and talked about his life. While we talked, I turned on my tape recorder and preserved his words.

Dad talked about his youth and about the little community of Evangeline, Louisiana, where he grew up and still lived. I learned all sorts of things about him that day. More than anything else, though, I was reminded what a good man he was. I never think about Paul's words in today's reading without remembering my father: "I have fought the good fight, I have finished the race, I have kept the faith" (v. 7).

I want to live like that so that I can die like that.

Lord, thank You for the strength to continue on life's journey. Help me keep the faith and finish the race. For Jesus' sake, Amen.

NOVEMBER 23

PRACTICAL ATHEISM

Titus 1:16

The church is filled with people who are practical atheists. What do I mean by that statement? They talk about faith, go to Bible studies, even give money to religious causes, but, in the end, they deny their faith by living according to standards other than the gospel.

One man is a church leader who knows all the right words to say about love and forgiveness. But if you disagree with him, he will turn on you in an instant and treat you like his worst enemy. Another guy lets a leadership position go to his head and seems to forget about fairness.

Paul ran into his share of such folks. That is why he could write, "They claim to know God, but by their actions they deny him" (v. 16). He was not interested in the opinions of the guys on the sidelines, those Monday-morning quarterbacks who can win every game from their Lazyboys. He wanted to know that when the whistle blew at game time, he could count on them.

An unknown poet put it this way:

I would rather stumble a thousand times
attempting to reach a goal,
Than to sit in a crowd
In my weather-proof shroud,

A shriveled and self-satisfied soul.
I would rather be doing and daring
All of my error-filled days,
Than watching, and waiting, and dying,
Smug in my perfect ways.
I would rather wonder and blunder,
Stumbling blindly ahead,
Than for safety's sake
Lest I make a mistake,
Be sure, be safe, be dead.

Let's be alive in our faith, remembering to live with an assurance that God is with us as we make daily choices for Him. I don't want to live as though God did not exist. Do you?

Father, forgive me for learning to make all of the right sounds while at the same time denying You with my choices. Help me bring everything in my life together under one Lord and Master—Jesus Christ. In His name, Amen.

NOVEMBER 24

To Be a Man

Titus 2:1–2

Bill Galston once took a job as deputy assistant to the president of the United States for domestic policy. The job was challenging, exciting, and demanding. Although Galston found the job enjoyable, he also found that it took him away from what he loved best—his family. His nine-year-old son, Ezra, enjoyed baseball but realized that his father could not be there to watch him play. Ezra wrote his father a letter in which he said, "Baseball's not fun when there's no one there to applaud you." Galston knew what he had to do. He resigned his high-profile job and got his life back in balance. He said of that experience, "It wasn't as if I were giving up something I didn't care about. But I was giving it up in favor of something I cared about even more. Fatherhood is the prism through which I see the world. Nothing else is even a close second."[1] This wise man had the patience to struggle through the complexities of life until he could find what he knew was the right path for him and his family. I think he is a real man.

Paul listed various aspects of what godly men should learn. "Temperate" is a lifestyle of moderation. Sure, there is plenty of room for celebrations and joy, for intensity and passion. But overall, we learn discipline. "Worthy of respect" is a life that is worth someone else's copying. "Self-controlled" is our ability to say yes to the better things of life and no to the lesser things. If we do not control ourselves, who will? "Sound" in faith, love, and endurance is wholeness and strength in each of these areas.

This is a short list of manly characteristics, but it strains at the seams of importance. Learn these well, and be a man.

Lord, all throughout this year I have been working better to love You and to grow as a man. Help me each day as I continue making progress. In Jesus' name, Amen.

NOVEMBER 25

TRANSFORMED
Philemon 8–16

How does another man become my brother? This is not a trick question but a theological reflection. Think about some of the relationships in your life. Some are relationships of convenience, such as the one you might have with a person at a service station or a grocery store. Others are relationships of necessity, such as with people at your work. You might be closer to them, but they are not necessarily your closest friends.

Once in a while, though, relationships click. You find yourself drawn into close friendship with someone. I have several friendships like that. One, in particular, has lasted more than half of my

---

1. Bill Galston, quoted in "Get a Life," by Michael Warshaw, *Fast Company*, June–July 1998, 140.

life so far. We have gone through our ups and downs in our families and careers. We have visited in each other's homes and have called throughout the years to keep up with each other. One of the strongest of the elements that draw us together is our commitment to Christ. Both of us try to live out our faith and to become men that God can use.

In today's Scripture reading, Paul sent a runaway slave named Onesimus back to his owner, Philemon. The slave had found Paul and had become a valued help to him. But Paul knew that the legal situation had to be resolved, so he sent Onesimus back. In writing a letter to accompany Onesimus, Paul told Philemon that Onesimus was once "useless" to him but is now "useful." In fact, the name Onesimus means "useful." Paul urged Philemon to take him back, not as a slave but as a brother.

What would transform a slave into a brother? The only thing I can think of is the living power of Jesus Christ. It puts all men on the same level and shows us all to be needy at the same place—our soul.

Look around you. You might find a brother.

Help me, Father, to see others as my potential brothers. In Christ, Amen.

LISTENING FOR GOD
Hebrews 1:1−4

Does God still speak to men today? Is His voice still evident in the chaos of everyday life? Do we need some special "receiver" to pick it up? The writer of Hebrews began his book by answering these questions.

A long time ago, he wrote, God spoke through the prophets. We have read about them in the Bible. Men such as Isaiah, Jeremiah, Elisha, Jonah, and others were spokesmen of the Lord. They opened their mouths and their lives because of their conviction that God was actively communicating to humankind through them. Hebrews says that after speaking through the prophets, God changed His tactics; He spoke through his Son, Jesus.

I believe that Jesus is still the avenue through which God speaks to us. How does He do so? As we read the words that Jesus spoke, we come to realize that they represent reality. They give us life and hope. They point the way to eternal life. Take, for example, Jesus' teaching about following Him. He once said, "No one who puts his hand to the plow and looks back is fit for service in the kingdom of God" (Luke 9:62). We understand that message and see those words as an encouragement to go straight ahead as best we can. If we spend our lives turning around to see what we have left, we will not get very far.

You are reading this book because you want to listen for God's voice. I hope that you are also reading the Scripture passages that Mark and I have been providing with each devotional throughout this year. They represent God's intention to speak to you not only here and now but also to all ages and in all circumstances. We might have to quiet some of the noise around us to hear Him.

In a sense, Jesus is our "hearing aid" for God's voice. What do you hear?

Lord, I want to listen as You speak to me. Help me to distinguish Your voice from those of others, and give me the courage to follow You. In the name of Jesus, who helps me hear, Amen.

NOVEMBER 27

PAY ATTENTION
Hebrews 2:1–4

"Pay attention!" That is what I sometimes have to tell children when I speak to them (and to adults, too!). Children wiggle and giggle and have a hard time focusing on anything. But are we adults much different?

I know a man who owns three boats. He is always working on them, taking them out for recreation, going somewhere with them, or coming back with them from somewhere. His life is a blur of activity. I wonder when he sleeps. Mostly, though, I wonder when he has time to pay attention to the most important things in life.

The writer of the book of Hebrews says to "pay more careful attention, . . . so that we do not drift away" (v. 1). The image is not of a person who intentionally turns his back on God and goes off on his own. It is more a picture of someone who, like a grazing sheep, nibbles his way to lostness. When a ship comes into port, it is secured to the moorings by strong ropes; otherwise, the wind and the tide would move it into a position that the captain does not want. Our lives are similar. They are to be guided, moored, and cared for. In other words, we need to pay attention.

Today's Scripture asks, "How shall we escape if we ignore such a great salvation?" (v. 3). Part of our salvation involves listening to what God has to teach us. But how can we learn anything if we are always running away from Him? He sometimes has to say to us, "Pay attention!" I admit, that is difficult for me. Is it hard for you, too? I get busy and take off on a course that I might even believe is of God, but I sometimes forget to check my progress along the way. Getting off course is so easy.

Let us make up our minds that we are going to pay attention to our Lord. He is worth listening to.

Lord, You know me and my tendency to get involved in all sorts of things that might have little to do with You. Help me, when all is said and done, to pay attention to You. In Jesus' name, Amen.

NOVEMBER 28

FACING DEATH DOWN
Hebrews 2:14–18

It is a great thing to face death and survive. I am not being silly about this; I am very serious. As a pastor, I have counseled with many people who were facing death and have conducted numerous funerals. I have seen death take infants, young children, middle-aged parents, and aging seniors. Sometimes death arrives on the scene almost like a friend and escort. At other times, it sneaks in through a crack in the window and strikes when you least expect it.

I am speaking personally when I say that it is a great thing to face death and survive. That is exactly what I did in the summer of 2000. Lying in the ICU one evening after a bad accident, I faced the possibility that I might not make it out of the hospital alive. Although death had waltzed around me many times before, that was the first time that it had ever asked me to dance. I learned that night what I have seen others learn—every individual has to come to grips with his own death. Some men never deal with this issue. They flit from one thing to another, always trying to keep one step ahead of mortality. Others calmly stare death in the eye and face it down, at least for a while.

Today's Scripture instructs us about this matter. Jesus knew our dilemma, being both physical and spiritual. Through His death and resurrection, He changed death itself. His work was to "free those who all their lives were held in slavery by their fear of death" (v. 15). Jesus looked death in the eye, and death blinked first.

Since that evening in the ICU, I realized that life is fragile and that one day I will take that dance with death. But I no longer fear it. I don't have to. My Lord Jesus Christ has gone before me and awaits my arrival. That fact is enough to give all of us courage.

Free me from all fear, Lord. Fear of living and fear of dying. Your Son paved the way, and we follow Him anywhere. In Christ's name, Amen.

HEROES GALLERY
Hebrews 11

Hebrews 11 is a look at the heroes gallery of the Bible. Person after person is lifted up as being someone worthy of copying because of that person's faith. Abraham, Isaac, Joseph, Moses, and others are lifted as if to say, "Look here, follow these men and women; learn from their lives."

I have my own gallery of heroes. Maybe you do too. Everyone in my group has taught me something. I have mentioned my father several times in this book. He had a profound effect on me by his quiet but strong life. Brother Sam, the pastor who baptized me, and Brother Bob, who took me under his spiritual wing to teach me, were two pastors who shaped my young life. John, a college roommate whom I helped lead to Christ, and Brother Perry, a pastor during my early college days, drew things out of me that I did not even know I had in me. They belong in my heroes gallery.

There are many others. Jim, the best college teacher I ever had, is in there. George, Earl, Tom, and Fisher, professors in seminary, all gave something of themselves to me. Esther and Harry, members of two of my early churches, showed me things about courageous, faithful living that still inspire me more than a quarter century later.

Authors whom I have never met reached out from their pages to help mold me. People I don't know have supported the churches I have served and have helped me to grow in my faith. Person after person after person has added his or her touch to my life, and I am the richer for it.

You could list some of these people who have done that for you. But think about this—you can *be* that person for someone else. Would you like to have your name listed in their gallery of heroes?

Lord, help me to give of myself to others in such a way that my life of faith might inspire and instruct their life of faith. In Christ, Amen.

NOVEMBER 30

ENDURE
Hebrews 12:7–12

My middle name is not Atlas. I am not like the mythical ancient who carried the world on his shoulders. Unless I miss my guess, you are not either. Yet, part of our lot in life is to carry some heavy loads. In the words of today's Scripture, "endure hardship." Is this simply a call to buck up and take whatever life dishes out? Not exactly. We need to read the rest of that verse: "endure hardship *as discipline*" (v. 7).

Discipline is the lessons we learn that add strength and courage to life. A setback might be bitter to go through, but it is discipline in that it teaches us patience and the ability to come through the experience a better man. I agree with the CEO of a large company who was once asked, "How do you make good decisions?" He answered, "By experience." The questioner followed up, "Okay, but how do you get experience?" The CEO replied, "By making bad decisions!"

You might not have thought that hardship is the entrance exam to the university of hard knocks. If we pay attention and learn from our experiences, we will find that we change. Today's reading continues, "No discipline seems pleasant at the time, but painful. Later on, however, it produces a harvest of righteousness and peace for those who have been trained by it" (v. 11). The promise is that when we endure our hardships, we will emerge more Christlike. That makes the ordeal worthwhile.

As we end this month, I invite you to take a few moments and think back over the past thirty days. What hardships have you faced? What crises? What events seemed so big as to wash you away? Now ask yourself, What did I learn from this experience, and how can I use it for God's glory?

Father, whatever I face, let me face it all with
Your Spirit within me. Discipline my life for Your
sake. In Christ Jesus, Amen.

THE SECRET TO BECOMING WISE

James 1:4–8

When was the last time you did something really boneheaded— something, perhaps, like the guy in the following story?

A man left work one Friday after being paid. Instead of going home, he decided to spend the whole weekend the way he wanted, partying and having a good time. Unfortunately, he neglected to tell his wife about any of this!

When he got home Sunday night, his wife was livid. She tore into him, raking him up one side and down the other. Finally she said, "How would you like it if you didn't see me for two or three days?"

By this time, the man had had enough. So he came back with, "I'd like that just fine!"

The wife gave him his wish. Monday, he didn't see her. Tuesday and Wednesday passed without his seeing her. By Thursday, however, the swelling had begun to go down, and he could see her a little bit out of one eye!

Why do we involve ourselves in unwise things when God has told every one of us that wisdom is ours for the asking? The answer is that for some people the price of obtaining wisdom is too high.

God wants to make us wise, but we must come to Him, asking in faith and with consistency. Proverbs further tells us that we must be willing to steep ourselves in God's Word, where wisdom lies.

Much time spent in the Bible and much time spent in prayer—is that too much for you to do to obtain wisdom? I encourage you to raise your goals—make the standards for your life higher. Ask God to help you become wise, then pay the price for that wisdom by learning from His Word.

Wisdom is like water released from its banks. It has a tendency to spread everywhere. Your godly wisdom can touch the lives of many people, blessing them and helping them to grow in Christ.

Decide today that you will ask God to help you become wise.

Dear Lord, I humbly ask You for wisdom. Give me the faith to believe that You'll answer this prayer and the discipline to spend much time in the Bible. May I become wise so that I can honor You and enrich Your kingdom. In Jesus' name, Amen.

DECEMBER 2

RESISTING TEMPTATION

James 1:12–15

What does temptation look like in your life and mine?

For some of us, temptation resides in a bottle. Others of us have a problem resisting the lure of money. Pornography draws some of us like a moth to a flame. And more of us than we'd like to admit are battling substance abuse habits that enslave us.

For all of us, the first step to overcoming temptation is to admit that what we're doing is a sin. God can't help us with what we won't confess. We must also realize that we need help in staying away from the temptation. An accountability group of fellow believers is a great way to get the strength we need to overcome our weakness consistently.

Finally, if we're "tempted" to play down the seriousness of our giving in to temptation, we might want to read today's passage again. A careful study of temptation's progress shows us the end result—death.

It's time for us to quit playing games with temptation. The moment has come for us to turn from sin and get serious about living for Jesus Christ. Not tomorrow but *now.* Not halfway but completely sold out for God.

Dear God, I don't want temptation to rule my life any longer. I confess that I've sinned, and I ask for forgiveness. Please cleanse me, strengthen me, and give me the wisdom to change my habits to avoid these old temptations. I want to live for You, not continually give in to sin. In Jesus' name, Amen.

GETTING THE MOST FROM BIBLE STUDY
James 1:22–25

James tells us that it is vital that we not forget what we read in God's Word. Reading is important, but if we don't follow through with changed actions, we've really accomplished nothing. Early in my Christian life, I developed the habit of reading the Bible daily. But I must confess that often I came away from my time spent in the Word not really having absorbed what I'd just read.

The key that made my Bible study more effective can be summarized in one word: *meditation.* I began this practice more than twenty-five years ago, and it still works for me today. Here's what I do.

When I read a passage of Scripture, I turn my eyes from what I've just read and ask myself several questions, including the following:

1. What did I just read? If I can't remember, I read it again!
2. What lesson did I learn that I need to implement in my life?
3. What promise did God give me through this Scripture?
4. Is there a verse in this passage that I need to memorize?

In Psalm 1, we are told that the godly man meditates on the law "day and night" (v. 2). I encourage you to use the preceding questions as a guide to creating your own "meditation motivation." The more you remember of God's Word, the more you can put into practice.

Heavenly Father, I want to make my devotional time as meaningful as possible. Help me to understand and digest what I read in the Bible. May I apply Your truths to my life today. In Jesus' name, Amen.

DECEMBER 4

FAKE GOLD AND REAL JEWELS

James 2:1–8

Tillman Franks, before he retired, was one of country music's great agents to the stars. His son plays guitar in our praise band, so when Tillman published his autobiography, I bought it to learn as much as I could about the early years of country and rock music.

After a horrific wreck that injured him and killed one of Tillman's friends, the agent found himself in the hospital. For a number of years, he'd worn a diamond ring on his hand that was the envy of all of his friends. When someone from the local mortuary came to the hospital to talk to Tillman about the funeral, the man was so kind that Tillman took off the diamond ring and gave it to the guy!

"Everybody thought I was out of my mind. . . . They thought it was a $10,000 ring that I gave away," Tillman remembers. In reality, the diamond was big—but fake! It was worth a few dollars at the most.[1]

Sometimes the biggest and the flashiest doesn't always mean the best. Fake jewels and fake people can sometimes hide their lack of worth behind a glittery façade.

James warns his readers not to judge people on their wealth or lack of it. He also demands fair, impartial treatment to all who enter the church.

How do you treat the members and guests at your local church? Do you offer the same kind words to everyone? Or do you have a certain crowd you hang out with to the exclusion of nearly everyone else?

Limiting your time and attention to only the chosen few means that you're missing out on the real jewels hidden from your narrow sight. It also means that you're not fulfilling God's commandment concerning how to treat other believers!

This next Sunday, look around for new people with whom you can interact. Take an interest in even those who have few people skills. In doing so, you will both be blessed and strengthen the body of Christ.

Lord, may I not be guilty of judging people by
their wealth or their power. I want to love and be
kind to all of those at my church. Help me to see
others as You see them and love them as You do.
In Jesus' name, Amen.

---

1. Tillman Franks, *I Was There When It Happened* (Many, La.: Sweet Dreams, 2000), 120.

DECEMBER 5

ARE YOU A LAW BREAKER?

James 2:10–13

I must have been about nine years old when I got into trouble for breaking the law.

Mom had baked some cookies for her Sunday school class meeting and had laid them on the kitchen table to cool. "Touch one of those cookies," she warned, "and you die." Unbelievably, I managed to leave the cookies alone—even when Mom put the cookies in a cookie jar, planning to store them there until the fellowship that night.

I resisted temptation—until she went to the back of the house to lie down.

"She'll never miss one or two cookies," I reasoned. Carefully climbing up on a chair, I managed to reach the cookie jar, where it rested on top of the refrigerator. I took the top off, set it down, got out my first cookie, took my first bite, and—*crash!*

The top of the cookie jar rolled off the refrigerator and hit the floor, shattering completely. In what seemed like one five-millionths of a second, Mom was standing in the doorway of the kitchen scowling at me. There I stood with my accomplice, the chair. Cookie crumbs surrounded my lips, and broken pieces of cookie-jar lid surrounded my feet.

Mom was right. I died that day! My heart jumped into my throat, and I could see my brief life flash before my eyes. I won't talk about the punishment, but it was a long time before I could sit down.

Was my Mom all that upset over the loss of one cookie? Of course not. It was the principle of not obeying her that got me in trouble.

It's the same with God.

James reminds us that if we break any part of the Law, we are guilty of breaking the whole Law! In other words, when we break any of God's commandments, we have chosen to follow not God but our lusts. The principle of disobeying God holds true whether we murder or tell a "white lie." The earthly consequences are certainly worse for some sins rather than for others. But it is the concept of sin, in any form, that keeps us out of fellowship with the Lord.

Today, let's ask God to help us honor Him by keeping every part of His Law. The Lord doesn't need lawbreakers, He desires His children to obey Him completely.

Dear God, I want to honor You by being the best Christian possible. I don't want to turn a blind eye to anything in my life that displeases You. Help me to follow Your commandments and live in Your grace today. In Jesus' name, Amen.

DECEMBER 6

FAITH AND WORKS

James 2:14–18

If you went to see Russell Dunham today, you'd find a placid, eighty-one-year-old gardener enjoying his forty-acre spread. In January 1945, however, young Sergeant Dunham found himself and his platoon in a desperate situation. Pinned down by withering machinegun fire, trapped at the bottom of a steep hill, hindered by snow all around and a barrage of artillery fire behind, Dunham made a life-changing decision.

He charged the hill—alone.

A bullet slashed across his back, sending him tumbling. He got back up and charged the first machinegun nest. Kicking aside a grenade that landed at his feet, he shot the machine gunner and his assistant.

Then his rifle jammed! Dunham never hesitated. He jumped into the machinegun nest, grabbed the third gunner and hurled him down the hill. "The captain said we needed prisoners," he explained later.

The second machinegun nest, about fifty yards away, trained its fire on him. Dunham responded by grabbing an M-1 rifle from a wounded soldier and advancing toward the nest. When he was close enough, he lobbed two grenades into the enemy emplacement, wiping out the crew. Then he started for the last enemy stronghold, sixty-five yards above him. When Dunham had crawled to within fifteen yards of the machinegun, he stood up and lobbed his last two grenades, wiping out the crew.

All told, Dunham single-handedly destroyed three fortified positions, killed nine of the enemy, wounded seven more, and captured two.

Why did Dunham risk his life like that when others wouldn't? He loves his country. And on that day, Russell Dunham *proved* it. His act of courage earned him the Congressional Medal of Honor— and the gratitude of millions of Americans.[1]

James tells us that faith without works is dead.

Even non-Christians say the same thing: "If you're gonna talk the talk, you've gotta walk the walk." "Practice what you preach." "Put your money where your mouth is." "The proof of the pudding is in the eating."

Let's ask ourselves: What deeds am I doing that reveal my faith in God? Do I follow through on my promises to others? Am I taking an active role in my church? Do I give at least 10 percent of my income to the work of the Lord as He commands?

If we claim to be believers, let's act like believers! Let's let our actions be consistent with our faith in God.

Heavenly Father, I want my life to make a difference for You. I want to do more than talk a great game. Please help me to live actively for you through my giving, my church involvement, my witnessing, and my helping others. In Jesus' name, Amen.

DECEMBER 7

PROFANITY OR PRAISE?

James 3:5–12

I walked out of a movie recently. It's something that I haven't done in ages, but the rating had led me to believe that it would be okay for me to watch it. Long ago, I decided not to go to R-rated movies. But after about fifteen minutes of this particular movie, I realized that our country's standards had slipped lower once again.

---

1. *Reader's Digest*, June 2001, 122–23.

Profanity spewed from the lips of the characters. Not just one or two words, but nearly every other sentence contained graphic cursing. As my wife and I walked out of the theater, we saw children and young teenagers sitting with their parents listening to and absorbing what I call "speech pollution."

I can't control what happens at a theater, but I can control what I see and hear in my house. I have a device called "TV Guardian" installed between my VCR and my television. It deletes almost 100 percent of the profanity in films and television shows. In addition, I don't think my children have ever heard me or my wife utter a word of profanity. They get enough of it at the school's lunchroom and in the halls.

How is your speech? Is profanity a part of your life? What are you teaching those around you about how to speak?

You can have a "potty mouth," or you can have a "praise mouth." But you can't have both. Listen to what verses 10–12 from today's passage say to us: "Out of the same mouth come praise and cursing. My brothers, this should not be. Can both fresh water and salt water flow from the same spring? My brothers, can a fig tree bear olives, or a grapevine bear figs? Neither can a salt spring produce fresh water."

The Bible clearly says that your mouth will reflect what is in your heart. Your coworkers, your family members, your teammates will learn about your walk with Christ through how you express yourself.

If profanity is a part of your life, confess it as a sin and ask God's forgiveness. It's a habit, but it's a habit that can be broken.

Lord, I confess that sometimes my mouth doesn't honor You. I ask You to help me give any profanity in my speech to You and allow You to cleanse me completely. Help me change my vocabulary into words that honor You. In Jesus' name, Amen.

THE PRAYER THAT GOES UNREWARDED

James 4:1–3

When it comes to the theology of prayer, many believers have the mistaken impression that if we simply have enough faith, we will receive that for which we ask. They will cite several Scripture passages to prove their point, but we ignore other Scripture passages that give a balanced approach to prayer. For example, 1 John 5:14 says, "This is the confidence we have in approaching God: that if we ask anything according to his will, he hears us."

James concurs with the apostle John. He writes bluntly to his audience in verse 3 of today's passage, "When you ask, you do not receive, because you ask with wrong motives, that you may spend what you get on your pleasures."

Prayer asked with selfish motives that do not honor God will not be answered. These are prayers that are not according to the Lord's will. Because God loves us, He will not give us that which He knows would harm us or be a temptation to us.

We have a lottery in my state. I've (kind of) jokingly said there are thousands of people across my state praying on Saturday night, "Please, God, let me win the lottery. If you'll answer this prayer, I'll even give part of my winnings to the church!"

That's not the kind of prayer God is going to honor because it is not God-honoring. The Lord desires to hear our problems, our longings, our hopes, and our needs. But as we lift our petitions to God, we also need to remember that our reason for asking must be pure and the request something of which our Lord will approve.

Dear God, as I bring this prayer before Your throne, I humbly ask for a powerful prayer life that will honor You and grow me spiritually. May I learn how to ask for things that will please You and strengthen Your kingdom. In Jesus' name, Amen.

BRING 'EM BACK ALIVE

James 5:13–20

Charles Eastwood was an Army officer during World War II. He commanded a unit that was responsible for relieving the Marines on Iwo Jima after they had secured that important island. The fighting had been particularly fierce for the Marines 2d Battalion, 28th Regiment. Over the preceding six weeks, of the 250 Marines in the unit, only 27 remained alive. Among them were the survivors of the six men who had raised the flag in the now-famous photograph.

To this day, Eastwood remembers their posture and attitude as they prepared to leave the island. "Their features were darkened with gunpowder and severe strain. Many were injured. They had prevailed against twenty thousand defenders who fought to the last man. In watching the Marines, we sensed their courage and commitment by how they carried themselves: with spirit and strength. They faced the world straight on."[1]

They faced the world straight on. God needs Christian men who are not afraid to face the world "straight on." He wants you and me to look out for others, raising our eyes from our own needs and interests.

The Bible tells us that we are in a spiritual battle of horrific proportions. The casualties can be for all eternity, and our enemy won't give up until the Final Battle. Our home, our workplace, our team is the field of battle. Look at it carefully. Wounded men need our help.

Someone must tell those who don't know Christ how they can find hope and forgiveness. Christian men who are weak and struggling need a helping hand that will guide them back into the center of God's will.

Let's be willing to say, "I will be that man. I will pay the price to live for God and help others come to Him."

---

1. Robert K. Cooper, *The Other 90 Percent* (New York: Crown Business, 2001), 154–55.

Father, help me to stand firm for You in the middle of spiritual warfare. Please give me the strength and the wisdom to guide others to You today. In Jesus' name, Amen.

EVER-FRESH

1 Peter 1:1–5

My wife's car needed an oil change the other day, so I agreed to take it in. As we were moving things such as sunglasses and cell phones from her car to mine, I heard Susan say, "Eew! What's this?" I saw her pick up a grocery bag from the backseat and hold it as far from her nose as possible.

Uh-oh! I had made a run to the grocery store several nights earlier and obviously had not removed all of the grocery bags. Susan held up a sodden mass of what had been tomatoes but was now smelly garbage.

Nearly everything in our world eventually rots, deteriorates, wears away, or can be stolen. Delicious tomatoes become fuel for the compost heap. Clothes develop holes. Mountains are worn down by wind and rain.

Peter tells us in his first letter that there is one thing that will stay fresh forever. He says that, as believers, we have "an inheritance that can never perish, spoil or fade" (v. 4). I don't know about you, but it seems to me that making deposits into something I can never lose is the best use of my time!

Let's take a moment to thank God for the assurance of salvation in Christ. Let's also ensure that our priorities are geared toward helping others discover the way to heaven.

Heavenly Father, I thank You that I don't have to wonder if I will be able to go to heaven. I thank You for the knowledge that nothing can steal my salvation because I've committed my life to Jesus

Christ. Today, may I point the way to heaven through my words and actions. In Jesus' name, Amen.

BE HOLY

1 Peter 1:13–19

Someone sent me the following in an e-mail.

THINGS MY MOTHER TAUGHT ME:
My mother taught me LOGIC: "If you fall off that swing and break your neck, you can't go to the store with me."
My mother taught me ANATOMY: "If you don't stop crossing your eyes, they're going to freeze that way."
My mother taught me ESP: "Put your sweater on; don't you think I know when you're cold?"
My mother taught me about ROOTS: "Do you think you were born in a barn?"

And, finally, my favorite:

My mother taught me HUMOR: "When the lawn mower cuts off your toes, don't come running to me!"

We learn all sorts of lessons from all sorts of people. Some of what we pick up from others can have a major impact for good in our lives. Other examples may actually lead us down the wrong path. After we come to know Christ as Savior, however, one of the most important lessons for us comes from the throne of God. Our Lord tells us that we are to be holy because He is holy.

The word *holy* means "set apart." We must not be united with our culture and its values. Our ideas of right and wrong cannot be determined by the media or the latest fads. Although we certainly have to live in this world—and have an impact upon this world—

God tells us that the best way we can be effective for Him is to stay close to God and far away from the influence of society.

When we're set apart, we're easily identifiable. God needs more men who will identify with Jesus Christ. He wants you and me to be holy.

Father, I want to learn this important lesson for my own life. Help me to stay far away from sin and close to You. May I be holy and loving for You today. In Jesus' name, Amen.

DECEMBER 12

GOT MILK?

1 Peter 2:1–5

Several years ago, I took six weeks to visit some of the greatest churches in the United States. I attended services at Willow Creek, Saddleback, First Baptist of Daytona, and First Baptist of Orlando, among others. In some cases, I spoke with the senior pastor of the church. In a few instances, I talked with associate pastors or other staff members. My goals were to see different worship styles, observe why these churches were growing, and take a close look at staff dynamics.

An unexpected benefit of all of the time spent studying great churches was what I learned about the leaders. Each of them still wanted to learn. They all had a thirst for helping others, but they were also what I call "lifetime students." The desire to be the best servant of Christ possible drove these men to continue adding to their storehouse of knowledge and wisdom.

What about you? Are you still learning? If so, *what* are you learning? Some people think that they know everything, so no one can tell them anything. Those people, quite frankly, are losers.

If you want to make a difference in this world, you'll continue to grow in the knowledge of God. And Peter tells us that one of the best ways to do that is by consuming your daily supply of milk—the milk of God's Word.

Got milk? Every day, drink in the Bible and learn more of the Lord.

Lord, I want to have a thirst for Your Word.
Help me to read it daily and apply it to my life.
May I always be learning more of You so that I
might be used of You. In Jesus' name, Amen.

DECEMBER 13

THE GREAT SACRIFICE

1 Peter 2:6–10

Chuck Colson tells about visiting a unique prison in Brazil. Operated by Christians and based on Christian values, the prison consisted of clean rooms and an atmosphere of peace. Everywhere Colson looked, he saw Scripture verses decorating walls until he came to what used to be a notorious torture cell.

"What inmates reside here?" Colson asked.

"This is an isolation cell. There's only one prisoner in here now," the guide said as he opened the door. Colson saw nothing in the spare room but a cross with a carving of Jesus hanging on it.

"He's doing time for the rest of us," the guide explained softly.[1]

Because Jesus took the punishment for you and me, we can have freedom forever: freedom from sin, freedom from eternal death, freedom from loneliness, and freedom from purposelessness.

Remember: Jesus Christ is our reason for living—today and every day.

Lord, thank You for giving Yourself for me. What
love! I thank You for adopting me into Your
family and making me a place with You forever.
In Jesus' name, Amen.

---

1. Quoted in Max Lucado, *In the Grip of Grace* (Dallas: Word, 1996), 113.

CHRISTIANITY AND GOOD CITIZENSHIP

I Peter 2:13–17

Here is your trivia question of the day: About how many elephants are in Africa today? (A) 0, (B) 500, (C) 1,500, (D) 2,500, or (E) 3,500? If you guessed anything other than A, you would be wrong. There are no elephants in Africa! What we call the "African elephant" is actually a loxodont, a relative of the elephant. True elephants come from India.[1]

It's important for us to get our facts straight. After all, how can we make correct decisions in life with faulty information?

In today's Scripture reading, the apostle Peter reminds us that good Christians also make good citizens. They obey the laws of the land, pay their bills, and help their neighbors. One of the best ways we can be a witness to others is by helping make our nation a better place.

In the past, some Christian groups have withdrawn from their surroundings, completely ignoring the country in which they lived. The verses we've just read, however, tell us to set an example for other citizens by our good behavior and our ability to get along with others.

Our highest allegiance, of course, is to God. When the laws of the land interfere with our devotion to the Lord, we must always choose to honor Him. Except in those dire circumstances, however, we are to respect and obey our governmental authorities.

By your life as a citizen of your own city and country, how are you measuring up to Peter's commands?

Dear God, help me to be a good citizen. May Your wisdom fill me and guide me to get along well with my neighbors. May my actions as a citizen and neighbor point others to You. In Jesus' name, Amen.

---

1. Deane Jordan, *1,001 More Facts Somebody Screwed Up* (Atlanta: Longstreet Press, 1997), 3.

AFRAID OF DEATH?

1 Peter 3:8—17

As a boy growing up in Hot Springs, Arkansas, I had the privilege of knowing a wonderful missionary couple. John and Jewell Abernathy had already retired twice from the mission field by the time I met them, and their lifetimes of experiences and stories made my visits with them fascinating—even for a teenager.

The Abernathy's had been in China during the great Shantung revival. They saw mass conversions and powerful works of the Holy Spirit. At the same time, they were also in that vast country when the Communists swept through and began killing Christians right and left.

One day, Dr. Abernathy asked me if I'd ever noticed the indentation in the middle of his forehead. I nodded—it was impossible to miss! He smiled and said, "I and some other missionaries and pastors were rounded up and marched to the edge of a huge pit one night. When we refused to turn away from trusting in Christ, they shot us. For some reason, the bullet that hit me didn't kill me. It might have been a ricochet. Knocked unconscious, covered with blood, I must have fooled my captors into believing I was dead. When I came to, I managed to crawl out of the pit and on to safety."

I remember being amazed at this story. "Weren't you scared of dying, sir?" I asked this great man of God.

"Scared of dying?" he replied. "Actually, I was scared of *not* dying! At that moment when the soldiers trained their guns on me, I suddenly realized that being faithful to my Lord and Savior was infinitely more important than saving my life. I knew that if I died, my Jesus would welcome me with open arms into heaven. And I would face Him having been found faithful."

In verse 14 of today's scripture, Peter has these words for us:

"But even if you should suffer for what is right, you are blessed. Do not fear what they fear; do not be frightened."

Don't be frightened of this life or of the possibility of leaving this world. Jesus will take care of us, wherever we are.

Father, I place myself in Your care. I don't
want to be afraid of life or death. Please help me
face today knowing You are my strength and my
guide. In Jesus' Name, Amen.

FIRED UP—OR FIRED?

1 Peter 4:1–8

Four-year-old Emily didn't like having to go to bed. Her mother tried to explain that children required a lot of rest and that it would be good for her. Emily, however, was having none of it. She insisted on staying up. Finally, her mother said, "God gave me the responsibility of looking after you. He knows you need a mother. It's late, so you have to go to bed. I'm not trying to be mean, but this is the job that God gave me."

"In that case," Emily replied, "you're fired!"[1]

In the fourth chapter of 1 Peter, we see that the believer should fire his old, ungodly lifestyle. It has no place in a Christian's job description. On the other hand, those who know Christ as Savior must be fired up about being holy, staying away from sin, and loving others with a Christlike love.

As God looks at your life, would He say that you're fired up for Him, or would He be tempted to say, "You're fired!" Are you doing the job that God put you here on earth to do? Are you using your talents, time, and energy for Him?

Take a moment to ask God to remove from your life everything that keeps you from being fired up for Jesus Christ.

Dear Lord, I want to fulfill my calling to be
Yours in the best possible way. Keep sin out of my
life today. Help me to be "fired up" for You. In
Jesus' name, Amen.

---

1. Liz Curtis Higgs, *While Shepherds Washed Their Flocks* (Nashville: Nelson, 1998), 28.

PRIDE OR HUMILITY?

1 Peter 5:6–11

You've seen them on television. Their team is in the process of winning the ballgame. A camera focuses on a fan or a player, and they hold up their index finger while shouting, "We're number one! We're number one!"

Pride.

This emotion can quickly move from a healthy self-image to becoming a major stumbling block in relationships with both God and your fellowman. Take, for example, the professing Christian with whom I talked several years ago. Active in her church, she had come to me for counseling. It turns out that she was having an affair with another church member, often using the pretext of going to church activities to hide their adultery!

When I confronted the woman with the fact that God condemned this sort of behavior, her response was, "I believe God wants me to be happy. He's okay with what I'm doing." When I showed her Bible verses, she simply shook her head. When godly friends tried to show her the error of her ways, she said, "I feel good about this. It can't be wrong."

In other words, to her, her emotions were a stronger authority than was God's Word.

This woman went on to divorce her husband, throw her teenage children into turmoil, help wreck another home, and completely ruin her life. Pride can kill you.

When you place your happiness over the happiness of others, it's difficult to have a servant's heart. It's hard to have a spirit of humility when your center of attention is self. Ironically, God says that you will be happiest and most fulfilled when you take on Christ's spirit of humility and attempt to serve others in the name of your Savior.

How's your pride index? Where does humility before God and service to others rank in your priorities?

Heavenly Father, I want to remember that everything I have and am that's good is because of You. May I serve others today in Your name, humbly

*representing You in everything I do. In Jesus'
name, Amen.*

DECEMBER 18

EVERYTHING I NEED

2 Peter 1:1–4

Attention, Children: The Bathroom Door Is Closed.

Please do not stand here and talk, whine, or ask questions. Wait until I get out.

Yes, it is locked. I want it that way. It is not broken, and I am not trapped. I know that I have left it unlocked, and even open at times, since you were born because I was afraid that some horrible tragedy might occur while I was in here, but it's been ten years, and I want some PRIVACY.

Do not ask me how long I will be. I will come out when I am done.

Do not bring the phone to the bathroom door.

Do not go running back to the phone yelling, "She's in the BATHROOM!"

Do not begin to fight as soon as I go in.

Do not stick your little fingers under the door and wiggle them. This was funny when you were two, but not now.

Do not slide pennies, Legos, or notes under the door. Even when you were two, this got a little tiresome.

If you have followed me down the hall talking, and are still talking as you face this closed door, please turn around, walk away, and wait for me in another room. I will be glad to listen to you when I am done.

And yes, I still love you.

(Signed) Mom[1]

---

1. Packyhumor.dardan.com.

Sometimes we have such short memories. God does wonderful things for us, but when tragedy strikes, some of us become like little children standing outside the door, wondering if Mom still loves us because she's gone for a moment. We say things such as, "God, how could you do this to me? I don't deserve this. I thought You loved me!"

Again, how quickly we forget. Remember: we chose, through sin, to alienate ourselves from God. We earned God's condemnation for all eternity, and hell was our ultimate destination. In spite of our sinfulness, God chose to love us. He gave Jesus Christ, His only Son, to take our sins and our condemnation upon Himself. He forgave us of everything we've ever done, adopted us into His family, and is preparing a place for us with Him in heaven. Moment by moment, God listens to the prayers that we bring before His throne.

Isn't that enough? What else does God have to do to prove He loves us? But there is more. Verse 4 of today's passage tells us that we have been given "great and precious promises." Promises such as "Lo, I am with you always" (Matt. 28:20 NKJV). "If I go and prepare a place for you, I will come again and receive you to Myself; that where I am, there you may be also" (John 14:3 NKJV). "If you abide in Me, and My words abide in you, you will ask what you desire, and it shall be done for you" (John 15:7 NKJV).

The tragedies you face don't mean that God has abandoned you or that He no longer loves you. Focus on His mighty act of salvation on your behalf. Thank Him for His grace. Claim His promises. The tough times will pass. God's love lasts forever.

Dear God, help me not to lose my faith or give up during difficult times. Help me to remember all Your love toward me. Give me the wisdom and knowledge to understand and claim Your great and precious promises to all who believe. In Jesus' name, Amen.

THE SEVEN WAYS TO IMPROVE YOUR MEMORY
2 Peter 1:5–9

Remember the story of the old couple sitting on the front porch? They'd been married for ages. One evening, it was getting chilly, so the man said, "How'd you like for me to fix you a cup of hot chocolate?"

"I'd love some!" his wife replied. "And could I have some marshmallows on top?"

The husband nodded yes.

"And I'd also like a cookie or two on the side. Could I have that?"

Again, the husband said yes.

"You know, we're not getting any younger," she continued. "You'd better write all this down or you'll forget."

"I won't forget! I tell you, I won't forget." The husband slammed the door as he went into the house.

Thirty minutes went by. The door opened and out came the husband. "Here's your hamburger and milk," he said proudly.

The woman was disgusted. "You should have written it down. I knew you'd forget. Where are my french fries?"

How is your memory? I've said—only half-jokingly—that if I ever lose my Palm Pilot, I'll have lost half my mind.

Peter tells us of seven spiritual qualities that can improve our memory: goodness, knowledge, self-control, perseverance, godliness, brotherly kindness, and love. Without these qualities, we become forgetful of what God has done for us. A proper spiritual diet, however, can provide these necessary ingredients that will help us become effective and productive for our Lord and Savior.

Dive into the Word today and begin improving your memory!

Father, I do not want to be an ineffective disciple.
Help me develop these seven spiritual qualities to
where they are strong in my life. In Jesus' name,
Amen.

READY OR NOT, HERE HE COMES!

2 Peter 3:9—14

No one knows the exact moment, day, month or year the second coming of Christ will occur. But you do know this: you're closer to that momentous time right now than you were yesterday.

When Jesus returns, what will He find you doing?

The other day I came into the house and found my oldest daughter on the phone. Though she's married and lives in another part of our city, Amy still finds time to drop by and check on me every few days. When I walked into the living room, she held up a finger to keep me silent. I soon understood why. My daughter was busy sharing the gospel of Jesus Christ with someone who didn't have a relationship with the Lord.

Before she got off the phone with her caller, Amy had given an excellent defense of the faith. She had also invited the person to church the next Sunday and had offered to pray with them about giving their life to Christ.

As a father, how do you think I felt? If you said proud, you'd be right! To hear my daughter being faithful to Jesus, even when no one else was around, was a wonderful blessing.

You need to bless God in the same way. In other words, you need to be found faithful. And since no one knows the moment of Christ's return, you must dedicate yourself to living every moment for Christ.

He's coming. Are you ready?

Lord, I know You can come at any moment—even right now as I'm praying. Help me to be consistent in my walk withYyou, so that no matter when You return, I'll be ready. In Jesus' Name, Amen

CAN I GET A WITNESS?

1 John 1:1–5

"Did you see the defendant commit the crime with which he's charged?"

Silence fills the courtroom. The defendant, on trial for his life, leans forward nervously as he awaits the answer. The judge and the jury know that this testimony could free or condemn the prisoner.

"No, I didn't see him do anything. In fact, I was nowhere near the scene of the crime. But I did read about it in the newspaper, so it seemed to me that I should come to court and give you my opinion."

We know that a court would never allow such a testimony! Only those who have personally witnessed something in relation to a case may testify.

The apostle John is just such a witness. As Gnosticism, the first heresy of the Christian church, tried to sidetrack believers, John came to the rescue. One of the tenets of Gnosticism was that a person's body was inherently evil. If that was true, Gnostics reasoned, Christ could not have had a real body. They surmised that His body was only an illusion, like a ghost.

With that background in mind, read again today's passage. John is saying, in effect, "Hold on a moment. I'm a personal witness to the fact that Jesus Christ inhabited a *real* body. I heard Jesus, I saw Him, and *I've touched Him!*"

John's personal testimony helped squelch Gnosticism and keep Christianity on the right doctrinal path.

Your personal testimony might not be quite as dramatic, but God can still use it to touch lives. If you don't share, however, no one will know what you've experienced. Decide to be like John. Share what Christ has done for you as the Lord opens doors today.

Father, thank You for men and women throughout the ages who have been willing to be a personal witness for Christ, no matter what the cost. Help me to be a part of that glorious fellowship. As You

give me opportunity today, may I be bold to share
what You mean to me. In Jesus' name, Amen.

MIXIN' IT UP
1 John 1:5–9

I'm not much of a cook, but, having lived in Louisiana for years, I do know this: add a little Tabasco sauce to whatever you're cooking and it'll be a lot spicier! I love it on scrambled eggs, in hamburger meat, and *especially* on top of red beans and rice. Hey, let's go eat!

As a joke last year, one of my staff members (who shall go unnamed, Jeff Jones) made some fudge at Christmas time. At this time of the year, our office is flooded with peanut brittle, fudge, fruit cakes, divinity (appropriate), and a lot of candy. Jeff's fudge blended in with all of the other goodies—until I put a piece of his "Tabasco fudge" in my mouth. Whoooeeee! It got my attention, and not because I liked it! Jeff and I don't disagree about many things, but we're far apart when it comes to peppers and fudge. They just don't go together.

Christians and sin don't mix, either.

John reminds us that "God is light" (v. 5). In other words, no sin can exist in His presence. The apostle goes on to say that we cannot claim to be in fellowship with God and allow sin to continue unchecked in our life. If we've convinced ourselves that God overlooks the one or two little sins that we enjoy, we're fooling ourselves. God hates sin. After all, sin cost Jesus Christ His life.

Ham and eggs are a good mix. Chex is a good mix (sorry). Oreos and milk are a good mix. But Christians and sin are diametrically opposed to each other.

Don't mix it up with sin. Stay away from it.

Heavenly Father, I know that You are the "Father
of Light." You dwell in such pure brightness that
no man can approach. May I allow You to keep
the darkness of sin out of every nook and cranny

of my life. Today, may I walk in the light as You
are in the light. In Jesus' name, Amen.

LOVE AND HATE:
WHERE DO YOU STAND?
I John 2:6–11

Do you hold grudges? If I ask the question, "With whom are you angry?" how many people come to mind?

It's possible to fall into a trap of being easily offended and then staying angry. While in college, I knew a guy who stayed angry at the world. He used to say, "I don't have to have a reason to be mad at somebody. I have to have a reason to *like* them."

The problem with anger and hatred is that they put you outside the fellowship of God. John probes this theme over and over throughout his first letter. He states the spiritual truth this way: "Anyone who claims to be in the light but hates his brother is still in the darkness" (v. 9).

At this point, perhaps you begin to play a semantics game that goes like this: "I don't really hate people; I'm just angry with them. I don't have a problem with forgiveness; I just have a good memory." Be honest with yourself. This kind of attitude is displeasing to God and creates problems among believers.

If this devotion has hit home, do something about your attitude. Begin by acknowledging your hatred and lack of forgiveness toward others as sins. Ask for forgiveness, and let God begin giving you a new heart filled with the love of Christ. If necessary, talk about your anger with a trusted, wise Christian. That person might be able to give you some valuable insight about reasons for that anger.

Love God, and you'll love your fellowman. It's as simple as that.

Dear Lord, I don't want anger to consume me or
keep me from Your love and forgiveness. Please
cleanse me of my wrong attitudes and begin
creating in me a new heart that loves and forgives
easily. In Jesus' name, Amen.

CHRISTMAS EVE
I John 3:1–3

Tomorrow is the day we celebrate the incarnation of Jesus Christ, the Son of God. Fully God and fully man, the creator of the world came into this world to show us how much God loves us. As John says in verse 1 of today's passage, "How great is the love the Father has lavished on us!"

You're probably planning on opening gifts either tonight or tomorrow morning—or both! In any case, remind your family of the true meaning of Christmas. This time of the year is not about spending money and getting presents. It is about men and women lost in the darkness of sin and desperately needing help. Christmas is about a Son away from home and a Father who loves us so much He is willing to give up that Son.

"Peace and goodwill," the television specials proclaim. But how can those qualities come from hearts made angry and selfish by sin? Only a heart change—a life change—will allow us to have peace on earth and goodwill toward men.

You hold in your life the greatest gift anyone in this world could want. This season of the year, share the gift of Jesus Christ with someone. Do your part to improve this world by telling your friends how to get to the next world.

May this be a wonderful day for you and your family.

Dear God, thank You for sending Jesus Christ to teach us about You. Thank You for living among us and showing us Your love. Above all, thank You for the greatest gift of all, the gift of salvation. In Jesus' name, Amen.

A Christ-Filled Christmas

I John 4:1–9

On this day, I gather my family around me, and we do two things. First, we talk about the great memories of past Christmases. It always provides moments of both tears and laughter. It's also a great way of helping your family put down strong roots.

The second thing we always do is open the Bible and read the Christmas story. Then we share about what Christ means to us.

Whatever your traditions on this day, make sure, above all, that Christ is in the center of everything you do. Thank Him for His birth, death, and resurrection.

> *This is how God showed his love among us: He sent his one and only Son into the world that we might live through him. (v. 9)*

If you are alone on this day, thank God that He has adopted you into His family. Remember that in heaven you'll be part of the greatest family reunion in the history of the universe! If you are with your family, thank the Lord for them, and make the most of the time you have with them today.

Don and I wish you a wonderful, Christ-filled Christmas.

> *Heavenly Father, thank You for the gift of Your Son. May we honor Him on this, the day when we celebrate His birth. In Jesus' name, Amen.*

How Is Your Building Coming Along?

Jude 20–25

I drive my youngest daughter across town to school several days a week. On the way, I've noticed a house being built. I've seen the project progress from a bare slab, to a wooden frame, to a nearly completed, brick two-story home. It looks as if whoever oversaw the construction did a good job.

How is your building project coming along? I'm talking about your life, not your house. Jude admonishes the Christian to "build yourselves up in your most holy faith" (v. 20). And it doesn't matter if you're a klutz when it comes to driving a nail or if you could build a dream home all by yourself. When it comes to your life, God has given you all of the abilities and tools you need.

For example, Paul tells us in Galatians 2:20 that Christ lives in the believer. The Architect and Builder of the universe—the One who dug out and filled the oceans, the One who sculpted the mountains of the world—is ready and available to help you build up your life!

At this point in your journey, what does your spiritual house look like? Is it strong and sturdy with new rooms being added regularly? Or is your life a mess of sticks and stones that barely hang together?

Jesus Christ wants to help you succeed in your building project. He is ready to transform your life—beginning today—if you'll make Him foreman of the construction team. Give Him complete control, and Jesus will make you happier, more at peace, and stronger than you ever thought possible.

Get started on your life's building today by handing the project over to the Lord.

Dear Lord, I confess that this life of mine isn't all You desire it to be. I do want to be built up in the faith, constructing a life that will please You. Please take control of my life from this day forward. Change me for Your glory. In Jesus' name, Amen.

LOSING YOUR FIRST LOVE
Revelation 2:1–5

Ginger (name changed to protect the innocent) stands out as my first love during my teenage years. She lived in my neighborhood, and I was at her house nearly every day. Her mom made sure she was always in the house with us, which created some pretty interesting conversations between a weary adult and two stubborn teenagers. How much did I care for Ginger? So much so that I made a decision that changed one habit of mine for a lifetime.

I had been invited by Ginger's mom to stay and eat lunch with them one day. She served ice tea, and I asked for some sugar. "Mark, at our house we don't put sugar in our tea," she explained. "If you want to keep coming here, you'll have to drink your tea unsweetened."

Well! I really liked sweetened tea. But then I looked over at Ginger—and I said, "Ma'am, I'll be happy to drink my tea without sugar."

Ginger and I went our separate ways later that year. But to this day, decades later, I still drink my tea without sugar. Ah, the power of love!

For we who are believers, our first love needs to be Jesus Christ. In John's letter to the church at Ephesus, the ancient apostle shocks his audience with a piercing message from the Lord. He says that good works, correct doctrine, and endurance in the face of difficulties are not enough. We must be ever vigilant to fiercely love Jesus Christ and the church, His body.

The Ephesian Christians had become cold and sterile in their faith. They valued correctness over a vibrant relationship with God.

John's remedy for his first-century audience also holds true for us today: "Remember the height from which you have fallen! Repent and do the things you did at first" (v. 5). Has there ever been a time in our lives when we loved Christ more than we love Him today? Did our ministry to the body of Christ, over time, diminish because of fatigue or apathy?

Let's return to our first love. Let's ask Jesus Christ to forgive our coldness and allow Him to fan into a blaze the fire of our love for

Him and His church. It's the kind of life-changing decision that can help us forever with our first love!

> *Lord, I don't want to stray from the center of Your fellowship. Help me to have a living, vibrant relationship with You. Help me to love You as I should, and give me the desire to minister to Your people, the church, in Your name and with Your love. In Jesus' name, Amen.*

DECEMBER 28

THE DANGER OF "NICE"
Revelation 3:14–20

Nice.

It's a dangerous word. In the third chapter of Revelation, John uses another word for "nice." He calls the church at Laodicea "lukewarm." It means the same thing—and God hates it. It makes Him nauseated.

What's wrong with "nice?" God says that He would rather the local believers and their church be cold—dead—than be "nice." Cold is recognizable; so is hot. But "nice" just blends in with its culture, not causing problems, but not changing lives, either.

God has put us here on earth to make waves in our culture. We are the "salt of the earth" (Matt. 5:13). Our presence is supposed to spice up life. We are to be noticed, as in a "city . . . set on a hill" (Matt. 5:14 NKJV). Jesus Christ and His apostles showed us the way. Their way of living for God got them beaten, imprisoned, and killed.

But they changed the world.

Today, we Christians are in grave danger. We are being seduced into thinking that we should adopt a "nice" attitude and "nice" tolerance for those around us. We never make the front page of the paper, never make anyone mad—and never challenge anyone with the claims of Christ.

Quite frankly, I believe that Jesus Christ is looking for fanatics. Not the wild-eyed kind that foam at the mouth. Jesus wants men who will lovingly—but firmly—share an uncompromising gospel with everyone. Men who won't back down in the face of adversity, water down their stand on biblical issues when peer pressure comes to bear, or cave in to "niceness" so that everyone will get along with them—those are the men who will one day hear, "Well done, my good and faithful servant."

Don't be "nice." Get on fire for God.

Heavenly Father, help me not to compromise my convictions by trying to be nice to everyone. I want to love everyone with a godly love, but I also want to present them with a true example of what it means to be a Christian. May I be on fire for You today. In Jesus' name, Amen.

DECEMBER 29

"YOU ARE WORTHY"

Revelation 4:8–11; 5:11–14

Before this year ends, let's take a trip. Using today's passage of Scripture as our means of transportation, let's travel to the throne room of heaven.

What a marvelous place! More beauty than we could ever imagine surrounds us. Hundreds of thousands of mighty angels gather before the throne. A tremendous throng of believers who've gone into heaven before us spreads out as far as the eye can see. And every eye is focused on one person: Jesus Christ.

"Worthy is the Lamb!" roars the holy assembly. The twenty-four elders fall before their Lord and Savior. We also find ourselves on our knees, stunned by the joy and love we feel. From every corner of the universe, we hear singing more beautiful than any artist who ever recorded. And we find ourselves joining in the universal praise of Jesus Christ: "To him who sits on the throne and to the Lamb be praise and honor and glory and power, for ever and ever!" (5:13).

It's time to go home. We sigh, close the pages of God's Word, and return to this life.

One day, though, we'll be right there in the throne room. And when that moment occurs, we'll never have to leave again. We'll always be a part of that joy, love, peace, and incredible experience of seeing God face to face.

Until then, remain faithful.

Dear Lord, You are worthy to receive all praise. In everything I do today, help me remember my future destiny and my reason for living. Until the day I stand before You in heaven, help me to remain faithful to You. In Jesus' name, Amen.

DECEMBER 30

THE END OF EVIL
Revelation 20

I hate cancer.

Cancer has robbed me of my friends in an untimely manner. It has fractured families in my church. My wife, during the writing of this book, died due to a battle with this terrible disease.

I hate child abuse.

Hundreds of victims of this pernicious crime have come to me for counseling over the years. I've seen the mental scars that selfish guardians have inflicted on innocent children—scars that last well into adulthood, robbing the victim of normal emotions and a healthy self-esteem.

I hate sin.

Satan, the father of lies, has seduced billions of people to turn from God and follow their own path. On that path, beautiful and wide though it might be, these men and women are led to their doom. Eternal separation from God is the price we pay for the temporary benefits received from sin.

One day, however, sin will be no more. Before the judgment seat of God, all evildoers are punished and all evil is destroyed. As the saints and angels watch, Satan, his fallen angels, and all of his followers will be thrown into the lake of fire—forever.

In light of this coming event, let's be sure of two things. First, we need to be certain that our names are written in the Lamb's Book of Life. Jesus Christ must be our Lord and our Savior. Second, we must endure. The knowledge that unjust deeds and debilitating disease eventually will be destroyed should give us the courage to stand for God, no matter what is currently happening to us.

One day—perhaps today—evil will be destroyed. We know that Love has already won the battle.

Dear God, help me to keep my eyes on heaven. Help me to remember that all injustice will one day be judged, punished, and destroyed. Until then, may I not grow discouraged in serving You. In Jesus' name, Amen.

DECEMBER 31

TOMORROW: A NEW BEGINNING
Revelation 20:1–7; 22:16–21

Don and I want to thank you for allowing us to spend this year with you. We want to remind you that although today is the last day of the year, tomorrow holds a new beginning. You might want to read this book of devotionals again. If you've not yet read the first volume, *God's Man* (also published by Kregel), we encourage you to use that book as a guide next year.

In Christ, every end holds a new beginning.

Perhaps you have lost a friend or loved one to death this year. Maybe you, yourself, are facing some physical challenges that force you to contemplate your mortality. Remember that, for the Christian, death is simply a way of God's bringing you home to be with Him forever—a new beginning.

Some of you reading this book lost your job during the last twelve months. We want to remind you that God can use losses such as that to move you into an exciting, new area you otherwise never would have explored—a new beginning.

Perhaps separation or divorce has ripped apart your heart and your marriage. Remaining faithful to Jesus Christ in the face of such difficulties means that God can take those sorrows and make you stronger. He can use your experiences to touch the lives of others—giving you a new beginning.

Finally, if you do not know Christ as your Savior, the invitation that Jesus extends at the end of the Bible is directed to *you!* He wants to come into your life and forgive you of everything you've ever done that's wrong. Christ will live in you forever, give you fellowship and guidance, and one day bring you home to be with Him. Some of you need salvation—a new beginning.

On this last day of the year, we are offering you two different prayers. The first one is a model prayer that you can use to invite Christ into your life. The second one is a prayer of devotion to God.

May you grow in the Lord during this coming year!

Dear Lord, I know I've done some things that are wrong. I'm sorry for my sins, and I want to turn from them. I understand that Jesus Christ died on the Cross to pay for my sins and take the punishment for them. Right now, in the best way I know how, I open my life to You. Please come into my life, forgive me of all of my sins, make me clean and pure, and take me to heaven when I die. As best I can, I now give You complete control of my life from this day forward. Thank You for coming into my heart. Thank You for cleansing and purifying me from all sins. Now, help me to live for You. In Jesus' name, Amen.

Heavenly Father, thank You for being with me during this past year. In the coming twelve months, help me to remember that You are always with me. Also, help me to grow closer to You every day. In Jesus' name, Amen.

An Ideal Companion Book!

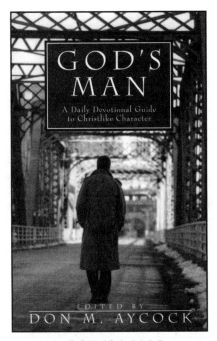

GOD'S MAN
A Daily Devotional Guide to Christlike Character

Edited by Don M. Aycock

This daily devotional provides practical help for men who want to build solid spiritual lives. Each of the readings includes a discussion of a Scripture passage and how that passage relates to a man's emotions, employment, finances, relationships, sexuality, temptations, and more.

The contributors come from all walks of life. Some are retired, some are middle-aged, and some are beginning their careers as businessmen, writers, physicians, pastors, professors, organizational leaders, and counselors. In spite of their differences, they all have a common goal: to be God's man for their families, their colleagues, their communities—and to help you be God's man, too.

ISBN 0-8254-2000-8 • 336 pp. • paperback

Also from Kregel Publications

AMAZING GRACE
366 Inspiring Hymn Stories for Daily Devotions
by Kenneth W. Osbeck

An inspirational daily devotional based on 366 great hymns of the Christian faith. Each day's devotional highlights biblical truths drawn from true-to-life stories behind the writing of these well-known hymns of the faith. Each story includes a portion of the hymn itself, as well a suggested Scripture readings, meditations, and practical application.

Your personal or family devotional time will be enhanced by the challenging and inspiring thoughts contained in this thrilling collection of classical and contemporary hymn stories.

ISBN 0-8254-3448 • 400 pp. • paperback

Kregel
Publications

Available from your local Christian bookstore, or
Kregel Publications, P.O. Box 2607, Grand Rapids, MI 49501